MA AND PA KETTLE ON FILM

BY
LON AND DEBRA DAVIS

Ma and Pa Kettle on Film
By Lon and Debra Davis
Copyright © 2021 Davis House, LLC

Published in the USA by:
BearManor Media
1317 Edgewater Dr., #110
Orlando, FL 32804

BearManor Media, Orlando, Florida
www.bearmanormedia.com
Printed in the United States of America
Book design by Robbie Adkins, www.adkinsconsult.com

Library of Congress Cataloguing-in-Publication Data
Ma and Pa Kettle on Film / By Lon and Debra Davis
Paperback ISBN 978-1-62933-682-4
Case ISBN 978-1-62933-683-1
1. Ma and Pa Kettle (film series) 2. Comedy films—history and criticism.

Cover photos courtesy of Steve Cox.

Marjorie Main and Percy Kilbride as Ma and Pa Kettle, 1953.

*This book is dedicated to Scott H. Reboul,
with love, gratitude, and respect.*

Table of Contents

Acknowledgments vii

Foreword by Brett Halsey x

Introduction xii

Part 1: The Egg Came First

Chapter 1: Betty MacDonald and the Best Seller 3

Chapter 2: The Egg and I (1947) 11

Part 2: The Movie Series

Chapter 3: Ma and Pa Kettle (1949) 76

Chapter 4: Ma and Pa Kettle Go to Town (1950) 112

Chapter 5: Ma and Pa Kettle Back on the Farm (1951) 148

Chapter 6: Ma and Pa Kettle at the Fair (1952) 169

Chapter 7: Ma and Pa Kettle on Vacation (1953) 205

Chapter 8: Ma and Pa Kettle at Home (1954) 230

Chapter 9: Ma and Pa Kettle at Waikiki (1955) 265

Chapter 10: The Kettles in the Ozarks (1956) 297

Chapter 11: The Kettles on Old MacDonald's Farm (1957) 314

Part 3: The Legacy

Chapter 12: Losing Marjorie and Percy. 336

Chapter 13: The Kettles in Pop Culture. 340

Sources 351

Index 354

Acknowledgments

First, the authors would like to extend their gratitude to Ben Ohmart, the benevolent leader of BearManor Media, for giving them yet another excuse to write about classic films. This is most appreciated, particularly during the soul-killing pandemic of the *annus horribilis*, otherwise known as 2020.

The presentation of material is just as important as the material itself. That said, the authors struck gold the day they were first put in touch with Robbie Adkins, of Adkins Consulting. She is a true professional, as well as a delight to know.

And because motion pictures are a visual medium, illustrations—the more the better—are a necessary component of film books. In addition to using their own photos, the authors are fortunate enough to know some generous collectors of film stills, most notably the wonderful Steve Cox, who provided many beautiful, high-resolution scans. Jerry Murbach, whose domain name is doctormacro.com, kindly contributed several rare photos as well. In certain instances, when stills were unavailable to illustrate a given scene, Mark Pruett came through with the requested screencaps. Studio-placed ads in vintage trade magazines are culled from mediahistoryproject.org, a free online resource, featuring millions of pages of books and magazines from the histories of film, broadcasting, and recorded sound. This useful website is sponsored by the Mary Pickford Foundation.

For providing valuable assistance and encouragement, the authors are heartily indebted to two trailblazers in the field of film documentation, Leonard Maltin and James Robert Parish. In the early seventies, Leonard and Jim were among the first writers to consider Ma and Pa Kettle, the Bowery Boys, the Three Stooges, and Abbott & Costello suitable subjects for study.

Gratitude is also due Michelle Vogel, the capable biographer of Marjorie Main, for her open-handed approach with her hard-earned research material. Ted Okuda contributed an interview he had done with retired Kettle director Charles Lamont. Randy Skretvedt, the affable film-and-music historian, offered his insights and observations. And Samuel Stoddard, the online classic movie critic, granted permission to reprint his thoughtful, succinct reviews of the Kettle films.

The authors had the privilege of conducting telephone interviews with five of the surviving actors who portrayed the offspring of Ma and Pa Kettle. Contact information for these fascinating men and women, now in their seventies and eighties, was accessed by this book's most deserving dedicatee, Scott H. Reboul. As for the Kettle kids themselves, they are:

- Olive Sturgess Anderson, the charming actress who played Nancy Kettle in *The Kettles in the Ozarks*.
- Richard Eyer, former child star of the 1950s, who was Billy Kettle in two pictures, *Ma and Pa Kettle at Home* and *In the Ozarks*.
- Sherry Jackson, whose show business career began as Susie Kettle in the series' second, third, fourth, and fifth instalments.
- Joe Reiner, a retired detective sergeant, for sensitively relaying the on-set memories of his late wife, Lori Nelson, who portrayed Rosie Kettle in *Ma and Pa Kettle at the Fair* and *At Waikiki*.
- J. P. Sloane, the respected theologian, once known as Billy Kettle in *Ma and Pa Kettle Back on the Farm*.
- And finally, Brett Halsey, the fine actor and writer, who was Elwin Kettle in *Ma and Pa Kettle at Home*. Brett was also kind enough to provide this book with its foreword, which just happens to be up next.

Foreword

I was delighted to learn that Lon and Debra Davis were writing an entire book about the Ma and Pa Kettle series of films, which rank among the most important and most entertaining comedy movies of all time. This book is another welcome chapter in film history.

In 1953, I played Elwin Kettle in *Ma and Pa Kettle at Home*. It was my first leading role, and one that stands out among the many roles I have played in the succeeding years of my acting career.

I was still a fledgling student in the Universal-International Studio's New Talent Program when I was cast in the picture. As part of my studio training, I already had bit parts in ten or so U-I movies, but playing Ma and Pa Kettle's eldest son, Elwin, was my first big break and a terrific learning experience.

As in sports, music, and almost everything else, a person learns best by playing with those with more talent and experience. The Kettle series may have been regarded as B-films, but except for the relative newcomers like Alice Kelley and me, its principal cast was made up of A-class actors with long and respected careers in film and theater.

Marjorie Main, Percy Kilbride, and Alan Mowbray each had over fifty successful years of playing leading roles in Hollywood and on Broadway. Acting with them was like a gift from God, and just watching them perform together was a learning experience that could never be equaled in even the best of acting classes.

I have worked with many other great and notable actors in my own long career, but *Ma and Pa Kettle at Home* was my beginning, and I treasure every memory of standing in the shadow of the marvelous talents I appeared with in that film.

Brett Halsey
Laguna Woods, CA

Brett Halsey has had a prolific career as an actor, appearing in more than a hundred films; he is currently a novelist. For more information on this talented man, please see Chapter 8, "*Ma and Pa Kettle at Home* (1954)."

Brett Halsey, 2020.

Introduction:
What's So Great About Ma and Pa Kettle Anyway?

Will Rogers had it . . . Marie Dressler and Wallace Beery had it . . . and now Marjorie Main and Percy Kilbride as Ma and Pa Kettle seem to have it, too.

What is it? Well, it's hard to put your finger on it . . . but millions of movie patrons feel it the minute Ma and Pa Kettle appear on the screen. And with each new picture, added millions of "Kettle converts" trek to the nation's theaters to bask in that "indefinable something"—so real, so warm, so human, it has become a part of the very heart and humor of America itself.

So began a particularly insightful ad placed in various trade magazines in 1952 to promote *Ma and Pa Kettle at the Fair*, the latest installment of the wildly popular movie series. These unpretentious black-and-white films, made on Universal's backlot for a few hundred thousand dollars apiece, raked in $35 million at the box-office, the equivalent in 2021 of $350 million, effectively saving the studio from bankruptcy.[1]

The Kettles—a fictional family headed by Phoebe ("Ma") and Franklin ("Pa") Kettle of Cape Flattery, Washington—endeared themselves to movie audiences, those hardworking folks who simply wanted to laugh and forget their troubles for seventy minutes or so. And laugh they did—great shouts of laughter—whether it was at Pa starting up his ancient battery-operated radio by banging a chair on the wooden floor, or at Ma using a broom to clear the dinner table of squawking chickens.

"One of the theories for the Kettles' popularity is that the blowsy Ma and the ineffectual Pa . . . represent some sort of American myth," reads a Universal-International (U-I) report of April 6, 1953. "But that theory doesn't stand up when it's considered that the comedies are amazingly popular as far away as Australia." A prime reason for such widespread success was credited to the lead players: "It must be considered that Percy Kilbride does a very funny characterization, with his dead pan, outlandish dignity and nasal drawl, and that Marjorie Main knows her business equally well."

Truer words, as they say. The pairing of Main and Kilbride is a prime example of perfect Hollywood casting. Rarely have two actors had such onscreen chemistry; they belong in the same league as William Powell and Myrna Loy, Spencer Tracy and Katharine Hepburn, Stan Laurel and Oliver Hardy. In other words: On their own, they're wonderful; together, they're sublime. Critics, it is true, had few positive things to say about the Kettle films' uncomplicated stories and time-worn gags. But moviegoers pay to see actors, not critics, and they happily handed over their quarters to see Marjorie Main and Percy Kilbride.

In the coming pages, the spotlight will shine brightly on the ten low-budget films to feature Ma and Pa Kettle and their brood of fifteen. We will read what those who labored behind the scenes had to say about the films; we will also learn background informa-

---

1   The adjusted figures used herein are determined by the Inflation Calculator, which can be accessed at www.usinflationcalculator.com.

MA AND PA KETTLE ON FILM

tion on the stars and supporting players who so skillfully brought their characters to life.

So, join us, won't you? as we spend ten years on the backlot of Universal Studios in the forties and fifties. But bring along a sweater; it gets a mite chilly in the evenings.

Lon and Debra Davis
Lake Oswego, Oregon

Lon and Debra Davis have both been obsessed by classic films since childhood. A longtime married couple, they reside in the Pacific Northwest, due south of Cape Flattery, Washington.

Lon Davis. Photo by Greg Burns.

Debra Davis. Photo by Lon Davis.

PART 1:
THE EGG
CAME FIRST

Betty MacDonald seems a bit self-conscious as she sits at her typewriter while the press photographer snaps away, c. 1951.

Chapter 1
Betty MacDonald and the Best Seller

Betty MacDonald, the acclaimed author of *The Egg and I*, was born Anne Elizabeth Campbell Bard in Boulder, Colorado, on March 26, 1907. She had four sisters, Mary, Dorothea, Alison, and Sylvia, and one brother, Sydney. The family enjoyed a warm relationship throughout their lives. Although her name was Anne, she preferred Betsy, and later, Betty.

When she was twenty, she met the man who would be her husband, former marine Robert Eugene Heskett. That he was interested in her and not her thinner, prettier sister Mary confounded Betty. But Betty's infectious, toothy smile, hearty laugh, and sarcastic sense of humor apparently made the stronger impression on Bob, who was twelve years her senior, and gainfully employed as a life insurance salesman. Selling insurance, however, was not his driving ambition in life. For some reason, he was obsessed by the idea of raising chickens. Betty had been taught by her mother, Elsie, that it was a wife's duty to share in her husband's interests and support him in every way possible. So, when Bob spoke excitedly about combining their respective holdings and buying a tiny, run-down chicken farm in the logging town of Point Ludlow on the Olympic Peninsula, she went along with the idea. Betty and Bob were married in a small ceremony on the Bards' family farm in Seattle, Washington, on July 10, 1927. This was followed by a rather subdued honeymoon, in Victoria, Canada—an hour's ferry ride away—during which Bob seemed preoccupied with his new calling in life.

Although their days during the summer months were filled with backbreaking work—clearing the property of brush and tree stumps and trying to make the ramshackle farmhouse at least inhabitable—the Hesketts could safely be described as happy. Bob was, at first anyway, sympathetic and encouraging to his young, inexperienced bride, and Betty was a willing student. But as summer gave way to fall, there was more than a change in the air. It became dark early, it was freezing cold, and wet, the rain endless and distressing. Betty came to realize that she was little more than an unpaid farmhand, with her distracted husband more concerned about how much she could shoulder and not the least about her well-being.

No self-respecting farm wife, according to some unwritten law, should be in bed except between the hours of seven at night and four in the morning "unless she is in labor or dead." So, when that dreaded alarm clock would ring in the black of night, Betty staggered out of bed to face her day. And what days they were! Carrying heavy buckets of water from a well to the house; wrestling with an ancient, rusty stove possessed of its own malevolent personality; caring for hundreds of chirpy, smelly, maddening baby chicks. And then, twice a week, if she could get the strangely recalcitrant "Stove" hot enough to heat the water, she bathed her tall body in a tiny tin tub.

It soon became all too clear that the sullen Bob and the bookish Betty were a match made in hell. More than anything, she longed to devour the classics in front of a roaring fire. His idea of reading material was the latest issue of *American Poultryman*. Without a radio or a telephone, Betty grew increasingly lonely. The surrounding mountains began to close in on her, making her feel as though they were peering over her sore shoulder. Their nearest neighbors, Maw and Paw Bishop and their thirteen offspring, lived on a shabby farm about a mile away. Although their place was anything but clean, there was a feeling of warmth and hospitality. For Betty, a visit to the Bishops was a welcome respite from her otherwise harrowing existence.

By the end of 1927, Betty discovered she was "that way"— mountain code for pregnant. Having a newborn baby daughter to care for only magnified the situation. She felt as if she were fleeing down the track just ahead of a rushing locomotive. A year later, another baby was on the way—and in addition to caring for two infants, she was still responsible for the feeding and watering of the chickens, as well as keeping detailed records for each one. Finally, in 1931, four years after her sentence began, she reached the end of her tether. Oddly enough, it was not the chickens that had temporarily broken her spirit—it was Bob. A victim of shell shock from his time in the First World War (a condition now referred to as post-traumatic-stress disorder, or PTSD), he was also an alcoholic, turning physically abusive when consuming his own moonshine. The time had come for the now-twenty-four-year-old Betty to pack up her few belongings, bundle up her two daughters, and head, not for the mountains, but back to the safety of her immediate family.[2]

A genuine survivor, Betty went on to weather the Great Depression as a single mom with, by her own admission, no marketable skills. Still, she got by, taking any available job to put food on the table. With the aid of her always-encouraging sister Mary, Betty was able to obtain temporary positions as a secretary to a mining engineer and a lumberman; she also worked for a lawyer, a rabbit grower, a credit bureau, a florist, a dentist, a gangster, and a pyramid scheme, among other odd jobs. In the latter thirties, as prosperity was truly "just around the corner," Betty contracted tuberculosis, a lung disorder exceedingly difficult to treat in those days before the widespread use of antibiotics. She had to be separated from her family for over a year while she lay motionless in a sanitarium before

The Egg and I

Life on a wilderness chicken ranch told with wit and high humor

By Betty MacDonald

The cover for the book's first edition, 1945.

---

2 Bob Heskett never remarried, although he did become involved in a relationship with a newly divorced lady in 1951. When her angry ex came to their door, demanding to see her, fifty-five-year-old Bob told the man to leave. A fight broke out in the hallway of the new couple's home, during which Bob was stabbed to death. His assailant was charged with murder and sentenced to prison.

being pronounced well enough to return to her life. How did she manage to carry on despite such challenging circumstances? One word: *humor*. Betty was blessed with the uncanny ability to find something funny within virtually any situation. Even in the dreary, ice-cold sanitarium, she cheered up patients and staff members who daily were surrounded by illness and death.

When she was finally released from this isolated existence, she remarried, this time to a caring man named Don MacDonald. She doted on him, her children, and her extended family members. Her humorously exaggerated tales of chicken farming, devoid of the unpleasant truths of her disastrous first marriage, were a tonic to anyone fortunate enough to be in earshot when she told (or retold) them.

Predictably, Betty's friends and family encouraged her to put her story into book form. This was a tall order. Betty did not consider herself an especially gifted writer. For a full year, she spent every spare minute seated at the kitchen table, or perhaps in a corner of the living room, writing, rewriting, and rewriting some more. A genre of literature then in vogue were books in which people survived the hardships of the wilderness and seemingly loved every minute of it. Betty honestly believed that anyone who felt that way must also enjoy athlete's foot. She used her at-times caustic style, mixed with some poetically descriptive writing, to create a picture of the untamed Pacific Northwest. The result was a manuscript bearing the title "The Egg and I." After initially being considered by Doubleday and Co., it was published by J. P. Lippincott in 1945. After four long years of reading about the war in Europe, Americans wanted to curl up with a good book, one that would make them laugh. *The Egg and I* was that book. Within a year's time, it had sold an estimated one million copies.

Betty, who had struggled financially for so long, was now a wealthy woman, not to mention a famous one. And along with the rewards and blessings of newfound success came the inevitable headaches. A particularly serious one involved the Bishop family of Port Ludlow, Washington. Through their lawyers, they filed a lawsuit in the amount of $100,000 against Betty MacDonald. They were convinced, and for good reason, that MacDonald had based the Kettle characters on them. The author insisted that this was *not* the case; the Kettles, she said, were strictly a product of her imagination. The Bishops, however, doggedly set out to prove that they were indeed the template for those bumptious characters, and that MacDonald had exposed them to ridicule and scorn. They would have their day in court, beginning on September 27, 1947, with the honorable Judge William J. Wilkins presiding.

Betty was ill-prepared for the relentless interrogation by the prosecution. She became so distraught at one point that she abruptly left the witness stand in tears. Court was adjourned until the following day when her questioning recommenced. Several witnesses for the prosecution unwittingly helped the defense by pointing out the differences between the characters and the real-life protagonists, particularly in saying that the late Suzanne Bishop, the alleged inspiration for the rough-talking Maw Kettle of the book, *never* swore like her literary alter ego. Paw Kettle was described in the book as dark-browed, large-nosed, and wearing a black derby, an accurate description of Albert Bishop, judging by a photo taken

Betty on Puget Sound. This photo originally appeared in the Seattle *(WA)* News.

of him the previous year (at eighty-seven, Mr. Bishop was too ill to attend the trial). He was also said to be impractical, if not as downright inept and lazy as Paw Kettle; he even once accidentally burned down a barn, something Paw does in the book. Another member of the Port Ludlow community (referred to as the fictional Port Townsend), Raymond H. Johnson, a Native American, claimed he had been portrayed as Crowbar, one of Paw Kettle's overworked assistants. He was demanding $75,000 in damages. Forty-year-old Wilbur Bishop claimed that he had been the model for Elwin Kettle, a teenaged boy with striking blue eyes. Looking directly at the jury, he asked plainly if his eyes were not blue. The jury found this comical and could not suppress their laughter. Another point that struck them as funny was the difference between the number of children in the Bishop family (thirteen) and the Kettles (fifteen). An elderly woman named Annie McGuire, who resembled a lumberjack in her red-and-black-checked shirt, claimed that she, too, had been the object of libel. She clearly recognized herself as the character Mary McGregor, described in the book as having "fiery red, dyed hair, a large dairy ranch and a taste for liquor." This plain-spoken country woman could not contain her own laughter when passages

The farm where Betty MacDonald lived while writing The Egg and I *still stands in the picturesque countryside that is Vashon, Washington. It is currently an inn.*

of the book were read aloud in court. Still, she said that the first time she had read the alleged description of herself, she was prepared to "beat up" Mrs. MacDonald—if only she had known where to find her.

Given the hundreds of thousands of dollars at stake for both Betty and her publisher, she was in a state of acute anxiety throughout the trial and the deliberation process. After she had consumed countless cups of coffee and smoked just as many cigarettes, it was announced that the jury had reached a verdict. Betty was found "not guilty." But was she, really? It seems clear that she had indeed used these idiosyncratic individuals as thinly disguised characters. As she later pointed out: "*Every* book is based to some extent on facts, or else how could you write?" And, in truth, it did not appear that the citizens of Port Ludlow had been damaged by the book, although the moment they lost the case they immediately requested a new trial. The judge, while not granting their request, said that if he had to make a ruling without the benefit of a jury, he "might have allowed nominal damages to several of the plaintiffs and perhaps, in some cases, even more."

Betty MacDonald was no one-hit wonder; she wrote a series of books for children. Featuring her original character, Mrs. Piggle-Wiggle, the books found a large audience. And for her more mature following, there were inspirational memoirs, including the cleverly titled *The Plague and I*, which detailed her year at the sanitarium. Betty was generous with her family and friends, but she was never especially interested in having a lot of money. She once said that if she had to choose between being rich or poor, she would choose the latter. And fame was a burden she had *never* desired. ("I think fame is the most appalling thing that can happen to you," she said, frankly. "I certainly think the old saying is true—'Get your head above the masses and you'll get stones thrown at you.' You have to be thick-skinned to take it.") More than anything, Betty enjoyed being a wife and mother, staying home, taking care of the ones she loved. After living in Washington State most of her life, she decided to settle down with her husband (and her mother, who lived harmoniously with them) on a ranch in the picturesque town of Carmel, California, in the Monterey Valley. Sadly, her years of peace would be in short supply. She was only fifty when she died, of uterine cancer, on February 7, 1958.

The Betty MacDonald Network, a Literary Society, is quite active in 2021, with new members joining their ranks on a regular basis. Betty's daughters have seen to it that their mother's books remained in print, and these continue to delight readers both young and old. The Vashon, Washington, home at which Betty wrote her most famous works, is currently operating as a bed and breakfast, called The Betty MacDonald Farm. And there is a two-lane stretch passing the chicken farm where she and Bob lived for four backbreaking years. The street sign reads: Egg and I Road.

Chapter 2
The Egg and I (1947)

Poster for the theatrical reissue of The Egg and I *in 1954.*

Released by Universal-International on June 13, 1947. 108 minutes. Reissued on July 3, 1954. Produced and Directed by Chester Erskine. Based on the novel by Betty MacDonald. Screenplay by Fred F. Finklehoffe. Associate Producer: Leonard Goldstein. Director of Photography: Milton Krasner, A.S.C. Film Editor: Russell F. Schoengarth. Production Design: Bernard Herzbrun. Set Decorations: Russell A. Gausman and Oliver Emert. Music: Frank Skinner. Orchestrations: David Tamkin. Costume Design: Vera West. Make-Up: Jack P. Pierce. Hair Stylist: Carmen Dirigo. Assistant Director: Frank Shaw. Sound Department: Glenn E. Anderson and Charles Felstead.

Cast: Claudette Colbert (*Betty MacDonald*); Fred MacMurray (*Bob MacDonald*); Marjorie Main (*Ma Kettle*); Louise Allbritton (*Harriet Putnam*); Percy Kilbride (*Pa Kettle*); Richard Long (*Tom Kettle*); Billy House (*Billy Reed*); Ida Moore (*Emily*); Donald MacBride (*Mr. Henty*); Samuel S. Hinds (*Sheriff*); Esther Dale (*Birdie Hicks*); Elisabeth Risdon (*Betty's Mother*); John Berkes (*Geoduck*); Victor Potel (*Crowbar*); Fuzzy Knight (*Cab Driver*); Isabel O'Madigan (*Mrs. Hicks*); Dorothy Vaughan (*Maid*); Colleen Alpaugh (*Kettle Child*); Polly Bailey (*Reveler at Country Dance*); William Bailey (*Doctor at Country Dance*); Jack Baxley (*Judge*); Vangie Beilby (*Reveler at Country Dance*); Hank Bell (*Reveler at Country Dance*); Carl Bennett (*Attendant*); Earl Bennett (*Reveler at Country Dance*); Joseph E. Bernard (*Asa Pettingrew*); Robert Beyers (*Kettle Child*); Chet Brandenburg (*Reveler at Country Dance*); Judith Bryant (*Kettle Child*); Robert Cherry (*Goon*); William Desmond (*Spectator at County Fair*); Banjo the Dog (*Sport*); Diane Florentine (*Kettle Child*); Diane Graeff (*Kettle Child*); Jesse Graves (*Porter*); Herman Hack (*Reveler at Country Dance*); Herbert Heywood (*Mailman*); Joe Hiser (*Goon*); George Hoagland (*Reveler at Country Dance*); Jimmie Horan (*Reveler at Country Dance*); Teddy Infuhr (*Albert Kettle*); Jack Kenny (*Townsman*); Ann Kunde (*Reveler at Country Dance*); Nolan Leary (*Announcer*); Ralph Littlefield (*Photographer*); George Lloyd (*Farmhand*); Kathleen Mackey (*Kettle Child*); Louis Mason (*Bergheimer*); Sam McDaniel (*Waiter on Train*); George McDonald (*Kettle Child*); Howard M. Mitchell (*Announcer*); Gloria Moore

*Betty MacDonald, screenwriter Fred F. Finklehoffe (left),
and producer/director Chester Erskine (right) meet to
discuss the treatment for* The Egg and I.

(*Kettle Child*); Frank O'Connor (*Reveler at Country Dance*); Bob Perry (*Reveler at Country Dance*); Charles Perry (*Reveler at Country Dance*); Eugene Persson (*Kettle Child*); Joe Ploski (*Goon*); Joe Recht (*Goon*); Beatrice Roberts (*Nurse*); Hector V. Sarno (*Burlaga*); Sammy Schultz (*Goon*); Nella Spraugh (*Reveler at Country Dance*); Dorothy Vernon (*Reveler at Country Dance*); Robert Winans (*Kettle Child*).

With the end of World War II in 1945, Americans' moviegoing habits began to change. An estimated ninety million citizens were lining up at movie theaters, waiting to see the weekly offerings. But with ticket prices edging up to forty cents apiece (up from twenty-three cents just seven years earlier), patrons were demanding better entertainment than had been provided during the troubled war years. Those in charge at Universal Studios heard these demands and changes were soon on the way.

On November 12, 1946, Universal merged with International Pictures. A new regime was in place, led by the former president of RKO, Leo Spitz, and former production head at 20th Century-Fox (as well as MGM's Louis B. Mayer's son-in-law), William Goetz.

J. Cheever Cowdin and Nate J. Blumberg stayed on as heads of the studio's parent company, Universal Pictures. The main goal for Universal-International (U-I) was prestige. No more western programmers, serials, and quickly made pictures that clock in at under seventy minutes. It would be first-class all the way. We are talking more British films, starring British actors with real British accents. Stories by British writers like Charles Dickens, and a new version of *Hamlet*, this one starring British actor Laurence Olivier, and written by that most British of all British authors, William Shakespeare. Meanwhile, pink slips were issued to those whose luster had faded, including the youthful soprano Gloria Jean, cornball comedian Andy Devine—even two British actors, Basil Rathbone and Nigel Bruce, the once-popular onscreen incarnations of Sherlock Holmes and Dr. Watson. Escaping the dreaded axe were Deanna Durbin and the comedy team of Bud Abbott and Lou Costello. After all, the studio needed *something* to fall back on if Shakespeare and Dickens failed to pay the light bill.

The Screenplay

With *The Egg and I* an unqualified literary hit, it seems only natural that Hollywood would try to get in on the profit taking. U-I won the bidding war for the then-impressive sum of $100,000 (approximately $1.4 million by 2021's monetary standards). But considering what a hot property *The Egg and I* was in Hollywood circles, the novel has surprisingly little narrative. It was incumbent upon screenwriter Fred F. Finklehoffe and producer/director Chester Erskine to create a proper framework for a feature film. They also had to adapt the novel in a way that would pass muster with the Production Code. The first order of business was to christen the Bob Heskett character with his wife's second husband's last name, MacDonald, thereby hiding the fact that one of the film's principal characters had been divorced, a taboo of the time.

Although often criticized as a hindrance to artistic freedom, the Production Code, which was rigidly enforced beginning in 1934 and lasted well into the 1950s, contributed to what is now considered the Golden Age of Hollywood. Please hear us out. If *The Egg and I* were made today, without having to avoid the elements of the novel once prohibited by industry standards—vulgar language, references to do-it-yourself abortions, and the so-called "humor" associated with outhouses and other personal functions—it would be a different kind of film entirely.[3]

Betty MacDonald's tome is at times quite harsh, particularly regarding Puget Sound's local inhabitants, the Native Americans in particular. MacDonald attributed her disdain for these indigenous people, specifically the men, to the unkind way they treated their wives. The characters Geoduck and Crowbar of the film version would exhibit none of the drunkenness, abuse, or lack of basic hygiene ascribed to the Native Americans of the novel. Geoduck (named for a large saltwater clam native to the coastal waters of western Canada and the northwest United States) and Crowbar are comic characters, to be sure, but they were not designed by the screenwriters as racial stereotypes. Their tireless work ethic is a perfect counterpoint to the supreme laziness of their entitled White boss.

This brings us to the Kettles. It must be said that Maw and Paw (as the names are spelled in the novel) are, frankly, unappealing characters—crude, manipulative, filthy, and criminal in their cruel neglect of the animals in their care. Had the screenplay depicted the Kettles as they are in print, it is doubtful—make that *extremely* doubtful—that they would have been spun off into their own series. In addition to rounding off the Kettles' edges (and changing the spelling to the more agreeable Ma and Pa), Erskine and Finklehoffe wisely added some new characters: Tom Kettle, Ma and Pa's eldest, and most accomplished, son; "Smiling" Billy Reed, the roving salesman with his rhyming couplets; and femme fatale Harriet Putnam, who provides the ideal conflict between the newly wed Betty and Bob.[4]

The screenplay also contained elements that were necessarily cinematic. There is, for example, an entirely invented sequence

---

3   As if to prove our point, in 1980, well after the dissolution of any sort of production code, an ultra-low budget, independently made movie bearing the title *Loose Shoes* was introduced as fodder for the quickly diminishing drive-in crowd. One of its tasteless movie parodies is called "A Visit with Ma and Pa." The sequence is a sad foretelling of the kind of "gross-out," adolescent "humor" that would permeate teen comedies for decades. As portrayed in this dreadful film, Ma and Pa Kettle are reduced to crass caricatures.

4   Reportedly, Harriet was based on a woman named Lesley Arnold, who set her sights on the real Betty MacDonald's second husband, Don.

involving a forest fire that threatens the MacDonald farm. Shooting this spectacle would require five cameras, four of which were operated by remote control. The inferno was started by the special effects crew at sundown and raged until sunrise, with towering flames leaping more than 150 feet into the sky. The Los Angeles, Burbank, and Glendale fire departments received more than a hundred calls from concerned citizens.

Of course, a film needs more than just a good screenplay and plenty of action; it needs the right actors to fill the roles. And in the case of *The Egg and I*, the casting directors outdid themselves.

The Cast

Starring Claudette Colbert as Betty MacDonald . . .

Claudette Colbert.

Claudette Colbert (1903–1994), listed by the American Film Institute as the twelfth-leading female screen icon, was born Emilie (Lily) Claudette Chauchoin in Saint-Mande, Val-de-Marne, France. Thrice nominated for an Academy Award, she won the Oscar for her role as a spoiled, runaway heiress in the 1934 romantic comedy *It Happened One Night*, directed by Frank Capra and co-starring Clark Gable (both of whom also received Oscars for their contributions). That same year she starred as the Queen of the Nile in Cecil B. DeMille's spectacular *Cleopatra*. Equally comfortable with comedy and drama, Claudette gives one of her most winning performances in *The Egg and I*. This was due, in part, to her prowess at physical comedy. In the screen treatment, the forty-three-year-old actress is nearly dropped when her husband attempts to carry her over the warped threshold of their farmhouse; she is forced to wallow in a muddy pig pen that had been liberally sprinkled with powdered fish meal (something to keep her porcine co-star interested); she takes a fall off the roof while carrying shingles and—through the miracle of editing—lands unceremoniously in a water barrel. By the end of filming, Claudette had suffered a bruised shin, a wrenched shoulder, a stubbed toe, a burned arm, frostbite, and scattered bruises as reminders of her time as a screen farm wife.

Fred MacMurray as Bob MacDonald . . .

Fred MacMurray.

Colbert's co-star in this and six other feature films is thirty-eight-year-old Fred MacMurray (1908–1991). Best remembered as Steven Douglas, the befuddled single father on the CBS-TV series *My Three Sons* (1960–1972), MacMurray had been cast as romantic leads in light comedy roles in films beginning in 1935. By 1943 he was the fourth-highest paid star in Hollywood. Although he never trained as an actor, he thrived when portraying complex characters, like the passion-driven insurance agent Walter Neff in Billy Wilder's 1944 film noir *Double Indemnity*, who plots with his seductive girlfriend Phyllis Dietrichson (Barbara Stanwyck, another frequent co-star) to murder her husband and collect on his life insurance policy. *The Egg and I*, a soufflé in comparison, required far less acting ability from the affable MacMurray. Although he fared better than Colbert when it came to making this film, he did suffer one rather serious injury, ironically enough, at the hands of his co-star. In a rather frivolous scene, he and the seductive female owner of a neighboring farm are having what appears to Betty to be an intimate conversation. In a jealous rage, she takes off one of her high-heeled shoes and throws it at Bob's head. Colbert, a petite lady, underestimated her throwing arm, as the shoe's sharp heel punctured a small artery in MacMurray's scalp. Blood ran down his face, onto his neck and staining his white shirt. He was promptly attended to at the studio's hospital. As a precautionary measure, a sponge-rubber heel was used for the final take.

Marjorie Main as Phoebe Kettle ("Call me Ma!") . . .

Marjorie Main.

The actress who is still remembered as Ma Kettle came into this world (with the assistance of her maternal grandfather, Dr. Samuel McGaughey) as Mary Tomlinson on February 24, 1890, in the tiny town of Acton, located in rural Marion County, Illinois. Mary had an older brother, Samuel, and a sister who died at the age of twelve. Her mother's name was Jennie; she was a devoted housewife. Her father, the Reverend Samuel J. Tomlinson, was a Disciples of Christ minister. Due to Reverend Tomlinson's career, the family moved from church to church during the next several years. From Acton, they transferred to Indianapolis, Indiana, where he was the pastor of Hillside Christian Church. After four years in that post, he accepted two other positions: first in Goshen, and then in Elkhart. By the early 1900s, the family had managed to settle down on a farm in Fairland.

Mary, a shy little girl, had a typical country upbringing. A bit of a tomboy, she climbed trees and waded in the river. Shy or not, she also displayed a sense of theatricality, which struck some of her neighbors as strange. Dancing wildly and enacting scenes from plays was not the type of behavior usually associated with a minister's daughter. Without realizing it, her actions related directly to her father. On special occasions, the reverend would read aloud from the works of Charles Dickens. Had he known this would be the result of his entertaining readings, he might very well have stuck to the Bible.

Mary attended public schools in Fairland and Shelbyville. Her higher education (a rarity for young women in those pre-suffrage years) began at Franklin College in Fairfield, in 1905. But something vital was lacking in her curriculum. Mary was inclined toward the theater, a career choice deeply disapproved of by her strict father and members of their provincial community. The independent-minded young lady transferred to the Hamilton School of Dramatic Expression, completing a three-year course in 1909, at the age of nineteen. There would be no looking back. She accepted a position as an instructor at Bourbon College in Paris, Kentucky, only to be discharged a year later when she had the temerity to request a salary increase.

The classically trained tragedienne, c. 1920s.

Her fledgling career gained some momentum while studying dramatic arts in Chicago and New York City. She received her first salary for acting—$18 a week—for her portrayal of Katherina in *The Taming of the Shrew*. Although her stern father had softened somewhat concerning his daughter's career choice, Mary decided to use as her stage name Marjorie Main. This, she hoped, would be less likely to embarrass her family and, besides, her chosen moniker had a sense of importance to it. As she explained to an interviewer, "There's main entrance, main event, main street, main everything. Why *not* Marjorie Main? Besides, it's an easy name to remember."

Her next acting job was on the Chautauqua circuit. A typical Chautauqua bill might include a speaker touting patent medicines, guaranteed to cure everything from rheumatism to consumption. There would also be theatrical recitations from the works of Shakespeare or Dickens. More than anything, it was necessary that the actor project to the last row of seats in the tents or open-air venues. With her deepening, gritty voice, Marjorie never failed to capture and hold an audience's attention.

After a stint in vaudeville, Marjorie's theatrical career began to take off. In 1916, she toured in the play *Cheating Cheaters* with John Barrymore. Her Broadway debut followed two years later, with a role in *Yes or No*. One of her most fascinating opportunities came in 1921. "The Family Ford," a comedy sketch written by and starring W. C. Fields, was performed at vaudeville's mecca, B. F. Keith's Palace Theatre. The premise (which would be integrated in two of Fields's films) features a "typical American family" taking out their tin lizzie for a day of picnicking. Without being granted admittance, the henpecked husband and bullying father (Fields) blithely motors onto the grounds of an estate, where he, his domineering wife (Main), and their bratty kids make a mess of the manicured lawn. This was, in a way, a preview of the "fish-out-of-water" situations that Ma and Pa Kettle would later face.

During a five-month tour in Fargo, North Dakota, Marjorie was part of a traveling Shakespearean repertory company. It was at this time that she met a psychologist and lecturer by the name of Dr. Stanley LeFevre Krebs; the two were married on November 21, 1921. Dr. Krebs, a widower with a grown daughter, was substantially older at fifty-seven than his thirty-one-year-old bride. Marjorie, however, was deeply in love with this distinguished gentleman, so much so that she was willing to put her acting career on hold and devote her time and energy towards him. Tending to his every need and acting as his booking agent for his many speaking engagements, Marjorie was, for a while at least, as happy as she had ever been or would be. She also claimed to have been inspired by her insightful spouse: "I learned a great deal about people from my husband. An understanding of people is essential to any actor worth his salt."

Still, this subjugation of her own ambitions slowly began to wear on her.

"Dr. Krebs wasn't a very practical man," she admitted. "I didn't figure on having to run the show. I kinda tired of it after a few years." She claimed that she and the doctor separated, but that, in the eyes of the law, they remained husband and wife.

Returning to acting with renewed enthusiasm, she was cast in *The Wicked Age*, a 1927 comedy satire in three acts, by Mae West. The plot was conceived while the playwright was in jail after having been prosecuted on moral charges for her hit show *Sex*. Marjorie was exactly the type of woman West preferred to cast in her

Marjorie Main (right) had an uneasy working relationship with the Dead End Kids in Little Tough Guy, *a Universal offering of 1938. Pictured, left to right: Hally Chester, Gabriel Dell, and Billy Halop. Pictured at lower left (top row, left to right): Bernard Punsly, Billy Halop, and Hally Chester; (bottom row, left to right): Gabriel Dell, David Gorcey, and Huntz Hall.*

vehicles. Being rather matronly—even at thirty-seven—Marjorie would never be compared physically to the hour-glass-shaped comedienne. Playing La West's burlesque queen mother, Marjorie was only two years the star's senior, West having been born in 1892. Unfortunately, the reviews for the show were so bad that it closed after a run of nineteen performances.

Marjorie made the first of her eighty-five movie appearances in the 1929 Vitaphone short *Harry Fox and His Six Original Beauties.* Capitalizing on her homely, middle-aged appearance, Marjorie was one of the so-called "beauties." Her first feature was *A House Divided* (1931), which she had played on Broadway for exactly one performance prior to its closing in 1923. Directed by William Wyler and starring Walter Huston, the film version has Marjorie in what amounts to a walk-on as one of the gossipy townspeople. Still, it was a step in the right direction. Talkies had supplanted silent films, and stage-trained actors were much in demand. Marjorie rose to the challenge by recreating some of her other stage roles on film, including one as a servant in *Music in the Air* (1934), which stars former silent movie queen Gloria Swanson and features a score by Jerome Kern and Oscar Hammerstein.

Marjorie could only work part-time, especially when Dr. Krebs was stricken with cancer. On September 26, 1935, he died at the age of seventy-one. Losing her husband marked the lowest point of her life: "I was brokenhearted, and I desperately needed work as much to occupy my mind as to make a living."

One of the stage roles that sustained her was that of Mrs. Martin, a gangster's mother living in a run-down tenement in the groundbreaking Sidney Kingsley play *Dead End* (1935). The Broadway run lasted for 687 performances, of which Marjorie was in 460. When it was adapted for the screen, producer Samuel Goldwyn purchased the property for $165,000, a record amount at that time. He hired Lillian Hellman to write the screenplay, William Wyler to direct, Gregg Toland to shoot it, and filled the cast with heavyweights from the theater and motion pictures— Joel McCrea, Sylvia Sydney, Wendy Barrie, Claire Trevor, and Humphrey Bogart. Marjorie reprised her deeply moving role as the long-suffering mother of Hugh "Baby Face" Martin, played by Bogart, who had likewise appeared in the original Broadway production. At one point, she was directed to slap him across the face and call him a "dirty yellow dog." When it came time to put this scene on film, Marjorie was not about to be held back. According to Bogie, she had "slugged me raw-faced" by the final take. Also in the cast were some ragamuffin street urchins played by Gabriel Dell, Huntz Hall, and Leo Gorcey.[5] Marjorie kept to herself during the run of the play, avoiding confrontations with the abrasive juvenile actors. *Dead End*, a commercial and critical success, was nominated for four Academy Awards, including one for Best Picture of 1937.[6]Other pictures of note that year to feature Mar-

---

5   As breakout stars, they would go on to appear together in melodramas for Warner Bros., known as the Dead End Kids. Later, working at the poverty row studio Monogram, the team was identified as the East Side Kids; at Universal, they were called Little Tough Guys. Ultimately, the team's leader, Leo Gorcey, along with agent-turned-producer Jan Grippo, refashioned the group as a slapstick team called the Bowery Boys, and starred in a slew of low-budget comedies aimed at the youth market, beginning in 1946.

6   It lost to MGM's *The Great Ziegfeld* (1936).

Marjorie Main and Wallace Beery in a tense moment from Wyoming *(1940), the first of their seven co-starring films.*

jorie were *Stella Dallas* (with Barbara Stanwyck) and *The Man Who Cried Wolf* (with Lewis Stone, best known as Judge Hardy in the Andy Hardy series).

Marjorie was memorably teamed with Wallace Beery (1885–1949), replacing the late Marie Dressler, with whom he had starred in such classic early talkies as *Min and Bill* (1930) and *Tugboat Annie* (1933). Dressler died of cancer in 1934, leaving a gaping hole in the film industry. Beery was a one-of-a-kind screen presence as well, a rough-hewn, hard-drinking individual whose brash characters seemed to be in a perpetual (albeit comical) bad mood. Offscreen, the man was anything but funny. He was known for his cruelty to his co-stars, particularly when those co-stars were women. His relationship with Marjorie bore that out. The problems were evident during the shooting of their first film together, *Wyoming* (1940). Her performance as the town's blacksmith was considered by many critics to be her finest thus far. According to a 1941 review in the *New York Times*, "Wallace Beery has found the perfect foil in Marjorie Main, all right. And, perhaps more than either he or his Metro bosses bargained for, a competitor who comes close to stealing his best scenes in the film."

This obviously did not sit well with Beery. Neither did his co-star's formal approach to acting. Beery only learned his lines to

a point, ad-libbing the rest as he saw fit. Main, with her classical training, stuck closely to the script. When Beery would begin
to make up his own dialogue, Main was confused, which nega-
tively affected her timing. "I've always been extremely conscien-
tious in my work and his behavior sometimes unnerved me," she
later told an interviewer. As the crusty actor refused to discuss the
matter civilly with her, Marjorie appealed to Beery's close friend
Leo Carrillo. His advice: "Just look at him and listen to him, and
when he stops talking, say your line." It worked, and Main was
cast opposite Beery time and again, in *Barnacle Bill* (1941), *Jackass
Mail* (1942), and *Bad Bascomb* (1946). Their seventh, and final,
onscreen teaming was in *Big Jack* (1949). Speaking to a reporter on
the set, he made no bones about his dislike for his frequent co-star:
"She's blown her lines thirteen times on this one take. If I have to
make another picture with her, I'll have a heart attack." His words
proved prophetic. Wallace Beery died a few days later, on April
15, 1949, of a heart attack. He was sixty-four. Many years later,

*Although she had no children of her own, Marjorie Main (left) was often
cast in motherly roles. In this case, she plays Mrs. Fisher, a woman deeply
concerned about the welfare of her daughter, Amy (Marilyn Maxwell,
right). The Show-Off (1946).*

when being interviewed by Hollywood columnist Army Archerd, Marjorie said, "Don't go expecting me to say anything nice about Wallace Beery, because I won't."

Marjorie's celebrity in the early years of World War II was such that she was able to draw a stadium full of people when she revisited her home state of Indiana. A true patriot, she was there to encourage the sale of Series E bonds, issued by the U.S. War Department. By one account, she personally helped to raise a half-million dollars, an especially great sum in 1942. Metro-Goldwyn-Mayer, realizing Marjorie's unique appeal to moviegoers, signed her to a seven-year contract in 1940; that contract would be renewed for an additional seven years in 1947. Although she usually played a maid, a cook, or a farm wife, she was occasionally given an opportunity to do something different. In the busy year of 1941, she appeared in a supporting role in *A Woman's Face*, starring Joan Crawford. In that stark melodrama, Marjorie wears her hair slicked back and speaks with a heavy European accent. That same year she gave a bravura performance as a landlady in *The Trial of Mary Dugan*, a role she often professed to be her favorite. At one point in that turgid courtroom drama, Marjorie

As with her maternal roles, Marjorie (left) was hardly a cook in real life, but she played an outstanding one in film after film. Case in point: Summer Stock *(1950), with Judy Garland (right).*

dramatically throws herself to the ground to demonstrate the exact position in which she discovered a murder victim. In addition to her performance as Ma Kettle, she is fondly recalled by film buffs for her roles in some classic musicals made by MGM. *Meet Me in St. Louis* (1944), *The Harvey Girls* (1946), and *Summer Stock* (1950), all starring Judy Garland, benefitted greatly from Marjorie's adept comic skills.

One of the clauses of a studio contract was that an actor could be loaned out to competing studios for individual assignments. MGM loaned out the fifty-six-year-old actress for Universal's *The Wistful Widow of Wagon Gap* (1947). Set in 1880s Montana, it was a time and a place "where men were men—with two exceptions," a reference to the film's co-stars, Bud Abbott and Lou Costello. The wistful widow of the title is Marjorie as Mrs. Hopkins, a tough-talking farm wife with seven rowdy kids, whose husband is accidentally shot to death by the inept Lou. A local law states that "he who kills a husband becomes the guardian of his wife and

Lou Costello (center) tries to cozy up to Marjorie Main (right), the star of The Wistful Widow of Wagon Gap *(1947). Bud Abbott (left) looks on with disapproval.*

children."[7]Lou has no choice but to become an overworked farm-hand for the tyrannical Widow Hopkins. Costello was known as a cut-up on the sets of his movies and frequently ad-libbed when he went up on his lines. In the outtakes from the film, Marjorie serenely stands by as Costello makes one out-of-character joke after another. Apparently, her negative experience with Wallace Beery was paying off.

Her next film assignment was a loan-out to Universal to play Ma Kettle in *The Egg and I*. In preparation, Main stated that she had read the novel a dozen times through; she did the same with the screenplay, all the while making notes in the margins on how best to deliver each line. Her insights into the character of Ma Kettle gave Marjorie an opportunity to engage in one of her favorite professional pastimes. "I have a feeling for costumes," she said. "I read a script, confer with the producer or director about what kind of woman it is, and then usually ask for the right to work out my own wardrobe. On the majority of my films, I've done my own costumes, and for the Kettle series my motto was 'If it's wrong, it's right.'" As for Ma's hair style: "I figured out the owl's nest hairdo, calling on my girlhood memories of hundreds of overworked farm wives back home in Indiana."

Percy Kilbride as Franklin Kettle ("Pa's the name") . . .

Percy Kilbride.

The actor who made Pa Kettle a believable, beloved character was born Percy William Kilbride to Elizabeth (née Kelly), a native of Maryland, and Owen Kilbride, a Canadian, in San Francisco, California, on July 16, 1888. One of Percy's first jobs was as a theater usher when he was just eleven years old. A year later, he made his stage debut, playing an 18th century French dandy in a local production of Dickens's *A Tale of Two Cities*. When the United States joined the

---

7 The story is reportedly based on an actual law that existed in Montana in the 1800s.

war effort in Europe in 1917, Kilbride answered the call, serving as a private in the U.S. Army, Company B, 317 Infantry, 80 Division. Following this, he was back before the footlights, appearing with regional stock companies.

Kilbride made his Broadway debut in 1928 in *The Buzzard*, which closed after a handful of performances. Still, he was cast regularly; his stage credits stretch throughout the thirties. Like

The serious young thespian, c. 1920s.

many of his colleagues during the early sound era, Kilbride was called west by movie producers looking for actors who were comfortable with dialogue. His celluloid debut was in the Carole Lombard Pre-Code vehicle *White Woman* (1931). He was soon back in New York City, performing in one play after another.

Opening at the Lyceum Theatre on October 18, 1940 was *George Washington Slept Here*, a comedy in three acts by Moss Hart and George S. Kaufman. The story concerns a young urban couple who are seeking a more peaceful lifestyle in the country, only to find frustration and stress. Percy Kilbride is perfectly cast as Mr. Kimber, described by critic Bosley Crowther as "a dead-panned, laconic hired hand." It is Kimber's primary duty, it seems, to continually relay the bad news of the next needed renovation, all done in Kilbride's trademark slow-paced, lilting New England accent. Radio comedian Jack Benny had seen the show on Broadway and was so impressed that he returned to see it five additional times. It was purchased for him as a vehicle by Warner Bros., adapted for the screen by Everett Freeman, and directed by William Keighley. To make the film a Benny vehicle, his character of the husband, as opposed to the wife in the play, is the one to buy the old house in the hopes of bringing it up to code. The constantly mounting costs and frustrations inherent to a remodel perfectly suited the star's manufactured tightwad image. For added insurance, he insisted that Kilbride reprise his role in the movie version. Appearing in scenes with the seasoned comic actor proved extremely challenging for Benny. Every time Kilbride opened his mouth to utter one of his seemingly harmless lines, Benny would break up. It took innumerable takes to get each completed scene in the can. Benny later said that Kilbride was quiet, friendly, and a bit on the eccentric side. Principled to the nth degree, he would not accept a dollar less nor more than what he felt he was worth. One anecdote that adds credibility to this characterization involves a bill for $3.10 that he turned in to the studio's accounts department. As he quietly explained, the extra dime was used to purchase a soft drink on his way home from a shoot.

Once Hollywood heard the gales of laughter Percy Kilbride could evoke from the simplest scene, he was cast as variations of the same laconic character in other films, such as *State Fair*,

Two consummate actors at work: Percy Kilbride (left) and Charles Winninger (right) in the Rodgers and Hammerstein musical-comedy State Fair *(1945).*

released by 20th Century-Fox in 1945. The Rodgers and Hammerstein musical-comedy features Charles Winninger and Fay Bainter as Mr. and Mrs. Frake, an Iowa farming couple, whose adolescent children, Margy (Jeannie Crane) and Wayne (Dick Haymes), experience life's highs and lows while vacationing at the Iowa State Fair. Kilbride is Mr. Miller, a neighbor of the Frakes,

Percy Kilbride (center), Dana Andrews (left), and Linda Darnell (right) in the film noir Fallen Angel *(1945).*

and a bit of a crepe hanger. He can always be counted on to find the negative in any given situation. Kilbride perfectly embodies this character, with a face and voice that one columnist compared to "an old rusty gate in the summertime."

Although he was hilarious in these hayseed roles, Kilbride had proven that he could play disparate roles with equal precision. This is borne out in another offering from 20th Century-Fox in 1945. *Fallen Angel* is a film noir, starring Dana Andrews, Linda Darnell, and in her final role for nearly two decades, Alice Faye. Percy has a memorable scene as Pop, the owner of a roadside diner. After seeing his performance in *The Egg and I*, however, everybody came to know him only as Pa.

Johnny Berkes and Victor Potel as Geoduck and Crowbar . . .

Johnny Berkes.

Johnny Berkes (1895–1951) earned some acclaim as a baggy-pants comedian on Broadway in the 1920s. When stage roles dried up, he went to Hollywood, where he appeared in such low-budget features as *Mr. Celebrity* (PRC, 1941) and *Bowery at Midnight* (Monogram, 1942). He has the distinction of being the first actor to play Geoduck, one of Pa Kettle's two

Victor Potel.

Native American handymen. His all-but-silent cohort, Crowbar, is played by Victor Potel (1889–1947). Potel's career began in 1910, when he was employed by the Chicago-based Essanay Film Manufacturing Company to portray comic rubes in westerns in support of the screen's first cowboy star, "Broncho Billy" Anderson. Later, in the sound era, Potel was selected by Preston Sturges as a member of his stock company. In all, he appeared in an estimated 430 films during his thirty-eight-year career.

Esther Dale as Birdie Hicks . . .

Esther Dale.

Birdie Hicks is the quintessentially judgmental "Church Lady," and Esther Dale (1885–1961), the actress who portrays her, does so with almost frightening conviction. Born in Beaufort, South Carolina, Esther Dale began her career as a lieder singer in Berlin, Germany. In her first Broadway play she was cast in the title role of the holier-than-thou, real-life temperance activist Carrie Nation. Dale, with her haughty bearing and authoritative voice, must have been the ideal casting choice. She made her first film in 1934, *Crime Without Passion*, an existentialist story of a psychotic lawyer played by Claude Rains. The directors of this unusual film were Ben Hecht and Charles MacArthur. Following that success, Esther Dale became one of Hollywood's most in-demand character actresses. Not one to be typecast, she is perhaps best remembered as Shirley Temple's kindly Aunt Genevieve in 1935's *Curly Top*. Birdie's hypochondriac mother is played by Isabel O'Madigan (1871–1951). Born in St. Louis, Missouri, O'Madigan got her start in films in 1912.

Richard Long as Tom Kettle...

Richard Long.

Young Tom Kettle is the very antithesis of his parents. Where Pa is lazy and unambitious, Tom is hardworking, industrious; where Ma is boisterous and quick to anger, Tom is even-tempered, soft spoken. The actor who played him was Richard Long (1927–1974), a former Chicago boy. In 1944, the Long family relocated to Hollywood, where he was a senior at Hollywood High. A talent scout from Universal was told by some drama students of the new leading man in a play then in rehearsal. Despite having what might be described as natural ability, Richard had only taken drama because he needed the credits for his English requirements. Fate, however, has a mind of its own. Two years later, Richard Long was under contract to U-I.

Louise Allbritton as Harriet Putnam...

Another character missing from the novel but vital to the movie is Harriet Putnam, an incredibly sexy, independent woman who owns and oversees the premier Bella Vista Farm. She is played by the incredibly sexy Louise Allbritton (1920–1979). Louise was the only child of L. L. and Caroline Greer Allbritton of Oklahoma City. Soon

Louise Allbritton.

after her birth, the family moved to Wichita Falls, Texas. The girl's mother died when Louise was a child, and her father did his best to parent a beautiful daughter whose only ambition in life was to become an actress. He sent her to the University of Oklahoma, where she studied journalism. After two unfulfilling years, she quit and moved to California, where she joined the Pasadena Playhouse. While apprenticing there, she tried unsuccessfully to get film work, purportedly because she was too tall. Her luck changed when a scout from Columbia Pictures spotted the statuesque Louise. After making two pictures for Columbia, she signed a seven-year contract with U-I.

Donald MacBride as Mr. Henty . . .

Donald MacBride.

A dear friend of Miss Putnam's—and an important, potential business contact for Bob and Betty MacDonald—is the surly Mr. Henty, played by Donald Mac-Bride (1889–1957). Born in Brooklyn, New York, MacBride made his show business debut on the vaudeville and Broadway stages as a teenage singer in such shows as *George White's Scandals*. Taking a chance on Hollywood, he appeared in a few silents, then returned full-time to films in the 1930s, essaying a variety of interesting parts in more than a hundred comedies and dramas. One especially memorable role was in the 1938 Marx Brothers romp *Room Service*, in which he portrays Gregory Wagner, the exasperated supervising director of the White Way Hotel in New York City. Groucho, Harpo, and Chico (along with a twenty-two-member theatrical company) have run up an enormous bill and refuse to leave, causing Wagner to have a conniption fit. His quirky use of the epithet "Jumping Butterballs!" is among that film's few comic highlights. Other notable credits for MacBride include his role as a flustered hotel clerk in *My Favorite*

Wife (1940), an ex-con and ringleader in *High Sierra* (1941), and an Irish politico in *The Dark Horse* (1946). As a rule, he was usually cast as by-the-book police officers, such as Inspector Vance in *Murder Over New York* (1940).

Billy House as "Smiling" Billy Reed...

Billy House.

"Smiling" Billy Reed is an overly familiar, rhyming salesman who is nothing if not persistent. He is played most convincingly by the rotund William House Comstock, better known as Billy House (1889–1961). The Mankato, Minnesota–born actor, writer, and musician performed in minstrel shows, circuses, vaudeville, Broadway plays, motion pictures, radio, and television. While working as a clown for the Gentry Brothers Circus, the three-hundred-pound Billy entered a fat-man contest in Texas, easily winning the title. He was repeatedly used by Walt Disney animators as a live-action model for their cartoon characters. For example, he was filmed dancing, and his movements were studied to create the actions of "Doc" in *Snow White and the Seven Dwarfs* (1937). He was also the model for one of the pirates on Captain Hook's ship in *Peter Pan* (1953).

And Ida Moore as Emily.

Ida Moore.

A final character, a little old lady named Emily, may not have been especially significant to the story but she provided the film with one of its most vivid portrayals. Emily was played by Ida Moore (1882–1964), a tiny, elderly, twinkling-eyed actress, who came from Altoona, Kansas.

Although she made her film debut in 1925, she did not devote herself fully to acting until the mid-forties, when she was in her sixties. Her role as the delusional mountain woman who had occupied the farmhouse prior to the MacDonalds is a showstopper.

Promoting the Film

The real Betty MacDonald makes an appearance as herself in the trailer for *The Egg and I*. Despite a lack of experience before the camera, she seems quite self-possessed as she tells moviegoers how the film version of her novel is "perfectly wonderful" and "very, very funny." The music accompanying the trailer is the film's theme song, written by Frank Skinner; this later became the instantly recognizable opening theme to the Kettle pictures.

Pre-release buzz was also generated when Claudette Colbert and Fred MacMurray enacted their roles in a thirty-minute audio adaptation on the January 4, 1947 broadcast of *This is Hollywood*. A longer version, also featuring Colbert and MacMurray, could be heard on the May 7, 1947 episode of *Lux Radio Theatre*. The roles of Ma and Pa Kettle in that radio play were voiced by William S. John-

stone (1908–1996) and Elvia Allman (1904–1992). Johnstone, a distinguished radio actor, is perhaps best known for having portrayed the title character of *The Shadow* for five seasons, from 1938–1943. Elvia Allman is well remembered by classic TV fans for her many portrayals of harsh female authority figures, including the chocolate factory forewoman in the hilarious *I Love Lucy* episode "Job Switching" (originally aired September 15, 1952).

Elvia Allman.

The Carthay Circle Theater, Los Angeles, c. 1940.

She even shares a brief scene with Marjorie Main in *The Kettles in the Ozarks* (1956).

One publicity event for *The Egg and I* that was recorded for posterity by newsreel cameras was a beauty contest featuring chickens. Comic-actor Billy House (Billy Reed in the film) poses with the winner, seen unhappily wearing a tiny paper crown, which it quickly shakes off. The film's premiere was a much grander affair—but then, *anything* would be. It was held at the Carthay Circle Theater, located at San Vicente Boulevard in Los Angeles. The Carthay, built in 1926 by developer J. Harvey McCarthy, was one of the most ornate movie palaces of its time. The opening-night premiere of *The Egg and I* was held on March 27, 1947 and was also covered by the newsreels. A stylishly dressed Marjorie Main is shown arriving in a limousine at the theater's covered entrance. She briefly stops while walking the red carpet to acknowledge the hundreds of fans cordoned off behind velvet ropes. In the grand tradition of Hollywood premieres, searchlights scan the night sky.

And now, if you will please take your seat, the picture is about to start.

The Storyline

Our tale begins in a snug motel room, a corner of which is stacked with a mound of luggage and a hand-lettered sign, read-

Betty (Claudette Colbert) and Bob (Fred MacMurray) MacDonald.

ing "Hitched." Bob Mac-Donald attends to his nighttime ablutions while Betty is the picture of the nervous bride on her wedding night. Wearing a pretty (though Production Code modest) peignoir, she waits expectantly in bed. Meanwhile, her husband appears to have only one thing on his mind—chickens. He blithely tells her that he has resigned from his position as customer's man for Saddle, Finch, Tanner, Pease, and Stuck and purchased a farm, a chicken farm, high up in the mountains on forty beautiful, fertile acres. Right after their honeymoon, he tells her, they will be traveling to the farm where they will live full time, raising thousands and thousands of chickens all by themselves. So smitten is Betty that all she can say is, "Whatever my husband chooses to do, it's all right with me!"

Bob MacDonald's truck carries livestock and supplies to his newly purchased chicken farm.

Oh, you naïve girl, you.

In their old pickup truck, which is loaded down with crates of live chickens secured to the roof, and, in the back, a goat, a sheep, and a milking cow, the MacDonalds make the long trip to their new destiny. At one point, Betty's fashionable hat blows off her head, landing in front of the goat. The inevitable happens.

"*He's eating it!*" she says in disbelief.

"Don't worry," Bob reassures her; "it won't hurt him."

After a long, tiring journey, the couple arrives at their dream farm. Did we say *dream*? By the looks of it, a better description of it would be *nightmare*. The lot is overgrown, the buildings are in an advanced state of decay, and the ramshackle house looks like it hasn't been inhabited by anyone for decades—except for maybe a family of raccoons.

"Where's the house?" Betty asks, looking right at it.

"That's it right there!"

"Oh," she says, crestfallen. "It needs a new coat of paint."

"The agent told me there isn't another house like this in the whole county," Bob says, his wife's sarcasm sailing directly over his head. "Come on, I'll show it to you!"

Picking up his bride in his arms, Bob decides to carry her over the threshold. But then, things never go smoothly like they do in the movies. The door is jammed, and Bob nearly drops Betty, who says tactfully, "Darling, you'd better put me down." He does. Putting all his weight against the door, it begins to give way. He pushes again, and then again. A moment later, both the door and Bob land with a *bang* on the wooden floor.

The tour resumes, with the proud homeowner spouting such platitudes as "Hasn't it got a lot of *character*?" and "They sure don't build house like this nowadays!" and "This is the kind of place where you can *really* get down to living. No running water, no Frigidaire, just plenty of elbow room." Betty, meanwhile, is surveying the cobweb-strewn living room.[8] She also comes face to face with a memorable

---

8   No studio ever had more flair with cobwebs than did Universal. Their set designers became expert at replicating them while making classic horror films in the early thirties, including Tod Browning's *Dracula* (1931).

character from the book: Stove—a massive, foreboding antique cookstove. Adjusting one piece of it, another piece falls off, and then another. "You and I, my friend, are not going to get along *at all.*" Betty says before leaving to search for Bob.

On the first night in their "dream home," Betty and Bob face every homeowner's fear—a leaky roof.

That night, the rains come, and wouldn't you know? The roof over the bedroom leaks . . . everywhere.

"Some of the shingles must've come loose," Bob says, unfazed.

With buckets in place to catch the rain, Betty, sniffling like she's coming down with a cold, wraps herself in pillows and blankets while attempting to get comfortable in the old bed, with its worn mattress and loudly creaking springs. Bob snuggles in next to her and begins to plan ahead: "Just think, Betty, this is probably where we'll be spending the rest of our lives. Doesn't that give you a wonderful sense of security?"

Betty sneezes.

"Now then," Bob says, all business. "Everything's got to be scheduled. You can't leave farming to chance; farming is enough of a gamble as it is. By June we should have at least a half-dozen sucklings. We'll have a calf in July; and then, along about August," he says smiling sentimentally, "we can begin to think about more important offspring."

"Oh, darling," Betty says, delighted.

"Maybe five or six hundred of 'em."

She frowns. "Five or six hundred *what?*"

"Well, chicks, of course!" Bob says. "Maybe even *more*, if we're lucky!"

"I'd like to raise something besides *chickens*, you know," Betty says.

"Oh," Bob smiles. "We'll have plenty of those, too. I'm counting on at least five; three boys and two girls."

"*All at once?*"

"No, one at a time," he says generously. "Let's schedule that for a year from today." He picks up a day-at-a-glance calendar and points to the date: Sunday, May 11th—Mother's Day." Looking at each other with doe eyes, Bob lowers the lamp until the room is pitch black.

In the darkness, Betty sneezes again.

It is still dark as pitch when the alarm clangs at four thirty in the morning. A rooster crows in the distance. As Betty struggles to open her eyes, her wide-awake husband is in the kitchen, whistling cheerfully and cooking bacon. "Betty," he says, "come on, wake up! Are you going to lie there in bed forever? Come on, get out of there; I've got breakfast almost ready."

Betty looks out the window at the darkness. "It's still *night* out!" she protests.

"Whattya' mean, *night?* It's four thirty! Half the morning is gone!" He chuckles. "I let you loll in bed because it's the first day, but from now on you've got to be up in the morning at four o'clock sharp!"

As a counterpoint to Bob's deliriousness at having found his true calling in life, we see a rather predictable (yet mildly amusing) montage of Betty attempting to chop wood and saw a branch from a tree (while seated on it, no less), and collect eggs from the protective chickens—all without the slightest bit of success. It doesn't take long for her to realize that life on an egg farm isn't all it's cracked up to be.

Betty (right) and Bob (left) meet Pa Kettle (center).

One morning, while Betty is laboring in her well-tended vegetable garden, a dilapidated mule-drawn wagon rolls thoughtlessly into it. The man at the reins is sixty or so; he is also short, slight, and unshaven. His moth-eaten sweater is out at the elbows and held together by oversized safety pins, and his black trousers are held up with a loosely tied piece of rope. He is cordial, and has a highly distinctive, slow-paced delivery, with more than a hint of New England to it.[9]

---

9   In J. W. Williamson's study, *Hillbillyland* (Chapel Hill: University of North Carolina Press, 1995), he refers directly to this scene when he writes: "Colbert, as MacMurray's doubting but dutiful wife, struggles to do the right rural thing and plants her little perfect garden. But intruding into this symbol of conventional effort come the legs of mules and then a wagon wheel, which rudely tromp on the rosy expectations of capital investment. Pa Kettle has arrived."

"Just dropped in to say 'Howdy,'" he says, chivalrously doffing his derby.

"Howdy," Betty says, unenthusiastically.

"Howdy," he repeats. "Ma told me to come by to invite ya' on over to the house. We're your neighbors, just down the road a spell. Kettle's the name. Folks call me 'Pa,'" he says, offering her a dirty hand to shake.

Accepting the hand smilingly, she says, "Nice to know you, Pa."

Bob drives up and exits his truck. After being introduced by Betty, Pa says, "Just wanted to tell you that as long as we're neighbors, you can count on us for anythin' you might be needin'. Just step in and ask for it; be glad to lend a helpin' hand."

"Well, thanks, Mr. Kettle, that's very nice of you," Bob says.

Noticing the newly cut lumber stacked neatly in the back of Bob's truck, Pa asks casually if he might have one or two of them. "I'm fixin' the barn and haven't had the chance to get into town," he explains confidentially. "Won't be needin' more'n two—or so," Pa says. Bob is generosity personified as he slides a few boards out of the back of his truck. He looks a little less generous when Pa asks for just a few more, and a few more after that. In all, that makes nine two-by-fours. Of course, now that he has the boards, he needs some nails, say three pounds or so? Oh, and a hammer and a saw. "Kids been usin' my saw and plumb ruined the edge; couldn't cut butter with it now."

"Well, I'll give you a hammer and saw," Bob says, his ire beginning to show. "But I'll need them back after a couple of days."

"Send it back to ya' as soon as I'm through with it," Pa assures him.

As Pa steps onto his carriage to leave, Betty approaches him and says sarcastically, "Say, you'll have to paint the place, won't you? Have you got any paint?"

"Come to think of it, I ain't," Pa says. "Ya' got any red ya' can spare?"

"No, we've only got green."

"Green'll do," Pa says magnanimously. "I ain't particular." Saying which, he gives the signal to his mule and off they go.

Betty is happily putting the final polish on Stove and stands back to admire her work. "*There*," she says. "I'll bet you never looked this good in your *whole* life."

Just then, a pipe breaks open, and out pours enough soot to re-blacken Stove. Betty registers her disgust, yelling, "Oh—*you*!"

While in this frazzled state, she catches a glimpse of two Native American males, peering ominously through the kitchen window. "*Indians!*" she screams, making a mad dash outside to find Bob. "*Indians!*"

Bob is in the chicken coop, conversing with Tom Kettle, the eldest of the fifteen Kettle children. A bright, serious, clean-cut young man, Tom tells the hysterical Betty that the Indians are just Geoduck and Crowbar, two fish salesmen well known to the area. They are harmless, he insists.

"You've been seeing too many westerns," Bob laughingly says to Betty.

Bob attempts to give Betty a lesson in egg gathering, but she insists that the chickens won't let her; besides, she says, "It seems kind of cruel to break the family up so early." Bob escorts her to the chicken coop, where he has her attempt to take some eggs out from under the roosting chicks. Not surprisingly, there is plenty of squawking and wing flapping. Bob, who can remove the eggs with nary a peep from the mother hens, agrees to take over that chore on a regular basis. Betty is then assigned to feed the pig. This three-hundred-pound black Tamarack sow, who answers to Cleopatra, clearly has a mind of her own.[10] When she gets out of the pen, Betty tries to corral her back in by saying, in her sternest voice, "You get back in there *this instant!*" But her ineffectual words land on deaf pig ears. Betty pulls those ears instead, an action that only causes the neophyte farmer to lose her grip and fall backward into the muck. While she is in this highly undignified state, a station wagon pulls up in front of the house. Out from the car steps a

---

10 Naming the pig after the Queen of the Nile was an obvious wink at the role for which Claudette Colbert was best known.

Bob attempts to coach Betty on the fine points of gathering eggs from protective hens.

beautiful young lady, her blonde hair bobbed in the same style worn by Joan Crawford in *Mildred Pierce*; a fashionable tweed coat is perched jauntily about her enormously padded shoulders.

"Having trouble?" she asks in her melodious voice. "Maybe I can help."

Striding into the pen with utter confidence, she effortlessly leads Cleopatra back to captivity. Bob shows up just then and seems instantly captivated by this ravishing lady farmer. "Well, *that's* the idea!" he says admiringly. "You certainly have a way with pigs!"

"Hello," she says pleasantly. "I'm Harriet Putnam, Bella Vista Farm."

Before giving Miss Putnam his undivided attention, he gingerly assists his fetid wife back to a standing position. Harriet explains that she has dropped by just to "look around." Bob suggests a guided tour instead. And before escorting his elegant visitor away, he turns to Betty and suggests she get cleaned up: "That's not exactly *perfume* you're covered in."

The mortified Mrs. MacDonald makes her way to the house. Nothing will do right now except a hot, soapy bath. But another intruder is there to deter her from her quest: "Smiling" Billy Reed, a rotund, overly cheerful salesman, wearing a pinstripe suit and a straw boater. Blocking the front gate and lifting his hat, he says cordially, "How *charming* we look today, Madam!"

"We don't look anything of the sort," she says, absolutely defeated. "*Who* are you?"

"The best friend the farmer's wife ever had—'Smiling' Billy Reed!" And then, his slogan: "'Whatever you need, see Billy Reed!' That's me." He points to his truck, a traveling store, with its open, back panel revealing numerous built-in shelves and apothecary drawers, all filled with sundries of every description.

Betty is in no mood for hard-sell tactics. Telling this stranger to get out of her way, she adds, "Right now, I don't need *anything* except a bath."

"*Bath?*" Billy Reed says, raising an index finger. "Soaps of the Orient, perfumes from Paree, bath salts from the Isle of Capri!"

Betty asserts herself: "I don't have time—"

"*Time*, the lady says. I've got all the *time* in the world. I've got alarm clocks, grandfather clocks, wristwatches, pocket watches—"

Betty, who had rushed ahead of this predator, slams the screen door in his face.

Undeterred, he promptly lets himself in, one slogan after another emanating from his grinning face: "If at first you don't succeed, try again, says Billy Reed."

His persistence is matched only by Betty's resistance. "*Please!*" she says, "I've *got* to change my clothes!"

"*Clothes?*"

"I *know*," she says, interrupting his spiel. "'If it's clothes you need, see Billy Reed.' I don't *want* anything. Now will you *please* go away!"

This seems to do the trick. "You can turn me down and send me away," he says, smiling to the last. "I'll be back again—another day!"

Walking onto the back porch, Betty sees Bob pull up in his truck, but he's not alone. A scruffy, speckled dog is tied on the flatbed. Betty is thrilled. Bob, however, informs her that this dog

Despite Bob's warnings, Betty quickly bonds with their "vicious" dog Sport (played by Banjo).

is *not* a pet; in fact, he's vicious, but according to Doc Wilson, the one who sold the dog to Bob, he's a wonderful hunter.

"What's his name?" Betty asks.

"Sport."

"Hi, Sport!" Betty says affectionately as she reaches out to pet him.

The dog growls ferociously.

"Betty, don't touch him—I tell you he's *dangerous*. It takes a steady nerve to handle a dog like this. You'd better leave him to me and stay away from him."

Betty (and, later, Bob) learn soon enough that Sport is anything but vicious. In fact, he's a big old baby who wants nothing more than to curl up in Betty's lap.

Betty walks up behind Tom Kettle as he is tinkering with an unusual-looking addition to the chicken coop. She expresses interest in the young man's invention and listens attentively as he explains just how it works. Betty, impressed, compares him to

Betty makes friends with young Tom Kettle (Richard Long).

Thomas Edison, a compliment humbly brushed off by Tom. She then asks if he is currently in college, a question that immediately seems to depress him. He would like very much to continue his education—maybe even study to be an engineer—there just isn't any money coming in at the Kettle house, he says, and besides, he has to be there to help out his ma, given his pa's lazy demeanor.

"I think I'll have a talk with Ma one of these days," Betty says.

With the Kettles being their closest neighbors—just five miles up the road—Betty decides to pay them a visit. While making the long trek on foot, a Model T Ford pulls up alongside her. The driver is Birdie Hicks, a member of "the oldest family in the county." She is accompanied, as always, by her elderly, somewhat batty, hypochondriac mother. Betty explains that she was just on her way to visit the Kettles. Birdie insists that Betty get in the car; she'll drop her off. Seated in the back seat of this antique automobile, Betty listens as Birdie drones on about what a worthless bunch the Kettles are.

"Pa Kettle been borrowing things from you, has he? You'll never get it back, no matter what it is. Lazy, shiftless fools, the whole lot of them. A disgrace to the community." Birdie's mother constantly chimes in, talking nonstop about miracle pills and medical check-ups. Ignoring her mother, Birdie asks Betty if she and her husband are the young couple that took up that abandoned farm up in the mountains.

"It wasn't exactly *abandoned*," Betty says defensively. "We *bought* it ..."

"Well, *nobody* else wanted it; that's why I call it *abandoned*. What on earth did you buy it for? You'll never get it to look like anything; too run-down. As for farming, it'd be nothing short of a miracle if ya' get anything to grow up there. Better folks than you have tried it and failed."

Pulling up in front of the Kettles' farm, Betty gets out of the car.

"Eyesore of the community," Birdie opines. "I've tried my best to get 'em run outta the county, but it's no use. Are you *sure* you want to stop off *here*?"

"Positive," Betty says.

"Can't say you weren't warned," she says as she drives off, her mother still talking non-stop about her liver.

"Thanks for the lift," Betty calls out politely.

The Kettle farm looks as bad as Birdie says it does: a falling-down fence, a sagging roof, slanting porch, junk all over the yard, and a sign out front that reads: "Beware of the Childrun (with the "n" in the misspelled *childrun* drawn backward, Our Gang style). As she makes her way to the front door, she encounters one Kettle child after another: some are hanging from trees like monkeys; others are beneath the house, sawing the support beams; two giggling girls are on a makeshift seesaw; some boys are playing in a large hole they had dug in the dirt yard. They seem friendly enough, although they clearly lack a sense of direction. Betty next encounters a pack of dogs, barking and carrying on something awful. Ma Kettle comes running out the door and onto the porch. A sturdy, zaftig woman of about fifty, with a loud, raspy voice and a ready laugh, she is far too busy with her unruly brood to be anything but disheveled. Her hair is a mess, and she is wearing

The Kettle farm, described by Cape Flattery's Birdie Hicks as "the eyesore of the community."

a tattered house dress, over which is a sugar sack apron. In what Marjorie Main later described as "a grand entrance," Ma grabs a pan and whips it at the dogs (a quick yelp is heard). "Quit that dad-blasted noise! Clear outta here! Go on, you!" she yells at the top of her lungs. Then, in an abrupt change of manner, she laughs heartily and becomes the most hospitable neighbor anyone could hope to visit.

"*Well, well,*" she says welcomingly, "ain't this nice? I was won-derin' jes' how long it'd be 'fore ya' got so lonesome you'd just *have* to come pay us a visit! Come on into the kitchen so's we can talk a spell!" Shooing some chickens off the couch, Ma says, "Take a seat and make yourself to home."

"Thank you," says Betty politely.

"Just throw that stuff anywhere," May says, referring to the junk on the couch.

Betty carefully removes some old household items—a dirty pot, blankets, toys—before sitting down.

Ma tends to the enormous stew pot on the kitchen stove, stir-ring its bubbling contents with a wooden spoon. "So, ya' like your

Preparing to set the table for dinner, Ma first rids the kitchen of some unwanted guests.

place?" she asks the now-seated Betty. Ma gives her a once-over. "Ya' don't look like no *farmer* to me!"

Betty laughs. "I'm not, actually. But I'm learning!"

"Well, there ain't nothin' like it," Ma says, laughing, "if it don't *kill* ya! You're stayin' for dinner, of course."

"No, thank you," Betty answers pleasantly.

"Oh, *course* you will," Ma insists. "Enough here for an army. Now, if you'll just give a hand settin' the table."

Betty is only too happy to be of assistance. As Ma takes the dishes down off the shelf, she says, "Tom was tellin' me what nice people you was."

"We think a lot of him, too. Tom's a good boy, and he's so *clever.*"

"*Ain't* he, though?" Ma agrees wholeheartedly. "Not a mite like the rest of the Kettles—makes me . . . *wonder* sometimes," she adds, pregnant with meaning.

"Seems a shame he had to leave school," Betty says sympathetically.

"Well, you know how it is," Ma replies, reaching a hand inside her blouse to scratch, "we need Tom around the place. Pa ain't much for workin' and"—she pushes a cackling chicken off the table—"the rest of the young'uns seem to take right after him."

"Well . . . just the same," Betty says seriously, "he ought to go to college."

Ma is incredulous. "*College?*" she rasps, then sends another chicken flying. "What fer?"

"Oh, just so he can make something of himself," Betty says earnestly. "You wouldn't want to watch him go to seed around here, would you?"

"Course not," Ma says. Resignation sets in: "Tain't fer me to say."

Betty stands close to Ma, her enthusiasm mounting. "If he had a *little* help, he could make out all right at the state university. There's no tuition, and he could work."

"Ya' been talkin' to him?" Ma asks quietly.

"He wants to go *so bad*," Betty says.

Ma's eyes fill with tears and her usually loud, raspy voice becomes soft, tender. "Yes, I know he does. I can see it in his eyes." She seems to consider the idea for a moment: "Tom got good marks when he was in high school. Not much I can do about it." Ma then thinks it necessary to justify her position: "Goodness knows I couldn't git along without Tom. We ain't got a live buck 'cept what *he* brings in. The last money I saved up, Pa took and bought two minks that he was gonna breed an' make us all a fortune. Only they up and *died* before they got around to breedin'!" And then, downcast again: "Pa's a bit of dreamer that way." And then, back to business: "Now, if you'll just get hold of that bell, we'll let the varmints know dinner's ready."

"Oh, *sure!*" Betty says and stands in the open front doorway, ringing the large bell over her head.

"Ya' better stay out of the doorway, honey, 'fore ya' git trampled on!" Ma warns from across the room.

"*What?*" Betty says, the ringing and the sound of an approaching stampede drowning out Ma.

"I *said*, ya' better stay out of that doorway!"

A dozen Kettle kids, led by Pa, come through the door, nearly knocking down the bell ringer. By the time she regains her bearings, the entire family is seated quietly at the table.

"Sit yourself down anywheres," Ma tells their guest. "We don't stand on no ceremony."

But there is no available spot.

"*Henry!*" Ma says sharply, "move over, let the lady in! Where's yer manners anyways?" The boy to whom she is speaking ignores her. "*Henry!* Ya' hear what I said? Move over and give the lady a place to sit."

The boy looks up. "I ain't Henry, Ma—I'm *Albert*. Henry's over there," he says, pointing to his brother across the table. "Don't ya' remember?"

"Well, whatever yer name is, move over and give the lady a seat!"

The seating arrangement settled, Ma gives her husband the signal: "Okay, Pa," she says.

Pa, his head bowed reverently, lifts his derby and says—quickly slapping away a childish hand from the bread dish—"Much obliged for everything."

An instant later the family, every last one of them, is digging in, devouring Ma's home cooking.

Bob reminds a reluctant Betty that they had agreed to have lunch at Harriet Putnam's.

"Do we *have* to?" she asks, sounding just like a whiny kid.

"Yep."

Bella Vista Farm is as far removed from the MacDonalds' and the Kettles' places as one can imagine. The farm is new, its milking machines are shiny, and the Herefords are fat and healthy.

Bob (who is even wearing a suit for the occasion), and a rather bored-seeming Betty, are in their hostess's well-appointed living room. Bob looks out the window admiringly and says, "It certainly is a beautiful layout. Betty, maybe someday *we'll* have something like this. If we ever get a contract for our eggs."

"Well, I could speak to Mr. Henty for you, if you like," Harriet says helpfully. "He's the agent for Great Western Markets out here. They buy *all* my dairy products."

"Well, I'd certainly appreciate it," Bob says. "We're at the stage where we can handle a steady contract."

"I'll talk to him. He does almost anything I ask him to do," she says, taking a drag on her long cigarette. "He's *such* a dear."

"A *young* man, I take it?" Betty asks.

"Ah, he *used* to be," Harriet replies in that sultry voice, her red lips curling in a half-grin. "He's a little crotchety now, I'm afraid. Besides, he has a *wife*."

"Those were the *old* rules," Betty says.

An awkward silence follows her remark.

Bob asks Harriet if they could begin the tour.

"Of *course!*" she says graciously. "I *love* to show it off. Just wait till we get to the barn and I show you my Speckled Sussex."

"Her *what?*" Betty asks, alarmed.

"*Speckled Sussex,*" Bob explains. "That's a breed of hen. Very special, too."

In her well-organized barn, with all its ultra-modern farming equipment, Bob is clearly in his element. Betty, however, is clearly in hell. "I've got a headache," she says suddenly. Bob is reluctant to go, but Betty insists on leaving right away. She tells her husband to stay if he wishes to. "I'm sure Mrs. Putnam won't mind driving you home . . . once she's through with you." Bob resists that trap and agrees to take his ailing wife home to rest.

"Drop in sometime when you're driving by," Harriet tells Bob. "You haven't seen *anything* yet."

"I'll do that," Bob says. "Don't forget about Mr. Henty."

"I won't."

As Betty settles into the passenger seat of their truck, Harriet approaches the window. "I *do* hope you'll feel better," she says, not quite sincerely. "How often do you get these headaches?"

"Oh, often enough," Betty cheekily responds.

Harriet smiles knowingly. "*Very* interesting. Good-bye."

Back on the road, Betty asks Bob if he finds Harriet attractive.

"She knows an awful lot about chickens!" he says approvingly.

But Betty is convinced that Harriet is scheming to take her husband away from her. For his part, Bob insists he is *not* interested in Harriet Putnam's beautiful house, or her farming equipment, or her cows. He is only interested in chickens.

Oh, and Betty, of course.

Betty opens the oven to remove a large pan full of, not cookies, but live baby chicks! She is overcome by how cute these chirping yellow pieces of fluff are. Bob, as usual, brings her back to reality by saying that by the time she has fed and watered the chicks every three hours, she won't feel so sentimental about them. Betty looks solemnly at the chicks and says, "If you kids had any sense, you'd go right back where you came from."

Bob and Betty spend an elegant night in.

Poor Betty. Her life has no sense of romance. This hits her especially hard one day right after scrubbing the kitchen floor. Exhausted and feeling grungy, she stands up and stretches her overworked back. What a life. She goes into the bedroom to freshen up. Just then, an idea comes to her. With more of a spring in her step, she approaches what is her hope chest, from which she removes her bridal gown. The next scene has her wearing the gown while admiring herself in the mirror. At that instant, Bob returns home. He approaches the bedroom, to which the door is ajar. Espying his lovely wife, he smiles and quietly steps into the bathroom. When Betty leaves the bedroom, Bob sneaks in and decides to do some freshening up himself. A time lapse shows Betty lighting the candles on an elegantly laid table. She looks happy for the first time since she was married. Just then, the bedroom door opens and out walks a tuxedo-clad Bob, looking tall and handsome as can be. The two enjoy a wonderful meal and top it off with a slow dance around the house, while the old-fashioned gramophone plays a 78 of "Let Me Call You Sweetheart."

At one point during this dreamlike interval, the couple suddenly realizes they are not alone. A dour-faced older man, wearing a large, black fedora, is standing in their living room, looking on disapprovingly. He clears his throat, causing the newlyweds to look up.

"You the folks that live here?"

"Why, *yes*," Bob answers.

"I'm Henty," the intruder says. "Great Western Markets."

Realizing that an important business opportunity has just entered his living room unbidden, Bob goes to greet him.

"How do you do, Mr. Henty?"

"Knocked on the front door, nobody answered," the man says abruptly. "So, I come 'round by the back way." Looking at this formally attired couple, he asks, "*Interrupting* something, am I?"

Flummoxed, Bob says, "No, my wife and I were just, uh—*Oh, this is my wife.*"

Bob, and especially Betty, turn on the charm for this old curmudgeon, but nothing pleases him. He refuses a cigar like he was the surgeon general and turns down a drink with the disapproving look of a prohibitionist. Ignoring their nervous overtures to make him feel comfortable and welcome, Mr. Henty begins to sing the praises of Harriet Putnam. "*Wonderful* little lady, Mrs. Putnam," he says with deadly seriousness.

"Oh, yes, *wonderful*," agrees Bob.

Betty's smile is wider than ever. "She's my *dearest* friend."

"She told me you people might have some eggs to sell."

"That's right, Mr. Henty, we have," says Bob.

"Thought I'd drop 'round on the way home, look things over."

"Mighty glad you did," Bob adds, hoping to gain some control over this unexpected business meeting. "Of course, we're not up to full production yet, but I'll be glad to show you the layers we have."

"Won't be necessary. I judge my eggs by the people that produce 'em," says the unsmiling Henty. "'Like chicken, like master,' I always say."

After what seems an eternity, Mr. Henty abruptly asks for his hat. Betty, who goes to retrieve it, finds that Sport has curled up on it. As she removes the battered fedora from beneath their sleeping pet, Bob says uselessly, "Very friendly dog, Mr. Henty. He likes to sit on hats."

Henty leaves with barely a good-bye. Betty and Bob hear his car door slam shut, the engine start, and the motor rev up as he speeds away.

"Well, that's the end of Mr. Henty," Betty says fatalistically.

"Yeah," says Bob in agreement. "Gonna have to eat an awful lot of omelets."

Burrowing into her husband's chest, Betty laughs good naturedly. "Oh, *why* did he have to show up *tonight?*"

Walking toward the door, Bob suddenly realizes that he never *did* carry Betty across the threshold. Betty, recalling the initial failed attempt, opens the door first. And, to the strains of "Let Me Call You Sweetheart," the formally attired Mr. and Mrs. Bob MacDonald cross the threshold together.

To show that Pa has good intentions, he volunteers his "expertise" in helping Bob construct a water tower on their property ("He may not know about anything else," Bob tells Betty, "but he *knows* about water tanks.") Just then, Harriet Putnam's station wagon pulls up.

"Bob, I need your help," she says, sounding desperate.

"What's the matter?" Bob asks, leaning into her driver's side window.

"Just about *everything*. My generator broke down and everything is stopped." After detailing all the work that has gone undone, she says that her foreman has not the slightest idea of what to do. She says this in her softest, silkiest voice, all the while flashing those doe eyes at Betty's husband. Bob quickly agrees to go with her.

"Why don't you get Tom Kettle?" Betty suggests. "He's a genius with machines."

"Oh, I couldn't possibly trust *him*," Harriet says dismissively. "He's such a *boy*. This is a *man's* job."

"I see what you mean," says Betty, folding her arms.

"Mm-hm," Harriet says, her grin resembling the proverbial cat that ate the proverbial canary.

Ma is putting the finishing touches on a quilt when Betty shows up at the front door.

"Come right on in!" Ma says welcomingly.

"I came to bring you something," says Betty. "It's a present."

"For *me*?"

"Yep."

"Jim-in-y *whiz*!" Ma exclaims, opening a box and taking out a garish-looking dress loaded down with ruffles.

"I made it myself," Betty says proudly. "Do you like it?"

"Drat my hide and call me possum! Ain't this sumpin'?"

"I thought you might like to wear it to the dance tonight, so I kind of rushed it at the last minute. You might have to do over a couple of seams."

"I ain't never been so surprised since I don't know when," Ma says gratefully. "First new dress I've had since way back before the war." Holding the Whistler's Mother–type garment against herself, she says admiringly, "Stylish too, ain't it?"

"You'll be the best-dressed girl at the ball."

Ma gives Betty a warm, affectionate hug.

Time to put the coffee on. Ma asks Betty to get some cookies out of the pantry closet. "All right!" she says cheerfully, opening the double doors. Out crashes a mess of household items and jars, making enough clatter to set off the chickens. Betty looks horrified by what she has done. "Oh, I'm *so* sorry!" she says helplessly.

"Pay it no mind," says Ma resignedly. "Just leave it. Might as well be one place as another."

As Betty tries to shoo the chickens out of the pantry, Ma begins to reminisce.

"When I was first married, I was as neat as the next woman. Tried to keep my house and kids clean. But *Pa's* such a lazy old so-and-so. It was *fight, fight, fight* all the time, so finally I gave up. I said, if I can't make Pa change and be neat, I'll have to change and be dirty. Been peace in the house ever since."

Ma shows off her quilt. "Say, ain't this comin' along pretty?"

"It's perfectly beautiful," Betty agrees.

Ma (left) shows off her quilt-in-progress to an appreciative Betty (right).

"Made one every year since I was married. Got 'em in the closet in the spare room—I figger it'll be somethin' real nice to leave the kids when I die."[11]

---

11 This line, incidentally, is one of the few taken verbatim from the novel.

Betty suggests that Ma raise some money by entering one of her expertly made quilts in a contest at the county fair. She could give the money to Tom for college.

Ma is strictly cool on the idea. "Tain't no use. Birdie Hicks'll win. She wrangles things around every year so one of her relations gets on the committee that judges 'em." Ma thinks about it for a moment. "Say, I've got a better idea," she says, her tone suddenly soft and gentle. "When it's finished, I'm givin' it to *you*."

"Oh, no, I couldn't," Betty objects.

"Oh, I got a whole parcel of 'em laid away. Can't think of anybody I'd rather see have it."

The friendship between these disparate women is so authentic, so affectionate, it is a privilege to witness.

Pa returns, perspiring from his brush with labor. The water tower is finished, he announces. Betty now has the luxury of running water in her house.

"Never seen the sense of running water in the house," Ma says, her pioneer spirit as strong as ever. "Rather get mine straight out of the ground, where the good Lord put it."

"I don't hold with too much water anyhow," Pa interjects. "Rusts the bones."

It is the night of the community dance, an event Betty has been looking forward to; goodness knows, there are few entertainments available to those living in the mountains, miles from civilization. That explains the size of the crowd: everyone and his uncle is there, dancing, laughing, eating—just having a grand old time. On the stage is a group of hard-working musicians, playing a forties-sounding dance tune. Ma is there, of course, wearing her frilly, new dress and surrounded by young'uns. She takes an entire roasted chicken out of a basket and proceeds to rip it apart with her bare hands, dividing up the pieces among the kids. Pa's doing his part for the community dance by serving glasses of punch—and something much more potent for those with a taste for it. Bob and Betty, meanwhile, trip the light fantastic. Bob, not exactly a Fred

Astaire (more of a Fred MacMurray), clumsily bumps up against the nearest couple, Harriet Putnam and Mr. Henty.

"I've been working on Mr. Henty here about taking on your egg account," Harriet tells him.

"A recommendation from Mrs. Putnam goes a *long* way in my book," Henty says in his customarily dour delivery. "Of course, we're not taking on new responsibilities just now . . ."

"Don't worry," Harriet says in her best stage whisper, "it's in the bag." And just like that, they disappear into the crowd.

"Quite a character," Betty comments sardonically.

"Yes, he is, isn't he?" Bob says.

"I meant *her*."

Crossing from one side of the dance floor to the other, Betty and Bob once again find themselves next to Harriet and Mr. Henty, only *this* time, they are standing at the desserts table, Mr. Henty bent over a homemade lemon meringue pie. Without looking where he is going, Bob again accidentally bumps into him. Mr. Henty turns around angrily, his nose white with meringue. Bob, more embarrassed than he can articulate, attempts to help the man clean up, but Mr. Henty is implacable: "Never mind! I'll *wipe it myself!*" he says indignantly and stalks away.

"You're certainly not helping me much," Harriet says smilingly to Bob. "I'll see what I can do."

Birdie Hicks, serving as the chairwoman of the refreshments committee, confronts Bob about what she had just witnessed. "You shouldn't have done that to Mr. Henty," she says, scolding him. "He's a very fine man and one of our leading citizens. One thing we don't stand for at these affairs and that's roughhouse. You want to stay around here, you'd better behave yourself, young man."

"Don't worry, Mrs. Hicks," Betty intervenes. "I'll keep an eye on him."

"See that you *do*."

The music suddenly stops. The sheriff has an announcement to make: "I don't like interruptin', folks," he says, "but we've got a little bit of trouble. Is Pa Kettle here?"

"Right over this way, sir!" Pa says amiably from the drinks table.

"Pa, you'd better git along home; your barn's on fire."

"*Jehoshaphat!*" Pa says, a look of pure astonishment on his face. "I *told* you that still of yours would blow up someday and, by golly, it did!"

This comment elicits loud laughter from those gathered.

"*Ma?*" Pa calls.

"We're comin', Pa!" Ma says, quickly gathering up the kids.

The sheriff continues: "That ain't all, folks. You see, a westerly wind blew up and carried the flames over to the woods just beyond. Now we've got a man-sized forest fire on our hands, movin' up the whole valley. We did the best we could, but it sorta got outta hand. Now, I want to suggest that all of you who have homes in that district, that you git along . . ."

"Come on!" Bob says, taking Betty by the hand.

Arriving at their property, which is surrounded by flames, Bob hooks up a hose to the new water tower. Thankfully, it was finished in time to meet this emergency. But when Bob turns on the pressure, the entire structure collapses. Now out of options, Betty and Bob stand by helplessly as all their newly refurbished outbuildings are destroyed.

The following morning, while surveying the still-smoldering embers of their combined labors, the heretofore optimistic Bob feels defeated. He tells Betty that there is nothing for him to do but return to working an office job. It's Betty's turn to step up, something she does admirably. They rebuilt Chicago after that major fire, she reasons; the same was true with San Francisco after the earthquake. If they can rebuild a couple of cities, why couldn't *we* rebuild a *farm*? Bob is overcome by this new side of his supportive wife. They embrace. At that moment, the engines of multiple trucks can be heard close by. Walking toward the sound, they are astonished to see the majority of the county's citizens parked on their property, with the sheriff as their spokesman.[12] In

---

12 The sheriff is played by Samuel S. Hinds (1875–1948). A graduate of Harvard University, he was a lawyer in Hollywood until the stock market crash of 1929 wiped out his savings. At this critical juncture, the distinguished-looking fifty-four-year-old changed his occupation to that of actor. Appearing in more than two hundred motion pictures and several plays, he was ideally cast as politicians, judges, doctors, and other well-spoken authoritarian figures.

The citizens of Cape Flattery converge at the MacDonalds' farm to lend their assistance, following a devastating forest fire. Look closely and you will see Bob and Betty (right, standing by a wood-paneled automobile); addressing the couple directly is the sheriff (Samuel S. Hinds, wearing a black Stetson hat); and to the left (in the wagon with the umbrella) are Pa, Ma, and the Kettle kids.

his speech, he says that everyone has faced tough times, and when they did, their neighbors were there to help. He then explains that every citizen present will donate either materials or labor to help the couple rebuild. The Kettles are there too, of course. Pa grandly offers to contribute nine two-by-fours, three pounds of nails, a hammer, a saw, and a quart of green paint.

Another big event: the county fair. Betty is excited about it, telling Bob she has never been to one.

"You haven't *lived*," he tells her.

"I'll never get a chance to if Ma Kettle finds out I entered her quilt in the competition." At the fair, the atmosphere is one of gaiety. Ballyhooed as "Hawaiian dancers from the island of Hawaii," a group of shapely hula dancers in gossamer skirts undulate provocatively. Geoduck and Crowbar amble by. They are wearing beanies and are generally weighted down with stuffed animals and other prizes they won at the shooting galleries; Crowbar even has a balloon on a stick. A merry-go-round, with its myriad lights and rousing calliope music, is loaded with kids riding colorfully painted horses that bob up and down as they make their endless rounds. At a livestock competition, Bob points out to Betty that the featured heifer is one of Harriet's.

"*Hello!*" they hear at a distance. It's Ma Kettle, once again wearing her new dress and a rather busy-looking hat, loosely adorned with feathers and flowers. She is complaining about the suffocating presence of the Hicks family, who seem to have entries in every contest. "Ya' can't fall down around here without landin' on a Hicks," Ma says, plain-spoken as always.

"I think I'll go along with Ma," Betty says, smiling. "I'm a little tired of cows. Even Harriet's."

No sooner has she left than Harriet Putnam shows up to keep Bob company. Amid the frumpily dressed farm women at the fair, Harriet stands out like a fashion model. She asks Bob to come

Ma (left), Betty (right), and Bob (center) meet at the county fair.

with her to her private box so that he can hold her hand during the judging. Bob readily agrees.

Meanwhile, Ma and Betty are taking their turn on the merry-go-round while chatting and laughing. This is interrupted momentarily by one of the kids, asking Ma for a nickel. Ma rustles around inside her purse until she finds one. Without another word, the girl jumps down from the carousel, eliciting a rebuke from her mother. Ma confides in Betty that she's got so many kids, she can hardly keep track of them. She then looks at Betty purposefully. "Just wait'll you have your'n—you'll see what I mean. How many you countin' on?"

"Oh, just one to begin with," she answers. "But not for some time yet. It's not on our schedule."

"*Schedule?*" Ma repeats, wide-eyed. "They're havin' 'em by *schedule* these days?"

While enjoying lunch with Ma on the fairgrounds, Betty suddenly says, "Hmm, say, we don't want to be late for the prizes."

"You ain't gone and entered somethin', have ya'?" Ma asks.

"Oh, no!" says Betty. "I'm just interested."

Billy Reed saunters by, wearing a black derby, a black jacket and tie, and sporting an ornate-looking ribbon with the word *chairman* printed on it. Betty asks, "Are you *really* as important as all that?"

"Vice president in charge of practically the whole works," he answers boastfully.

Betty is intrigued. "You don't *say!*"

"*Top* man," he reiterates. "Anything you need, ask Billy Reed."

"I'll see ya' later, Ma," Betty says, standing up to leave. "I've got some business to discuss with Mr. Reed."

"You gonna buy something?" he asks, hopefully.

"You come along with *me*," she says as the two leave together.

"Don't let him sell ya' nothin'!" Ma calls after her.

Arm in arm, Bob and Harriet are looking over her Hereford, which has just taken first prize in the livestock contest. As they discuss the modern workings of Bella Vista, Harriet says that farming has left her feeling empty, lonely for companionship. When Bob suggests she sell the farm, she immediately asks him to make an offer. Bob demurs, saying the price would be way over his head. How can you know until you've tried it? she asks seductively. Well, of course, Bob will have to have a closer look at the property; how about next week? How about *right now*? she counters.

What man with a pulse could refuse?

"Ladies and gentlemen," Billy Reed announces grandiosely, "first prize of the patchwork quilt annual contest goes to Mrs. Kettle, better known as 'Ma.'"

Radiantly happy, not to mention shocked, Ma says, "Well, hack me down!"

On her way to congratulate her, Betty stops and says to Billy Reed, *sotto voce*: "You can send over that portable billiard table anytime you're ready."

"Set of encyclopedias, don't forget," he adds just as quietly.

"And a set of encyclopedias," Betty confirms.

Hugging Ma, Betty exclaims, "You *won!*"

"Leapin' Lena, you went and entered that quilt I give ya'."

"I *told* you you'd win!"

"I can't understand it, with all them fine quilts from all over the county."

"Well, yours was the best, that's all."

"*Hmph*," says a disgruntled Birdie Hicks.

Billy Reed approaches Ma, saying, "Here's your ribbon, and here's your check—which I will keep for you in full payment on a brand-new electric washing machine, something you can't do without, Mrs. Kettle."

"No, you don't either," Betty says firmly, taking the check from Billy. "This is for *Tom*. I just saw him . . . Tom! *Tom!*"

She successfully hunts him down and hands him the check. "Now you can go to college! Isn't that—" Suddenly, Betty collapses in a faint. By the time she comes to, she is lying on a cot with a cool cloth covering her forehead. Ma is close by, holding her hand.

"There now, honey, ya' feelin' better? I sent Tom to look for Bob."

"I can't imagine what happened to me," Betty says groggily. "I've never fainted before in my life."

"Ya' better stop in at Doc Wilson's on the way back to town."

"What for?"

Ma looks at her knowingly and says, "Honey, ya' sure ya' looked at that *schedule* lately?"

It is now six thirty in the evening. Betty is back at home and radiantly happy. She is bustling about the kitchen, making another marvelous meal for Bob. Even Stove is cooperating; the meat she is cooking looks succulent and tender. She pours some au jus over it. A half-hour passes, and then another. Before long, it is nine o'clock, and the meat—and everything else on top of Stove—has become dried out, unappetizing. Still no word from Bob, and only Sport for company. At one point he barks, startling her.

She looks up to see an odd, unfamiliar face peering at her through the backdoor's glass panel. Betty welcomes the elderly, uninvited guest in and asks her to sit with her at the kitchen table. The lady identifies herself as Emily. She then introduces

A strange visitor named Emily (left) introduces Betty (right) to her husband Albert (center).

her hostess to her husband, Albert, seen apparently only by herself. Betty is justifiably unnerved by the presence of this mystery guest, not to mention Albert. Emily tells a story about how happy she and Albert were when they had *their* chicken farm. "It was *so* nice," she begins. "Everything was so happy until Charlotte came. She was just a plain, ordinary little white leghorn when she was hatched. But as time went on, she got bigger, and bigger, and *bigger*, and *bigger*, until she was *this high*, higher than a man! And that's when I begun to notice she wasn't friendly. She used to look at Albert and me as if she could peck us right to pieces. It made me nervous, I don't mind telling you. Why, once, when I was getting into bed, I heard a scratching noise and I looked up. And there she was, staring at me through the window. The wickedest look in her eye that I ever saw. Then one night, Albert and me was sitting in the kitchen, having a cup of coffee, just like we are now, when I heard a noise on the porch. Before we could take any notice of it, there was a knock at the door. Knock, knock, knock."

Suddenly, there is an *actual* knock at the door. Betty jumps up, screaming in terror.

In walks the sheriff and a deputy. "Oh, *there* you are, Emily," he says pleasantly enough. "I *thought* I'd find you here."

"Hello, Sheriff. I've been expecting you."

"You've been a bad girl again, Emily."

She giggles like a child and prepares to leave. As she reaches the door, she turns and says lovingly, "Come along, Albert. It's time to go now."[13]

The sheriff stays back for just a minute to make sure Betty has not been unduly disturbed by her encounter with Emily. He explains that she "walks out once in a while and it's up to us to come and fetch her. But it's never any trouble finding her. She always comes to *this* place. She used to live here."

"Sh-She lived *here*?" Betty says, chilled to the bone.

"Yes, she and her husband used to raise chickens. Made a very nice thing out of it, too. Then one day Albert ran off with another gal. We've never seen hide nor hair of him since then. Drove poor Emily plumb loco. Well, good-night, ma'am."

---

13 Director Erskine rather ingeniously uses the P.O.V. of the invisible man as he rises from his chair and exits with his wife and the sheriff's deputy.

Betty, worn out by this strange encounter, sits down and continues to wait for Bob to return. Her eyes grow heavy and, before long, she dozes off, only to awaken with a start. Was that a car pulling up?

"*Bob!*" she calls out.

No, it's not Bob; it's a messenger with a note *from* Bob, stating that she shouldn't wait up; that he would be delayed even longer. As the messenger drives away, Betty sees that it's the station wagon for Bella Vista Farm. So—he's with Harriet Putnam at this very minute! How *could* he, after all she had done for him! Why, she'd given him the best year of her life! Well, that's that. She packs her grip and leaves, but not before taking a brush and some paint (likely green) and writes I'M THROUGH! in all caps with an exclamation point and underscores it for emphasis. Slamming the door behind her, she boards a train and heads home to Mother.

During the couple's extended separation, Betty takes to bed. As the months slowly pass, she is at first besieged by letters from her abandoned husband, all of which she returns unopened. When she does see fit to take the train trip back to Washington State, with her newborn baby girl safe in her arms, she finds that Bob no longer lives in the house they had shared during the first year of their marriage. No, ma'am, the cab driver informs her; *this* is where he lives now. Saying which, he points to the opulent home marked by the sign reading "Bella Vista Farm." Betty is crushed. Harriet Putnam got her man, after all. Leaving Baby Ann with the curious driver, Betty stomps up the walkway and pounds on the door. A bathrobe-clad Bob appears, wondering who could be making such a racket at this time of night. With a minimum of dialogue, he assures his wife that he lives alone, and that on the night she left, he was in tense negotiations with Harriet Putnam to buy her farm as a gift for his wife.

Betty feels like a heel for having so misjudged Bob. Suddenly, she remembers the baby and heads for the door.

"Where are you going?"

"I'll be right back!" she tells Bob gleefully. "I've got a surprise for you!"

Bob *is* surprised—surprised and delighted. All is right again for the MacDonalds. At least it is until one of Bob's employees rushes in the back door to say that the water pipes in the chicken house have "busted wide open again, and them hens is goin' crazy!" Slipping on a hat, Bob says to Betty and Baby Ann: "Don't go away, you two!" and disappears out the door.

Betty makes eye contact with the camera and says, "*See* what I mean? I could write a *book!*"

The Payoff

Released to the nation's theaters on June 13, 1947, the film version of *The Egg and I* was, if anything, an even bigger sensation than the book. Made for a mere four hundred thousand dollars, it grossed $5.75 million (or more than $66 million by 2021 standards), making it the eighth-highest grossing film of the year. The reviews were favorable, for the most part, and virtually every critic singled out Ma and Pa Kettle as the highlight of the picture. *Variety*, for example, raved: "Top laugh-getters of the piece are indisputably Marjorie Main and Percy Kilbride in the main character roles of Ma and Pa Kettle. Both parts present constant temptation to burlesque and hamming. Miss Main and Mr. Kilbride resist the temptation and give an honest interpretation that simultaneously rouses the merriment and tugs at the heartstrings of the audience." On the strength of her textured performance, Marjorie Main was nominated by the Academy of Motion Picture Arts and Sciences as Best Actress in a Supporting Role.[14] The film was also one of Claudette Colbert's most financially successful; she even reprised her role as Betty MacDonald on an episode of *Hollywood Playhouse*, on January 5, 1950. Despite her strong association with the role, she later made it clear that she did not care for it. The reason seems obvious: she and Fred MacMurray were completely upstaged by those damned Kettles. And to think that Ma, Pa, and their brood occupy only twenty-one of the film's 108 minutes!

In the summer of 1950, *Granby's Green Acres*, a summer-replacement for *Lux Radio Theatre*, ran for eight episodes on the CBS network. This was reportedly an unauthorized version of

---

14 She lost to Celeste Holm for *Gentlemen's Agreement* (20th Century-Fox, 1947).

The Egg and I, created by Jay Sommers. The premise of the show has Gale Gordon as a former banker "who knows little about farming and proves it every week." His wife was played by radio (and, later, TV) veteran Bea Benaderet.[15]

In 1951, a daytime television serial version of *The Egg and I* debuted on CBS. Starring Pat Kirkland as Betty, and Bob Craven as Jim (not Bob), Doris Rich as Maw Kettle (a much more sedate interpretation of the role), and Frank Tweddle as Paw, the afternoon serial garnered high ratings, handily beating its competition, *Search for Tomorrow* and *Love of Life*. Proctor and Gamble sponsored the daily

There were the inevitable commercial tie-ins, including sheet music for a song entitled "The Egg and I," and an official, "egg-citing" board game for families to play together.

---

15 Fifteen years later, this radio show would be adapted by Jay Sommers as *Green Acres*, a television sitcom produced by Filmways. For more on that, please see Chapter 13, "The Kettles in Pop Culture."

fifteen-minute-long telecast once a week, but no other sponsors were forthcoming, despite the much-touted ratings. This was most likely because the serial contained primarily humorous content, not the dramatic (and romantic) situations usually associated with, and embraced by, fans of daytime soap operas. As a result, *The Egg and I* was pulled after one season.

The feature film of *The Egg and I,* however, had staying power. It generated so much fan mail that it was reissued theatrically on July 3, 1954. By that time, U-I had cranked out other rustic comedies, including *Feudin', Fussin' and a-Fightin'* (1948), directed by George Sherman and starring twenty-two-year-old Donald O'Connor. The versatile song-and-dance man shows off his abilities while performing a dance to "Me and My Shadow," written in 1927 by Billy Rose and Dave Drewer. O'Connor also revives the 1929 Andy Razof–Paul Denniker song "S'posin'," performed as a duet with the film's perky romantic interest, Penny Edwards. The main draw, however, was the reteaming of Marjorie Main and Percy Kilbride—not as Ma and Pa Kettle, perhaps, but close enough. The story involves a traveling hair-tonic salesman named

Marjorie Main and Percy Kilbride demonstrate their unique onscreen chemistry, even when playing characters other than Ma and Pa Kettle. Feudin', Fussin' and a-Fightin' *(1948).*

Wilbur McMurty (O'Connor), whose ability to run like lightning makes him an asset to the tiny town of Rimrock. The tough-talking mayor of this backwater community, Maribel Mathews (Main), her cohort Billy Caswell (Kilbride), and the inept sheriff (Joe Besser) hold Wilbur prisoner so he can compete in the all-important annual foot race against a rival town. The screenplay, by D. D. Beauchamp, is based on his fictional work "The Wonderful Race at Rimrock." Despite its thin storyline, the film has some entertaining moments. Maribel and Billy even end up as an engaged couple by the fade-out.

Something magical happened whenever Kilbride and Main appeared on the screen. Audience members sat up a little straighter, their smiles became a bit broader, and they could hardly wait to hear what they would say next. Witnessing this reaction numerous times during regular screenings of *The Egg and I* at Los Angeles movie theaters was the film's producer, Leonard Goldstein (1903–1954). By all accounts, Goldstein was a dedicated, enthusiastic man who simultaneously oversaw numerous low-budget films for Universal-International, beginning in 1946. A true visionary as

Joe Besser (left), Marjorie Main (center), and Percy Kilbride (right) infuse some genuine comedy into the Donald O'Connor vehicle, Feudin', Fussin', *and a-Fightin' (1948).*

well, it was he who determined that Ma and Pa Kettle should have a series of their own.

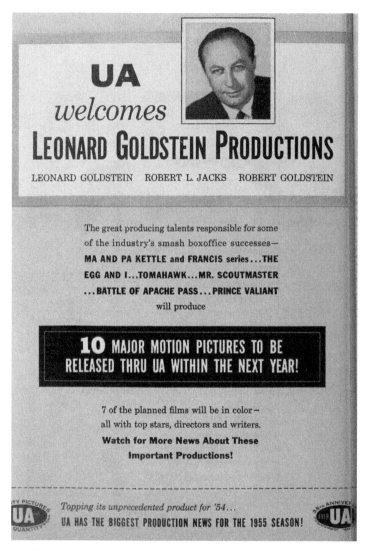

Independent Exhibitors Film Bulletin, *1954 (Vol. 22).*

Illustration by Bob Moore, c. 1949.

PART 2:
THE MOViE
SERiES

Chapter 3
Ma and Pa Kettle (1949)
a.k.a. *The Further Adventures of*
Ma and Pa Kettle

Released by Universal-International, April 1, 1949. 75 minutes. Directed by Charles Lamont. Produced by Leonard Goldstein. Production Management: Howard Christie. Screenplay by Herbert Margolis, Louis Morheim, and Al Lewis. Based on the characters from "The Egg and I" by Betty MacDonald. Music Arranged and Directed by Milton Schwarzwald. Director of Photography: Maury Gertsman, A.S.C. Film Editor: Russell F. Schoengarth. Production Design: Bernard Herzbrun. Art Direction: Bernard Herzbrun and Emrich Nicholson. Set Decorations: Russell A. Gausman and Oliver Emert. Sound: Leslie I. Carey and Richard DeWeese. Wardrobe: Rosemary Odell.

Cast: Marjorie Main (*Ma Kettle*); Percy Kilbride (*Pa Kettle*); Richard Long (*Tom Kettle*); Meg Randall (*Kim Parker*); Patricia Alphin (*Secretary*); Esther Dale (*Birdie Hicks*); Barry Kelley (*Victor Tomkins*); Harry Antrim (*Mayor Dwiggins*); Isabel O'Madigan (*Mrs. Hicks's Mother*); Ida Moore (*Emily*); Emory Parnell (*Billy Reed*); Boyd Davis (*Mr. Simpson*); O.Z. Whitehead (*Mr. Billings*); Ray Bennett (*Sam Rogers*); Alvin Hammer (*Alvin*); Lester Allen (*Geoduck*); Chief Yowlachie (*Crowbar*); Rex Lease (*Sheriff John*); George Arglen (*Willie Kettle*); John Beck (*Party Guest*); Dale Belding (*Danny Kettle*); Ralph Brooks (*Workman Carrying Sign*); Margaret Brown (*Ruthie Kettle*); Melinda Casey (*Susie Kettle*); Harry Cheshire (*Fletcher*); Jack Curtis (*Party Guest*); Russell Custer (*Party Guest*); Paul Dunn (*George Kettle*); Diane Florentine (*Sara Kettle*); Lloyd Ford (*Party Guest*); Jack Gordon (*Townsman*); Teddy Infuhr (*Benjamin Kettle*); Ann Kunde (*Townswoman*); Donna Leary (*Sally Kettle*); Nolan Leary (*Minister*); Wilbur Mack (*Diner on Train*); George Magrill (*Deputy*); Merrill McCormick (*Party Guest*); Sam McDaniel (*Dining Car Waiter*); George McDonald (*Henry Kettle*); Beverly Mook (*Eve Kettle*); Gloria Moore (*Rosie Kettle*); Richard Neill (*Party Guest*); Bob Perry (*Party Guest*); Eugene Persson (*Ted Kettle*); Rose Plumer (*Party Guest*); Snub Pollard (*Townsman*); Dewey Robinson (*Giant Man*); Walter Rode (*Party Guest*); Sherman Sanders (*Square Dance Caller*); Elana Schreiner (*Nancy Kettle*); Charles Soldani (*Indian*); George Sowards (*Party Guest*); Lem Sowards (*Party Guest*); Ted Stanhope (*Dining*

Car Steward); Burk Symon (*Doctor*); Harry Tyler (*Ticket Agent*); Dorothy Vernon (*Party Guest*); John Wald (*Dick Palmer*); Eddy Waller (*Mr. Green*); Robert Winans (*Billy Kettle*).

When Marjorie Main was sent the script for this sequel to *The Egg and I*, she turned it down flat. No use in playing *that* role again, she no doubt thought. But MGM, the company that held her contract, had other ideas. They benefitted financially from her being loaned out, and there was not a thing she could do about it. For the six Kettle films made between 1949 and 1953, Marjorie was still making her standard MGM salary while Universal-International raked in millions in ticket sales. She was entitled to none of the enormous profits, nor did she receive any much-deserved bonuses. Although initially bitter about this iniquitous arrangement, she became aware of the public's deep affection for her signature character. And she frequently said that she would "rather make people laugh than anything else."

James Whitmore and Marjorie Main make an unlikely—and, apparently, uncommercial—team in the 1950 MGM comedy Mrs. O'Malley and Mr. Malone.

Marjorie committed to the project despite being quite ill at the time. A serious sinus condition, one that plagued her for most of her life, had flared up, leaving her feeling weak and uncomfortable. Physicians were brought in to treat her and they agreed that the only way she would improve was to take a long break. Realizing that her absence from the set would cost the studio dearly, however, she agreed to inhale powdered penicillin at frequent intervals during the shoot. When filming stopped for the day, she immediately went home and straight to bed. Watching her performance in the completed film, no one would guess that she had been laid so low. And trouper that she was, she did not miss a single day of work.

Marjorie had another, ongoing issue making life difficult for her. This had to do with her germaphobia. Between shots, she could be found compulsively washing her hands and practicing what would later be known as "social distancing." Stories about her terror of germs were legion in Hollywood. On the day *Meet Me in St. Louis* went into production on the MGM lot in 1943, Marjorie was in her dressing room when she overheard one of her co-stars, Lucille Bremer, sneeze. According to Bremer, the older actress became quite hysterical, crying out, "*Who* is that *sneezing?*" Bremer also recalled that when Marjorie spoke on the telephone, she always wore a surgical mask. Another MGM co-star, James Whitmore, who shared top billing with Marjorie in *Mrs. O'Malley and Mr. Malone* (1950), told an interviewer for Turner Classic Movies that, between takes, the hairdresser had to—in front of her, no less—take out a new comb to fix Marjorie's hair.

In Allan R. Ellenberger's 2011 interview with Margaret O'Brien, the former child star who played Tootie Smith in *Meet Me in St. Louis*, recalled Marjorie as eccentric, but also "fun and nice." While the two were on location for *Bad Bascomb* (1946), both actresses did their best to contend with Wallace Beery. O'Brien also observed that, on location, Marjorie was so fearful of the mosquitos and other bugs that she wrapped toilet paper around her arms to protect herself. Working with one child in a film was apparently fine with Marjorie. It was when she had to share the shot with a group of them, particularly in the Kettle pictures, that she began to worry about contagions. On those days she had to share the set with a dozen or so young actors, Marjorie would alert the crew to "open the doors, air out these sets—ya' never know what these kids are carryin'!"

James Whitmore also recalled that his quirky co-star had the unsettling habit of speaking to her dead husband, sometimes during a take. "Yes, doctor?" she would say to seemingly no one. "Yes, darling, I know, I know, I understand." Following this bit of ghostly advice, she would give an expert reading of any line. Actress/entertainer Debbie Reynolds, then an ingénue at MGM, was another witness to this strange phenomenon. In her autobiography, *Debbie: My Life* (New York: Morrow, 1988), written with David Patrick Columbia, she remembers Marjorie as a consummate professional, but also acknowledges that she was a "funny one." Reynolds writes that on the set of *Mr. Imperium* (1950), Marjorie referred to her husband as "Horace," one of her many arbitrary names for him. While seated next to Marjorie on the set one day, Reynolds heard her say, "Horace, this is a very warm day and I'm tired. Why don't you get me a glass of water?"

She does not record whether he did or not.

On another occasion, Debbie walked past Marjorie in the studio commissary. There she was, seated at the lunch counter, and beside her was an empty stool, reserved apparently for the late Dr. Krebs.

"Say hello to Horace," she told the waitress.

"Uh . . . hello, Horace."

Marjorie continued, "I'll have the ham and swiss on rye toast and Horace will have the egg salad."

Reynolds believed that Marjorie Main was "off her rocker. But she could put on a costume and know her lines, and that was all that counted." She also had this to share about her one-time co-star: "Marjorie was an older woman, who, it so happened, had a real-life bladder problem. She'd be saying her lines on camera and nature would call. Continuing on with her lines, as if it were part of the movie, she'd walk right off the set into her dressing room. You'd hear the toilet seat go up, the toilet seat go down, the flushing, and Marjorie was still saying her lines. Then she'd come right back on the set, as if we hadn't cut, and finish the scene."

Despite her idiosyncrasies, Marjorie was well liked and respected by her co-workers. According to an October 13, 1954 U-I production report, before one early-morning call, Marjorie entered the sound stage, saw a dignified-looking man, possibly a producer, and asked, "Where did I park my car? I know I left it between two sound stages, but I don't remember which ones. Please go and find it for me like a good fellow." Leaving this man perplexed (but willing to do her bidding), she went into her dressing room, calling, "Yoo-hoo!" and "Honey!" thereby summoning hairdressers, wardrobe mistresses, and make-up artists. Minutes after doing this, she spotted the dialogue director, to whom she shouted, "I need to practice my lines. Help me, won't you?"

Charles Lamont (1895–1993) the director of the first, and four subsequent, Kettle films, had this to say about the orderly confusion generated by "Cyclone Marjorie," his nickname for her. "When she squints up her eyes and smiles," he said, "she can get away with *anything*. I don't know of any star who can get so much out of people without ever really demanding anything."

Director Charles Lamont behind the camera.

When film historian Ted Okuda spoke with the retired director, Lamont said that he had a good working relationship with Marjorie Main and Percy Kilbride and praised their professionalism (as opposed to his often-contentious working relationship with Lou Costello). Lamont said that Marjorie and Percy always got along well, although there was an aspect of Marjorie's on-set conduct that puzzled him. When actors film close-ups for two-person dialogue scenes that are to be intercut with medium shots, an assistant director, script girl, or whomever, usually reads the other actor's dialogue offscreen, to help with the cues and pacing. But Percy would graciously read his lines off-camera when Lamont was filming Marjorie's close-ups. Afterwards, Marjorie would start to leave the set and Lamont would say, "Marjorie, aren't you going to read lines for Percy's close-ups?" And she was always willing to do so. Yet Lamont remarked, "I was puzzled why I always had to remind Marjorie. She was a nice woman and great to work with, but I had to keep reminding her to return the courtesy. She didn't take the initiative to do this on her own. I didn't understand why. She wasn't a prima donna, and she liked Percy."

That she did. "Percy is the best deadpan actor in the business, and a true gentleman," Marjorie said. "I can't think of anyone else I respect more than my partner." As for Kilbride: "Marjorie's too busy for temperament. Her gusto and versatility are fascinating." Both had enjoyed long careers, and both relished their rather low

To help promote the March 1949 fifty-city territorial premiere of Ma and Pa Kettle *in Missouri and Kansas, Marjorie Main and Percy Kilbride made a joint radio broadcast over Kansas City's WHB.*

profiles within the industry. "Character actors from the New York stage don't have to die to go to heaven, they go to Hollywood," Kilbride told an interviewer. "After all, when a picture doesn't work out too well, the character actor is never blamed. It's always the producer, or the director, or the stars who take the criticism."

Now, at this late stage in their careers, Main and Kilbride were bona fide stars and, as such, they were expected to help promote a film. The year the first Kettle film was released, the Midwestern Practical Nurses Association bestowed the title "The Most Eligible Bachelor of 1949" on Percy Kilbride. When asked for his response to this honor, the perplexed sixty-two-year-old actor asked, "What woman would want to marry *Pa Kettle*?" As for Main, she was branded the "Most Untidy Housekeeper of the Year" for three years running. In response, innumerable household gadgets and appliances arrived at the studio, including an automatic bed maker. Most were from appliance firms, looking to have their products appear onscreen.

On the set, Marjorie was generally quiet and kept to herself; Percy was outgoing and friendly, although every so often he would go off on his own somewhere, smoking his pipe and studying his lines. When the director returned from a break, it was Marjorie's job to call for her missing-in-action co-star. And she did, Ma Kettle style:

"HEY, PERCYYYYYYYYYYY!" she hollered.

In no time he would show up with a smile, ready for the next take.

The Supporting Cast

Characters from *The Egg and I* who had proven to be either good foils, straight men, or adversaries, were brought back for the sequel. Ma's sworn enemy Birdie Hicks is back, as is the actress who played her, Esther Dale. Richard Long also returns as Tom Kettle. In addition, there are some new actors in now-familiar roles.

Lester Allen and Chief Yowlachie as Geoduck and Crowbar . . .

Chief Yowlachie.

Lester Allen.

Bug-eyed Lester Allen (1891–1949), a veteran of New York's vaudeville and burlesque houses, replaces Johnny Berkes as Geoduck. Sadly, Allen died the year the film was released, making way for yet another actor.

Taking over for Victor Potel as Crowbar is Chief Yowlachie (1891–1966), the stage name of Daniel Simmons. A genuine Native American, he was born on the Yakima Indian Reservation in Kitsap County, Washington.

Emory Parnell as "Smiling" Billy Reed . . .

Born in Saint Paul, Minnesota, Emory Parnell (1892–1979) was originally a concert violinist, but the young man put away his instrument to become a booking agent. In 1930, he officially began his forty-two-year career as an actor, appearing in and narrating industrial films made in Detroit. A tall, rugged individual, he was

Emory Parnell (left) and Percy Kilbride (right).

nicknamed "The Big Swede," and was routinely cast in Hollywood's endless supply of B-pictures.

And Meg Randall as Kim Parker.

Meg Randall.

A new character, Kim Parker, is introduced as the romantic interest for Tom Kettle. Kim is the film's spokesperson for the story's message that a healthy environment can greatly affect growing children, something the Kettles had heretofore known little about. The young lady cast in this thankless role was born Genevieve Roberts in Clinton, Oklahoma, on August 1, 1926. An aspiring actress, she attended the University of Oklahoma's School of Drama as an undergraduate, completing only her freshman year. Taking the stage name Gene Roberts, she was briefly under contract to MGM and 20th Century-Fox. Upon signing with U-I in June 1948, her name was changed to Meg Randall (1926–2018).

The Storyline

We open on a bustling day in Cape Flattery, Washington. The June sun is shining on this picturesque little town in the United States' Pacific Northwest. But in a conference room at the city hall a meeting is being held, one that is not without controversy. Ten citizens are present, each with his or her distinct opinion on the topic at hand. And what, pray tell, *is* the topic at hand? Why, Ma and Pa Kettle, of course. Or, more specifically, their run-down farm.

Mayor Dwiggins turns the floor over to Mr. Simpson. "For the past fifteen years, Pa Kettle's house has been a disgrace to our community—and an unfit place to be lived in. The back yard looks like the city dump."

"*Ain't it?*" another man asks innocently.

"This being the finding of this committee," Mr. Simpson continues, "I therefore move to condemn the Kettle house and to—"

"Hold on a minute, Simpson," interrupts another committee member. "There's a family of fifteen living in that house—or is it *sixteen?* I don't see how we can throw them all out in the wilderness. I think we should give them another chance. Tell them to spruce up the place a bit so that it looks presentable."

"Pa'll *never* spruce up that place and you *know* it," Birdie Hicks says acidly. "He ain't lifted a hand since he moved in, unless it was to borrow something."

The Kettles, meanwhile, are going about their lives. Ma, wearing her sugar sack apron, is at the sink, washing dishes. She carries a stack of plates to the table to set it. As usual, this involves brushing aside squawking chickens, with a loud "*Scat!*" As for Pa, he's in the bedroom, looking for his long underwear.

"They're hangin' on the clothesline," Ma informs him. "I just washed 'em."

"What'd you wanna go and do that fer? I just put 'em on the other day."

"Ya' put 'em on last winter."

Pa is perplexed by what he considers his wife's quest for perfection. "Well," she reasons, "*somebody* has to keep things neat around here."

"Gotta hand it to you, Ma," Pa says admiringly. "You've done wonders with the place." The "place" is its usual mess, with a clothesline suspended across the living room and livestock asleep on the couch. Ma lets Pa know that it's not easy taking care of fourteen kids.

"*Fifteen*, ain't it, Ma?"

Ma stops, puts a finger to her mouth and says, "Oh, yeah. I keep forgettin' about Benjamin."

One kid she never forgets about is their eldest, Tom. She and Pa are proud beyond measure of that boy. He has just graduated from Washington State University, where he majored in animal husbandry. He has even designed a revolutionary chicken incubator he hopes to patent and market. Yes, sir, that's one apple that fell far from the tree, not like the other bunch of ruffians. "There's a boy you can *really* call a self-made man," Ma says.

"Yes, indeed," says Pa, feeling prideful. "Like father, like son." He stands up, posing nobly in profile. Looking about the house, he reaches out his arms histrionically and exclaims, "Carved this out of the wilderness."

Ma looks downright irritated.

Time for a little entertainment. "Think I'll turn on the radio," he says, seated once again. The radio looks to be a mid-twenties model, with a large, circular speaker. Pa lifts his chair and lets it drop with a *bang*, causing the kitchen window to go up and slam shut, which in turn sends a cloud of dust everywhere. The radio, as it does every time Pa goes through this ritual, blares out "Tiger Rag."[16] Meanwhile, he takes out his tobacco pouch and begins to fill his pipe. He lifts his chair again, landing with another *bang*, as the window once more goes up and slams shut, emitting more dust. The radio stops.

"*Too* loud," he says, as he continues fidgeting with his pipe.

"What about the roof on the henhouse, Pa?"

"What *about* it, Ma?"

"You said you was gonna fix it one of these days."

"When did I say *that*?"

"Last March."

"Well, then I *will*."

"Will *what*?"

"*Fix it* one of these days."

"What about the well you was gonna dig in the back yard?"

"I'll do that *another* day. Can't do *everything* in one day, Ma," he explains patiently.

"Don't mess up my floor with that tobacco, Pa."

"Sorry," he says. "It's this old pouch. Ought to be getting my new one any day. Sent for it weeks ago."

"Where'd ya' get the money to send away for a tobacco pouch?"

"Oh, it don't cost no money. Just had to fill in the coupon with my name and address and write a few words about King Henry Tobacco. Ad said that *everybody* that answered would get a free pouch."

"Oh," Ma says, unimpressed. "I still think ya' outta fix that roof on the henhouse. How'd *you* like to sit in the broilin' sun all day and have to lay eggs besides?"

---

16 "Tiger Rag," a jazz standard, was first recorded by the Original Dixieland Jazz Band in 1917.

"I don't think I could do it," he answers, straight-faced as always.

Three Kettle boys—Benjamin, Danny, and Henry—come running into the house, eager to share some news with Ma. Danny's voice is the loudest: "Mayor Dwiggins and the whole town council and Birdie Hicks and her ma—they're havin' a meetin' right now!"

Ma, obviously concerned, says, "Wait a minute, uh, Billy—"

"I'm *Danny*," says Danny.

"Uh, Danny, what's this meetin' all about, son?"

"It's about *us*, Ma," Henry answers. "*This* place. They're meetin' to see about condemnin' it."

"*Condemnin'* it?"

"Yeah," Danny adds. "I just run into Mayor Dwiggins's boy, Fred, and he told me it wasn't his *pa's* fault. *Birdie Hicks* said this place was a menace to public health—and an eyesore to the town!"

Ma smiles sardonically. "We could've expected it. Birdie Hicks has been sore ever since I beat her at the quilt contest at the county fair."

"Where'll we *go*?" Benjamin asks in a state of panic. "Where'll we *live*?"

"Oh, calm *down*, Benjamin," says Ma, shaking him by the shoulder. "Votin' to condemn is one thing. Carryin' out the order is another."

"What can we *do* about it, Ma?" the frightened boy asks.

"I ain't sure yet, but if they *do* try to put us off this property, *we'll* be ready for 'em. Danny, go get the rest of the kids."

"Okay, Ma." The boys beat a hasty retreat.

With a determined expression on her face, Ma walks to a corner of the parlor and picks up a shotgun.

The town council meeting continues. A wire has just come through the Western Union office, informing Pa Kettle that he has won first prize in a slogan contest for King Henry Tobacco: a brand-new model house of the future, with every modern convenience. The mayor is thrilled. Why, this could put Cape Flattery on the map! In fact, he decides to deliver the extraordinary news himself, at the Kettles' front door. This is easier said than done.

Ma has arranged the house and front yard like a fortress, with the kids stationed at key locations to ward off intruders. The arrival of a cavalcade of black, official-looking cars puts every sniper, armed with either a slingshot or a BB gun, on high alert. While attempting to reach the house, the mayor and his assistant, Sam Rogers, are the targets of some expertly aimed projectiles.

"Say, wait a minute, kids!" the mayor says pleadingly. "All I want to do is talk to your pa!"

There is no cease fire. The two men make a dash for the door as shots ring out in quick succession. A pea shooter is added to the artillery. Realizing there is no way to safely reach the house, the two men hide behind a couple of barrels.

"Hey! *Hey*! *Pa Kettle*! Are you *home*?"

Cut to an open window. Ma appears, shotgun cocked. "Yes, *we're* home, and we intend to *stay* here!"

"Oh, no, you don't understand!" the mayor objects, standing up. *Bang!*

The two men dive under an old, discarded bed frame in the yard. "You don't understand, Ma!" reasons the mayor. "I got a telegram for Pa!"

"A *telegram*, huh?" Ma says suspiciously. "Why didn't *Alvin* bring it over? And what are those *others* here for?" she asks angrily, referring to the council members standing at the edge of the yard. "To *gloat*? This is *our* property, Mayor, and ya' ain't gonna trick us off it!"

"We're not tryin' to trick ya'," the mayor says sincerely while peering out from beneath the bed frame. "Will you let us come in under a flag of truce?"

"Might as well get it over with," says a resigned Ma. "HOLD YOUR FIRE, KIDS!"

His Honor is granted temporary asylum. Out from their hiding places emerge the various Kettle children, their weapons still in their grubby little hands.

"HEY, PA! *PA*! COME HERE A MINUTE," Ma shouts at the top of her lungs. "MAYOR'S GOT SOMETHIN' TO SAY TO US."

Pa walks into the scene with Geoduck and Crowbar not far behind. "Howdy," he says, as friendly as ever.

The mayor goes into politician speech mode: "(*Clearing his throat*) As mayor of this community, I deem it an honor and a privilege, Pa Kettle, to present you with this telegram."

Pa wordlessly accepts the communique and tosses it into a wooden box containing stacks of other unopened letters, bills, and items marked Western Union.

"Don't hold with readin' telegrams," says Pa blithely. "Might be bad news."

"Read it to him, Sam," the mayor instructs. Sam is already reaching into the box to do so.

"Dear Mr. Kettle," he reads aloud, "Your entry in the King Henry Tobacco Slogan Contest has won the grand prize: a prefabricated model house of the future, completely furnished. Congratulations. Signed, Victor Tomkins, President, King Henry Tobacco Company."

Pa seems completely unmoved, even disappointed.

"Congratulations, Pa," the mayor says, offering his hand to the new homeowner.

"That *all* it says in the telegram?" Pa asks, not making eye contact.

"Why, yes," Sam Rogers replies.

"Don't it say nothin' about my new tobacco pouch?"

"*Tobacco pouch?*" the mayor repeats questioningly.

"Never figured on winnin' a house," Pa says quietly. "The ad said *everybody* that wrote in would get a new tobacco pouch."

Ma, however, realizes their good fortune. "Well, if this ain't the age of miracles!" she laughs. "I never thought I'd live to see the day Pa'd get somethin' he didn't have to return!"

"What kind of a slogan did ya' write, Pa?" the mayor asks jovially.

"Can't rightly remember," Pa admits. "Wrote it on the back of somethin'. He begins to methodically empty his pockets, placing the contents in Sam's hands. One thing he doesn't hand over is a stick of dynamite. "Gonna blast a well in the back," he explains. Reaching into his pockets once again, he says, "I got it."

"Read it," the mayor says encouragingly.

Unfolding the well-worn page, Pa reads: "For smokin' or chewin', King Henry's most fittin'. It smells awful good, and it's dandy for spittin'."

The mayor and Sam Rogers are delighted by Pa's way with words. "Wonderful, Pa, just wonderful!" His Honor says. Turning to the council members standing nearby, he asks, "Isn't that a *wonderful* slogan, folks?"

Most of the men are smiling broadly, but Old Mother Hicks and Birdie look utterly unimpressed. "Great slogan, *hmph*," Birdie says disgruntledly. "I didn't even know Pa could *write!*"

The headline on the front page of the *Seattle Daily News* reads:

Cape Flattery Squatters Win
Palatial Modern Home in Slogan Contest
Winner Has Wife and Fifteen Children

Tom Kettle is on a train, heading home to visit his family. In the dining car, he is joined unexpectedly by a prim-looking young lady named Kim Parker. Kim is a magazine writer, whose most recent series of articles deal with the importance of hygiene in the home. Even though Tom and Kim eventually wind up as the film's romantic leads, it is anything but love at first sight.

Upon returning to his boyhood home, Tom is welcomed with open arms by his ma and pa. Before he can sit back and relax, however, Ma tells him it's time to go with the rest of the family for the official presentation of the new house. The next scene takes us to an upscale-looking neighborhood with modern homes and manicured lawns. The Kettles' new place is a large, two-story structure, with a myriad of front windows. A television crew, representing the ABC network, is in the front yard, as are numerous others, broadcasting the proceedings live. When he receives his cue, the president of the King Henry Tobacco Company, Mr. Victor Tomkins, formally presents Pa with "the key to your dream house."

Pa accepts the key and offers a subdued "Thanks."

After a brief silence, Tomkins says, "Oh, yes, I almost forgot. Our little extra surprise. A genuine oilskin tobacco pouch, filled with that good King Henry tobacco."

Pa, holding the shiny new pouch in his hands, looks happy for the first time since learning about the new house. "Now that's mite nice of you folks. For a while, I was afraid you wasn't goin' to come through."

Birdie Hicks and her mother stand by, disapproving as always. "A month from now," Birdie says, "those Kettles will have this place looking like the hog wallow they came from."

Ma and Pa seem awestruck by their "home of the future."

Before Ma and Pa enter the house, Tomkins asks if there is a little ceremony they might first like to perform.

"*Ceremony?*" Ma asks. "Oh, ya' mean like when we was first married? Yeah, I think that'd be real nice. Come here, Pa." And just like that, she picks him up and carries him over the threshold.[17]

---

17 In the original script, Pa is supposed to carry Ma over the threshold. But try as he might, Percy's 125-pound frame could not support his full-figured co-star. "*Shucks*," said Marjorie, "why don't we do it *this* way?" and *she* carried *him* into their new home. Director Charles Lamont reportedly commented, "That's funnier than the other way."

The model home is something to behold, not only for Ma and Pa, but for moviegoers at the time. It seems to have everything: doors with electric eyes that open automatically; a fully loaded entertainment center, containing a built-in stereo and a large, flat-screen TV, anticipating televisions of the early 21st century. An oddly discordant feature is a carousel bar with stylized horse stools; the bar can rotate to serve either the interior living room, or the exterior patio. There is a master control panel near the front door that operates virtually everything in the house. The bedrooms

THE PERFECT WORKSHOP

When the producers of the currently popular "Ma and Pa Kettle" outfitted a house with the latest and finest of everything, their natural selection for a home workshop was SHOPSMITH. Pa Kettle won the house in a slogan contest, and his son (Richard Long) seems to have won a pretty prize himself (Meg Randall).

Universal-International capitalized on the film by advertising the various luxury items included with the model home, in this case, the SHOPSMITH. Richard Long and Meg Randall unwittingly serve as the models for this print ad.

employ a modernized version of the "Murphy" bed, which fold up when not in use. The all-white kitchen has every imaginable appliance: an automatic dishwasher, an island housing a freezer, and foot pedals to operate the hands-free sink. One prophetic appliance is the Infra-ray oven, which supposedly cooks food in seconds. Behind the house is a large back yard, a barn, and a workshop.

No sooner have the King Henry Tobacco people left than the mayor arrives. And he has brought along a guest, Miss Kim Parker, who will be writing a series of articles about the Kettles for a national magazine. Tom, who is none too happy to see this lady journalist again, voices his objections to having his family held up for ridicule. Insisting that this is hardly her aim, she tells him that if he doesn't approve of what she's written, she will not send the pages to her publisher. He reluctantly agrees.

There follows a series of scenes in which Ma, Pa, and the kids attempt to get used to their new house and its many gadgets. Ma, for example, checks on the kids, all of whom are sleeping peacefully in their Murphy-style beds. She closes a window, adjusts a blanket on one, and generally sees to their comfort. Attempting to dim the light in the room, she flips a switch on the panel. The beds fold directly into the wall, kids and all! Momentarily panicked, she presses another switch, silently releasing the beds from their storage position. All is right with the world again.

Quiet time has finally arrived for Ma and Pa. Lounging in their immaculate, spacious living room (or parlor, as Ma calls it), they decide to listen to the radio. Harkening back to the old place, Pa takes hold of both sides of his easy chair and raises it slightly, only to drop it with a *thud*. Nothing happens.

"That's funny; it always worked in the other house," he says.

"Try it again, Pa," his wife says cheerfully.

The second he repeats the action of lifting and dropping the chair, Ma stealthily reaches a side panel on her chair and flips another switch, thus activating the radio. Pa looks as though he has triumphed over the electronics, and Ma lets him believe he has.

"Ah, *that's* better," he says, as a big band tune plays softly in the background. "Now I can make myself comfortable for a change." Taking out his pipe and new pouch, he carelessly spills some tobacco on the new easy chair.

"I never saw anybody as careless as you, Pa Kettle," Ma says, clearly fed up. "I've put up with your sloppy ways for the past thirty years just so there'd be a little peace around the house. But now the good Lord has provided a way so we can keep things in order, and I'll be *darned* if I'm gonna weaken."

"*Now*, Ma—"

"Don't ya' go 'now-Ma-ing' me!" she says firmly. "I'm puttin' my foot down. You're gonna learn to be neat even if it kills ya'!"

Pa may not like the new place and its attendant new rules, but Ma seems positively reborn. The all-white kitchen is immaculate, and a huge cake, covered in vanilla icing, sits on one of the counters. Tom is there, lending his mother a helping hand. The table is set, and nary a chicken needs to be swept off to complete the task. Even Ma herself looks better "put together" than she had at the old place; her hair is neat, she is wearing a clean dress and a regular, white apron. There is an extra spring in her step as she prepares the family's breakfast. Cupping her hands on the side of her mouth, she yells, "COME AND GET IT!"

"They can't hear you, Ma," says Tom. "The house is soundproof."

A split-second later, Pa and the kids come tearing in, their blurred images occupying the foreground of the shot. Even if they can't hear, they can still smell. As everyone seated at the table dutifully lowers their heads in prayer, Pa removes his derby and, looking heavenward, says, "Thanks a lot for what has been put before us."

On cue, everyone starts to grab for the serving dishes.

"Ah-ah-ah-ah!" he says, raising both hands. The kids retreat as Pa again removes his hat. "Guess I outta thank You for this brand-new house and all as well, but if You don't mind, I'll wait until we've lived in it longer. Amen. Let's eat."

And the feeding frenzy begins in earnest.

That evening, the Kettles host a housewarming party, and everyone is invited—even that wretched Birdie Hicks and her mother. In the spacious back yard, a square dance is in full swing, as the Kettles apparently hired a country band for the big event. Ma and Pa are both dressed to the nines, Ma looking especially nice in her new dress with a lace collar and a matching bow in her carefully coiffed hair; Pa is wearing a tailored suit, and his hair is neatly combed, with no ragged derby in sight. Everyone from the Kettles to their guests are putting their collective best foot forward for this once-in-a-lifetime shindig. Birdie and her mother, looking like two well-kept graves (to paraphrase W. C. Fields), make a solemn entrance. That is, Birdie does; her aged, ever-ailing mother cannot wait to join the revelers, kicking up her heels and dancing the night away. Pa is doing his part to help Ma: he carries in another huge cake, this one lavishly covered in chocolate icing.

As Pa manages to get soaked while attempting to fill a water pitcher with the pedal-controlled kitchen sink faucet, Tom walks through, conducting a tour. Some Kettle kids, a stray guest or two, and Geoduck and Crowbar are among his rapt listeners. A saturated Pa listens as well. Tom points out the clothes dryer, hidden behind a large white door. "You put the clothes in here, turn on the heat control, and in a few minutes they're all dry," he says pedantically. "Now over here is the thermostat for heating the entire house . . ."

As the group disappears, Pa has an idea. To dry off, he can stand for a moment in the drying chamber and be as good as new. Two of the kids—Benjamin and Henry—stay back for a bit after Pa has stepped into the closet. Locking the door from the outside, one of these young sociopaths turns up the heating element from Normal to 500 degrees, marked DANGER. They seem quite proud of what they have done as they join their older brother on another leg of the tour. Geoduck and Crowbar stay on, seemingly transfixed by the elaborate thermostat. Predictably, Pa begins to feel the heat. "*Help!*" he calls out. "*Get me out of this place!*" The two Native Americans immediately answer his cries by unlocking the door, preventing his being dried to a crisp. Pa walks out and, in a rather obvious visual gag, the suit he is wearing is ludicrously shrunken, his now high-water pants revealing white socks and black shoes.

"Used to be Tom's," Pa tells his rescuers. "Guess it'll fit Henry now."

The mayor and Kim Parker show up, and Kim is immediately hauled off by a square dancer without his even asking if he may have this dance. In the commotion, her right heel breaks off. Tom, ever the boy scout, volunteers to fix it. The two leave the party for the quiet of the house's fully appointed workshop. In addition to fixing Miss Parker's heel, he shows her his incubator and begins to demonstrate how the heating element is regulated. Kim leans over and asks if the chickens mind that this invention is taking away all their work.

"Uh, not the ones that believe in progress," he says awkwardly. Suddenly aware of his proximity to this predatory female, he begins to ramble a bit. Truly uncomfortable now, he suggests they go back upstairs. "They'll probably be looking for us," he says.

"You know, I wonder," Kim says, a smile plastered on her face.

"What?"

"I wonder whether *you* really believe in progress," she says, turning to leave.

Oh, *snap!*

Pa returns to the party, where Ma has been waiting for him to bring that pitcher of water. Pa is dressed in a different suit than the one that shrank; this one makes him look like he escaped from a tintype, circa 1890.

"Land sakes, Pa, *where'd* ya' get that *suit?*"

"*This,*" he says, posing proudly, "is the one I borrowed from your father when you and I were married, Ma."

Back on the patio, the mayor asks the guests for their attention. The music stops.

"I don't like to break up the party this way," he says, "but since nearly everyone in town is here tonight, I guess this is as good a time as any to elect a chairman for our county fair next month."

Tom whispers to Kim, "It'll probably be Birdie Hicks. She's been the chairman for the last ten years."

"Now, before we go to nominating," the mayor continues, "I think we ought to remember what Pa Kettle did for this town. His winning the house put us on the map. Keeping this in mind, I think it only fitting and proper that we pay tribute to Pa by unanimously electing him chairman of the county fair."

"I nominate Pa Kettle!" a guest yells out.

"I second it!" says someone else.

"All in favor, say 'aye'!"

"AYE!"

"Sounds unanimous to me," the mayor says. "Come over here, Pa, and say a few words."

Pa looks confused.

"Go on, Pa," Ma cajoles. "Go on. Go on."

Pa solemnly walks to the center of the group and says in his New England–accented, sing-songy way, "Don't know. Ain't much for runnin' a fair."

The crowd chuckles. Meanwhile, Birdie Hicks is fuming. "Come on, Mother. I've stood *all* I can stand."

"Oh, *Birdie*," her mother protests.

"We'll form a committee," the mayor explains. "You just preside over it."

"Take much work?"

"It's an honorary position; no work at all."

"*I accept!*"

The crowd cheers.

Walking toward their car, Mother Hicks says, "You're always ruinin' what little fun I have. My condition never bothers me when I'm dancin'."

Birdie isn't listening. "Just because a man writes a slogan ain't no sign he can run a fair. Why, Pa couldn't run water downhill!"

Just then, they are distracted by the sound of an approaching truck. It's that pushy, rhyming salesman Billy Reed.

"Ah, how *charming* we look tonight!" he tells the two old crones.

"Ma is giving a party," Mother Hicks complains. "And Birdie won't let me stay."

"'*Stay*,' the lady says? I was just about to join the party. But if you're leaving, I'll give you a little gift instead, a gift you can't resist—a hand-painted calendar to advertise that buying from Billy Reed is always wise!"

"Oh, thank you, Billy," Mother Hicks says graciously.

"Don't mention it. Just remember that I'll see you again, sell you my wares, and take your pay!" He walks toward the house, laughing at his own cleverness.[18]

"Aren't they pretty, dear?" the old lady asks her daughter.

Birdie reads aloud the slogan on the calendar:

For smokin' or chewin'
Reed's Hold All's most fittin'
It's handy for ashes
And dandy for spittin'

---

18 In this sequel to *The Egg and I*, the character of Billy Reed was written in the same flamboyant style used by the role's originator, Billy House. Emory Parnell's interpretation of Billy Reed, beginning with the next film, would be far more prosaic.

"Well, I'll be a turkey gobbler," she says, "if that ain't almost the *same exact* slogan Pa got this house with."

"Does that mean that Pa didn't come by it honest?" the old lady asks.

"It *sure* does, Ma," Birdie says. "And if *I* have anything to say about it, Pa ain't gonna get to *keep* this house. Come on, we got a lot of telegraphin' to do!"

The following morning, Ma tells Pa to go upstairs to the master bathroom and shave. She adds that Miss Parker is coming over, so he'll want to make a good impression.

"Why? *I* ain't courtin' her."

But Ma has spoken. The next scene finds him in their luxurious master bathroom, his face freshly lathered and a straight razor in hand. The shaving process, he finds, is rather a challenge given that the tri-fold mirror above the sink shows three different reflections. Perhaps more light would help. There are several directional lights above the mirrors. Pa pushes a button on a wall panel, not realizing he is activating the sunlamps. By the time he finishes, Pa realizes something is terribly amiss. With a towel covering his face, he yells for Ma, who comes running out of the kitchen.

"Why, *Pa!*" she says in shock. "What *happened* to ya'? Your face is redder than a fire engine!"

Tom and Kim enter the house together and are taken aback by Pa's five-alarm appearance. So is Ma, naturally. "Why, it looks like it might be *scarlet fever!*" she says.

"I'll call Doc Gruber right away," Tom says, rushing to the phone. "And, Ma, keep the kids out of the room. This'll probably mean quarantine if it *is* scarlet fever."

Cut to a close-up of Pa's deeply colored face: "*Scarlet fever?*" he says before falling back dramatically in his chair.

Ma is with Tom and Kim, waiting for the doctor's diagnosis. She is highly agitated, wringing her hands and pacing. The doctor exits Pa's room, chuckling.

Pa, fully believing he has scarlet fever, is sent to bed by Ma. Fortunately, he has a small jug of moonshine hidden in the headboard.

"Tell me what it is, Doctor," says Ma. "*Don't* try to spare me. Tell me the *truth*."

"Pa just has a bad case of sunburn," the doctor says cheerfully. "A real Fourth-of-July scorcher."

"I'll be right back," Tom says. He opens the door to the bathroom and sees that the sunlamps are on full blast. He shuts them off, along with the water still running in the sink.

"Rub his face with oil now and then and keep him cool," the doctor is telling Ma.

"Pa left on the sunlamps in the bathroom while he was shaving," Tom explains to those gathered outside the bedroom. "That's how he got sunburned."

"Good thing he wasn't takin' a bath!" Ma jokes, eliciting a laugh.

Once the doctor leaves, Ma tells Tom and Kim that she is reluctant to tell Pa the *real* cause of his discomfort—it's been one thing after another since he won the house. If he finds out the bathroom gave him a sunburn, he'll blow higher than a kite and will up and sell the place.

"Well, *don't* tell him," Kim suggests. "Just pretend he *does* have scarlet fever till he cools down."Tom objects to this form of duplicity, but Kim stands firm: "This house means a great deal to Ma and the kids, and I don't see why she shouldn't use a little strategy to keep it."

Kim is delighted when Tom approves of the feature article she has written about his family.

"It's up to you, Ma," says Tom.
"I'll *do* it!" Ma states with determination.

Tom, who has just learned that the Washington State Bank is considering backing his incubator, takes the time to read the first of Kim's articles about his family. He likes it very much, especially the part where she compares him to a young Thomas Edison. Delighted, she spontaneously kisses him on the cheek. When he goes to leave, he finally, *finally* gives her a real, honest-to-goodness kiss.

A day or so later, Pa is sitting up in the living room, a thermometer between his lips, with Ma and Kim doting on him.

The doorbell rings. Kim answers it, admitting Birdie Hicks and the president of King Henry Tobacco, Victor Hopkins.

"*There* he is," says Birdie accusingly.

"Mr. Kettle," Hopkins begins, "this is indeed unpleasant, but your entry in the King Henry Tobacco slogan contest has been disqualified."

"*Disqualified?*" Kim says in disbelief.

"If you'll remember correctly, the contest rules stipulated that all slogans entered must be *original*. Obviously, Mr. Kettle's was *not* original."

"Let me see that calendar," Ma says, snatching it out of Tomkins's hand. She quickly scans the rhyming slogan. "You mean we have to give this house *back?*"

"You didn't win it, and you're not entitled to it," says the pious Birdie.

"Tell the truth, Pa," orders Ma. "*Did* you copy that slogan from this calendar?"

"Can't rightly say," he answers truthfully. "Ideas just flit around my mind sometimes. Can't say *where* they come from."

"*Hmph*, listen to him," Birdie smirks. "He ain't got nerve enough to own up to it, and he ain't got brains enough to lie about it."

Ma approaches the nasty battle-axe: "You stop pickin' on Pa, Birdie. He don't need brains to lie." She turns to her husband and says gently, "Now think for a minute, Pa. Do ya' happen to remember *when* that slogan come to ya'?"

Pa seems to be straining mentally. "Month of April," he says. "I remember 'cause the rains came pourin' in and cut the whiskey in the still."

"Mr. Tomkins," Kim interjects logically, "I suggest before you start evicting people, you contact Billy Reed and find out who *really* thought up this slogan."

"*Nonsense*," Birdie says. "Pa ain't had an original thought since the day he was born. He borrowed that slogan from Billy Reed, just like he borrows from everyone. Besides, you can't check with Billy Reed. He's off on his route somewhere and there's no tellin' *when* he'll be here."

"I'm afraid Mrs. Hicks is right," Tomkins says. "We can't delay this any longer. You'll have to get out within forty-eight hours."

"*Forty-eight hours*," Ma says with distress. "But we can't! Pa's got *scarlet fever*."

"Scarlet fever, my foot!" Birdie snarls. "What he's got is a good, old-fashioned *sunburn*."

Cut to close-up of Pa, who says, "*Sunburn?*"

"Doc Gruber says Pa got it in the bathroom under that fancy new sunlamp," she adds.

Pa, in a fury, gets up and stomps out of the room.

"*Pa!*" Ma says, "Where're ya goin'?"

"Let 'em *take* this pesthouse," Pa says, stopping at the foot of the stairs. "I ain't stayin' in it another minute."

Seeing the forlorn expressions on Ma and Kim's faces, Tomkins says, "I'm sorry, but rules are rules, you know. Good day."

"Good day," Birdie adds with an evil grin.

Ma grabs her neighbor's arm roughly. "It may be a good day for *you*, Birdie, but it ain't for *Pa*. All the poor man wanted was a new tobacco pouch, and he ended up with a house he didn't want *and* a case of sunburn!"

"*Hmph*," Birdie says, exiting.

"I *knew* our luck wouldn't hold out," says an abject Ma to Kim. "I guess we'll have to move."

"Ma," Kim says, "you're not going back to that old house, are you?"

"I can't let Pa go alone," she says.

"What about the kids?" Kim asks. "This place is *good* for them. They're just now beginning to take an interest in it."

"I'll admit they haven't tore much of it down," Ma says.

"You have to think of their *futures*. If you let them go back to that old house, they'll go to seed there. At least *here* they have a chance."

"Well, I guess you're right," Ma admits. "But what can *I* do about it? Pa's dead set against stayin' here."

"Well, we have forty-eight hours," Kim says. "You wait right here, and I'll go and see if I—"

Suddenly, a stern voice intones: "Are you goin' with me, Ma?" It's Pa, wearing a bathrobe, his derby, and holding a suitcase and a coat. He looks fiercely determined, especially for him. "I asked you a *question*," he says.

"It's the *kids* we got to think of, Pa," Ma answers.

"Let's think of them in the old place," he says, unmoved.

"We ain't *goin'*, the kids and me," Ma says rebelliously.

Pa rushes over to his wife. "You ain't *goin'*?"

"We're gonna *stay* here till Miss Parker finds out about that slogan."

Pa leaves, stating, "I'm goin' home."

While in Seattle, Tom reads in the newspaper that Pa has been accused of plagiarizing the slogan, and that he must give back the model home. Although he is in a meeting with a loan officer at the time, Tom gets up and immediately heads back to Cape Flattery.

Meanwhile, Ma and the kids are peering out the front windows of the house as a car pulls up. A firm advocate of the Second Amendment, Ma has her shotgun in hand. "Here they come, the mayor and the sheriff," she says. "You kids know what to do."

Outside the house, handmade signs reading *No Trespassing* (with backward S's for comic effect) have been planted in the yard.

"I don't like the looks of this, Mayor," Sheriff John says.

"No need to worry, you've got the law on your side. Just follow me, John."

And then, reminiscent of the time the mayor approached the old place, BB guns are fired from unknown vantage points, knocking off His Honor's hat and hitting him on the backside, to the accompanying sounds of *"Ouch."*

"Can't ya' read those signs?" Ma says, charging out the front door.

"Put your gun down, Ma. We just came to talk."

"Ya' can talk from where y'are," she says stubbornly. "Just *shout!*"

"Forty-eight hours are up, Ma," the sheriff says, "and the law says you got to clear out."

"And I say I ain't settin' foot out of this house till I hear from Kim, one way or another."

"Oh, now, Ma, be *reasonable*," the mayor says pleadingly. "If you don't leave peaceably, we'll have to *force* you out."

Just then, Alvin the Western Union man shows up on his bicycle. But when Ma opens fire at the mayor and the sheriff, he wisely pedals away. The two officials, realizing the futility of the standoff, jump into their vehicle and drive off as well.

"John," the mayor says, "round up a couple of deputies; this is gonna be a fight to the finish!"

Back at the old place, Alvin is looking for Pa. Knocking on the house's screen door, he calls out: "Pa? *Pa?* are ya' home?"

Pa appears from around a corner of the house, carrying a lit blowtorch. "Howdy, Alvin," he says. This is immediately followed by the sound of an explosion.

"What was *that?*" Alvin asks, alarmed.

"Just blastin' a well in the back," Pa says.

"That *blowtorch!*" Alvin says. "*Turn it off!*"

"Oh, *that?*" Pa says, casual as ever. "Been workin' with dynamite all my life. Ain't never killed nobody . . . yet. What ya' got there?"

"Telegram," Alvin says. He then explains that he was originally going to deliver it at the new house, but a "fella'd have to be crazy to get anywhere near that fightin'."

"*What* fightin'?"

"Ain't ya' heard? The sheriff's tryin' to evict Ma and the kids from the model house. But they're holdin' out with shotguns."

"Ma and the kids—*again?* Gotta help Ma out, though."

Geoduck shows up, holding a shovel. "Time to dig well now," he says.

"No time fer diggin', Geoduck. Ma's just now fightin' the sheriff, and we're goin' back to give her a hand."

"You want Geoduck to get some help? I get many braves. Make it good and hot for John Law."

"*I'll* get the help," Pa says. "*You* get over to the house. And tell Ma I'm comin' with enough dynamite to scare off an army."

A cab pulls up at the new place and Tom quickly exits the vehicle. The sheriff and the mayor are parked out front.

"It's about time you came, Tom," the sheriff says. "Your ma's resisting a court order to give the model home back to those King Henry folks."

"Well, this is ridiculous," Tom says. "I'll go and straighten this thing out myself."

"I hope so, Tom. Your ma's a mighty stubborn woman."

"Ma!" Henry says. "Tom's comin' up the walk!"

Ma, seated in a hardbacked chair with her trusty shotgun across her lap, says, "Well, see that none of those varmints try to pussyfoot in with him!"

When he enters the fortress, Ma says, "Tom! I'm glad you're here in time to help us!"

"Ma, what are you *doing* this for?"

"Holdin' on to what's rightfully *ours*."

"Look," he says seriously, "this house *isn't* rightfully ours. Pa *copied* that slogan from Billy Reed's calendar."

"Won't say he did, won't say he didn't ... not till I get a telegram from Miss Parker."

"Well, what's *she* got to do with it?" Tom asks angrily. "Doesn't Pa *know* whether he copied the slogan or not?"

"Pa can't remember. And what's more, he don't give a hoot. He lit outta here to go to the old place the minute he found out it was a sunburn he had."

"You mean he's living there *all by himself?*"

"Oh, he'll get along all right ... *I hope.* But it's been a long time since he's been by himself."

"Oh, this is senseless, Ma, the whole thing. Get the kids outta here and go back to Pa."

"Go back to that broken-down junkyard? I should say *not.* I don't want to bring those kids up like a bunch of rag pickers."

"Now *that* sounds like Kim. *She* put you up to this, didn't she?"

"Now, don't get het up. For a young girl, she's got a tolerable amount of good sense."

"And a tolerable amount of theories. Don't ya' see, Ma, that theories are all right, but not when they break up families and endanger lives? You *have* to leave here, Ma."

"I ain't goin'," Ma says resolutely. "Pa's got to be taught a lesson."

In runs a panting Geoduck. "Message. Pa go to well with dynamite. He say you hold out till he bring it here."

"Did ya' hear that?" Ma says to Tom. "I *knew* Pa wouldn't let us down."

The sound of multiple explosions can be heard in the distance. "What was *that?*" Tom asks.

"Come from the old place," Geoduck says ominously.

"Did Pa have his blowtorch lit when he went for the dynamite?"

"Yeah. Pa have blowtorch lit."

Ma and Tom exchange concerned glances. "Come on," he says, "I'll get the mayor to drive us over in his car."

The situation at the old place is grim. A large tree has crashed through the house and refuse is everywhere. Geoduck then makes a frightening discovery: Pa's derby, its crown blown out by the explosion. This can mean only one thing.

"Pa's *gone*," Ma says mournfully. "And *I* killed him. Sure as I'm standing her, *I* killed him."

"It was an *accident*, Ma," Tom says, trying to comfort his mother.

But she will not be comforted. She blames herself for not having joined him; she was too busy fighting for the model house. And it was the fighting that led to Pa's demise.

Billy Reed pulls up in his mobile store, with Kim in the passenger seat. They come hurrying up to the others, their faces pinched with worry.

"Oh, Tom, what happened?" she asks, looking at the decimated house.

"They were trying to evict Ma and the kids, and Pa was gonna stop 'em with some dynamite." A pause. "But he never got there."

"Oh, *Ma*," Kim says. "What about the *telegram?* Didn't you show it to the sheriff?"

"*What* telegram?" asks Tom.

"The one I sent her telling her the house was really yours."

"It was Pa's slogan, Ma," says Billy Reed. "*I* borrowed it from *him*, not the other way around."

Ma, for once, has nothing to say.

"But I *did* send her one," Kim insists. "Don't you *believe* me?"

"Does it *matter* now?" Tom asks. "Look. You've got a climax for your article. Why don't you just go away and leave us alone?"

The family and their many friends and neighbors have gathered in front of the new house for a memorial service for Pa. A minister is speaking:

"Inasmuch as Pa's earthly remains consist of a derby, we'll dispense with a formal funeral. But I'd like to say here and now that Pa Kettle meant a lot to us. To *all* of us. Oh, his faults were many. But his virtues far exceeded them. He was a simple and unpretentious man, a man who felt more at home with what God gave him than with all the modern improvements of our age. *That* was Pa. So now, will you all bow your heads and join with me in a moment of silent prayer?"

Following a respectful silence, the mayor says, "Ma, I want you to know that if there's *anything* we can do—"

"There isn't anything *anybody* can do, Mayor," she says, her voice almost unrecognizably soft.

"If I had known this would happen, Ma," the sheriff adds, "I would have turned in my badge a long time ago. But if it hadn't been me, it would have been somebody else."

"I understand, John," Ma says in that same, understated manner. "You only did what you had to."

"Ma," says Birdie Hicks, both she and her mother dressed in mourning black, "there's no use in my tryin' to lie to ya'. I never liked Pa when he was alive. But now that he's gone, I—"

The peacefulness of the moment is destroyed by the war whoops of Indians. There must be at least a dozen of them, decked out in full regalia, with bows and arrows at the ready, riding in on a horse-drawn wagon. And *who* is leading this band of warriors? Why, none other than the man of the hour, *Pa Kettle*! "There

Although initially pleased to know that Pa escaped death by explosives, Ma does not appreciate all the worry he caused her, hence the raised board.

they are, boys!" he says. "Chase 'em outta town!" As the sound of shotgun blasts fill the air, the crowd disperses in every direction. Once Ma gets over the momentary shock that her beloved did *not* blow himself to kingdom come, she becomes incensed that he had caused her such worry and grief. Grabbing a board out of the wagon, she chases Pa down the street.

Tom is watching this tender reunion and chuckling like a simpleton. Seeing an unopened envelope lying near the wagon, he walks over to it and begins reading. Predictably, it is the telegram Kim had sent Ma, straightening out the slogan confusion.

The same minister who presided over Pa's memorial service is now performing a wedding, uniting Tom Kettle and Kim Parker in holy matrimony. Ma and Pa are among those gathered, unemotionally watching their first born becoming wed. Just as Tom says, "I will," Alvin quietly walks up to Pa to deliver a telegram.

"Whatcha waitin' fer?" Ma says. "*Open* it."

The contents provide a good idea of what fans could expect in the next series entry.

DEAR MR. KETTLE: YOU HAVE WON FIRST PRIZE IN OUR SLOGAN CONTEST: A TRIP TO NEW YORK WITH ALL EXPENSES PAID. CON- GRATULATIONS—THE BUBBLE COLA COM- PANY. WILLIAM JORDAN, PRESIDENT.[19]

The Payoff

The series debut was a hit, raking in $2.3 million at the box office. A critic for the *New York Times* wrote on August 12, 1949:

The powers at Universal-International, enchanted by those poor-but-happy, fecund rustics, Ma and Pa Kettle, obviously were right in transporting them from Betty MacDonald's book, "The Egg and I" and the film version thereof to a picture all their own. Reports in trade circles have it that this modest little number, "Ma and Pa Kettle" by title, which arrived at the Palace yesterday, is surprising and gratifying its sponsors by the very healthy business it is doing around the country. The answer to that phenom- enon is, however, not too obvious to judge by the comic goings-on at the Palace. For this yarn about the adven- tures of the Kettles—Ma and Pa and the fifteen pint-sized Kettles—in the electronic house Pa wins in a slogan con- test, is a mild entertainment depending almost entirely on its stars. That Marjorie Main and Percy Kilbride are not continuously funny is not their fault. The story framework built for them by the scenarists is a rickety affair not adapt- ed to sustain comedy. Chances for abdominal laughter are few but Ma and Pa have their moments in roles which fit them far better than their limp and tattered wardrobe. Pa's bewilderment at all the electric gimmicks, buttons, hidden beds and radios and Ma's genial but masterful domina- tion of her huge brood, whose names confuse her, makes

---

19 In the sequel, the product is referred to as Bubble-Ola.

for chuckles if not explosive guffaws. Acting honors are evenly divided too. Marjorie Main's Ma Kettle is a warm and natural character whose willingness to defend her new home with the aid of her trusted shotgun and numerous progeny is completely understandable. Rating equal sympathy, too, is Percy Kilbride's portrayal of Pa. A gent who shuns labor like the plague, he is content to return to his old squatter's shack after he is defeated by the gadgets in his new house and the accusation that he stole the winning slogan. As a cute twist, the film ends with Pa winning another slogan contest. Now a U-I troupe is hereabouts [in New York City] actually filming the second adventure in the Kettle saga. Good, bad, or indifferent, it looks as though the Kettles are here to stay.

Chapter 4
Ma and Pa Kettle Go to Town
(1950)

Released by Universal-International, April 1, 1950. 81 minutes. Directed by Charles Lamont. Produced by Leonard Goldstein. Story and Screenplay by Martin Ragaway and Leonard Stern. Music: Milton Schwarzwald. Director of Photography: Charles Van Enger. Film Editing: Russell Schoengarth. Art Direction: Bernard Herzbrun and Emrich Nicholson. Set Decorations: Russell A. Gausman and Oliver Emert. Costume Design: Rosemary Odell. Make-Up: Bud Westmore. Hair Stylist: Joan St. Oegger. Special Photography: David S. Horsley, A.S.C. Sound by Leslie I. Carey and Joe Lapis. Technician: Sherman Clark. Gowns: Rosemary Odell.

Cast: Marjorie Main (*Ma Kettle*); Percy Kilbride (*Pa Kettle*); Richard Long (*Tom Kettle*); Meg Randall (*Kim Parker Kettle*); Gregg Martell (*Louie*); Charles McGraw (*Shotgun Mike Munger*); Kathryn Givney (*Mrs. Victoria Masterson*); Jim Backus (*Joseph "Little Joe" Rogers*); Elliott Lewis (*Detective Sam Boxer*); Paul McVey (*Harold Masterson*); Bert Freed (*Dutch, Third New York Henchman*); Hal March (*Detective Mike Eskow*); Barbara Brown (*Elizabeth Parker, scenes deleted*); Ray Collins (*Jonathan Parker, scenes deleted*); Lester Allen (*Geoduck*); Leon Belasco (*Beauty Salon Manager*); Dale Belding (*Danny Kettle*); Stanley Blystone (*Train Conductor*); Leonard Bremen (*Tour Bus Guide*); Margaret Brown (*Ruthie Kettle*); George Calliga (*Party Guest*); Jack Chefe (*Nightclub Patron*); Charles Coleman (*Charles, the Butler*); Lynn Craft (*Nightclub Patron*); Helen Dickson (*Nightclub Patron*); Paul Dunn (*George Kettle*); Diane Florentine (*Sara Kettle*); Bess Flowers (*Party Guest*); Slim Gaut (*Bus Passenger*); Joe Gilbert (*Party Guest*); Dick Gordon (*Party Guest*); Maurice Gosfield (*New York Tour Ticket Seller*); Teddy Infuhr (*Benjamin Kettle*); Jackie Jackson (*Henry Kettle*); Sherry Jackson (*Susie Kettle*); John James (*Roberts, Masterson's Chauffeur*); Larry Keating (*Police Lt. Klein*); Douglas Kennedy (*George Donahue*); Donald Kerr (*First Cab Driver*); Mike Lally (*Counterman*); Donna Leary (*Sally Kettle*); Rex Lease (*Callan County Sheriff*); Peter Leeds (*Tall Beautician*); Wilbur Mack (*Party Guest*); John Marley (*Second Cab Driver*); Beverly Mook (*Eve Kettle*); Charles Morton (*Bus Passenger*); Forbes Murray (*Night Club Patron*); William Newell (*Horace "Hank" Hawkshaw, Police Desk Sergeant*); William H. O'Brien (*Waiter at Party*); Garry Owen (*Bubble-ola Delivery Man*); Eugene Persson (*Willie Kettle*); Elana Schreiner (*Nancy Kettle*); J. P. Sloane (*Billy Kettle*); Olan Soule (*Salon Technician*); Brick Sullivan (*Policeman at Station House*); Willard Waterman (*J. J. Schumacher*); James Westerfield (*Harvey, Zoo Attendant*); Chief Yowlachie (*Crowbar*).

As one U-I report (dated March 27, 1950) stated, the latest Kettle picture would be of "stouter thread and swifter pace" than the previous outing. It is, too. This is due in large measure to the talented writers of the screenplay, Leonard Stern and Martin Ragaway. Separately, Martin Ragaway (1923–1989) wrote television scripts for Lucille Ball, Jerry Lewis, and Red Skelton. Leonard Stern (1923–2014) is the co-creator of such television classics as *The Honeymooners* (1955–1956), *The Phil Silvers Show* (1955–1959), and *Get Smart* (1965–1970). In 1953, he and another writer, Roger Price, created the game *Mad Libs*. Ragaway and Stern set out to write a Kettle script that was funny, with less of the pathos found in *The Egg and I* and even *Ma and Pa Kettle*. They succeeded.

The Supporting Cast
Charles McGraw as "Shotgun" Munger, alias "Mr. Jones" ...

Charles McGraw (1914–1980) is well-suited to the role of bank robber-at-large "Shotgun" Munger, alias "Mr. Jones." A veteran of numerous Off-Broadway productions, Charles McGraw made a strong impression on fans of film noir in the opening sequence of *The Killers* (1946), when he and a fellow gangster (played by William Conrad) terrorize the inhabitants of a diner. McGraw's rugged good looks also allowed him some leading men roles in that same genre. During a career lasting three decades, he notched up numerous TV and film credits, portraying cops, military men, and hard-edged criminals.

Charles McGraw.

Jim Backus as "Little" Joe Rogers, another gangster ...

Jim Backus (1913–1989) attended preparatory school in his hometown of Cleveland, enrolling at the American Academy of Dramatic Arts. Typecast at first in roles as "rich types," he proved his versatility by portraying the milquetoast father of James Dean's character in *Rebel Without a Cause*

Jim Backus.

(1955). With his career moving forward at a good clip, Backus became the voice of the popular cartoon character Mr. Magoo; he also played opposite comedienne Joan Davis in the 1958 sitcom *I Married Joan*. The role that won him everlasting fame, however, was that of Thurston Howell III on *Gilligan's Island* (1964–1967).

Willard Waterman as J. J. Schumacher, the president of Bubble-Ola ...

Willard Waterman (1914–1995) is utterly convincing as the loquacious yet impersonal J. J. Schumacher, the vice-president of Bubble-Ola. Fans of old-time radio know Willard Waterman as *The Great Gildersleeve*, on which he replaced star Harold Peary during the height of the show's popularity. Waterman is likewise known for his many guest appearances on television sitcoms and in movies, the authors' per-

Willard Waterman.   sonal favorite being his portrayal of Mr. Vanderhoff, one of the morally bankrupt executives who use the bachelor pad of one C. C. Baxter for their extramarital trysts in Billy Wilder's *The Apartment*, the Best Picture of 1960.

Hal March as Detective Mike Eskow ...

Hal March (1920–1970) made his initial mark in 1944, teamed with fellow comic Bob Sweeney. Seeking a career as a solo act, he took small roles in such TV shows as *I Love Lucy* and *The Kate Smith Evening Hour*. His recognition factor rose significantly when he was hired as one of the four actors who played Harry Morton on *The George Burns and Gracie Allen Show* (he ultimately lost the part to noted stage and screen actor Fred

Hal March.

Clark). March used his personable approach to host the runaway hit game show, *The $64,000 Question.*

Larry Keating as Police Lieutenant Klein . . .

Larry Keating.

Announcer-turned-actor Larry Keating (1896–1963) was a dependable player on various situation comedies, including *The George Burns and Gracie Allen Show,* as the fourth (and final) Harry Morton, taking over for Fred Clark. He reprised the character on the short-lived sequel, *The George Burns Show,* following Gracie Allen's retirement. He was a regular on yet another Burns-produced sitcom, *Mister Ed,* from 1961 until his death from leukemia in 1963.

Olan Soule as a Salon Technician . . .

Olan Soule.

Olan Soule (1909–1994) may well be the most recognizable, yet completely unknown, character actor of his time. As a youngster, he got his first taste of show business working in a tent show out of Sabula, Iowa. Departing for greener pastures, he had been working regularly onstage in Chicago for seven years when he became involved in radio work in 1933. Upon relocating to California, Soule found work in film and television. His precise diction must have inspired the casting director to feature him in an additional, if unbilled, role in *Go to Town.* His is the voice of the radio announcer giving updates on the bank robber at large.

And Maurice Gosfield as a Tour Bus Ticket Seller.

Anyone who grew up watching *You'll Never Get Rich*—a.k.a. *The Phil Silvers Show,* a.k.a. *Sgt. Bilko*—will recognize the comical-looking Maurice Gosfield (1913–1964), who played Private Doberman on that classic 1950s sitcom. So popular was Gos-

field's misfit character that D.C. Comics published eleven issues of a Private Doberman comic book from 1957 to 1960. Despite his dumpy appearance, Gosfield thought of himself as a sophisticate and a ladies' man.

Maurice Gosfield and two of his babes.

With his escalating fame, Percy Kilbride was now the frequent subject of U-I's publicity items. One topic involved what had become his most-recognized trademark: a derby hat. According to the item (dated February 12, 1950), the hat was originally presented to him in 1930 at the Lambs Club by politician Al Smith. (Smith, who served four terms as mayor of New York City, was associated with that style of hat.) Apparently, it became something of a talisman for Percy; he wore that same derby in fifteen Broadway plays and twelve movies. For the latter, he was asked if he would permit having it dyed black, as its original color, brown, would not photograph as well; he gave his consent. Although the hat became battered and slightly moth-eaten as the series contin-

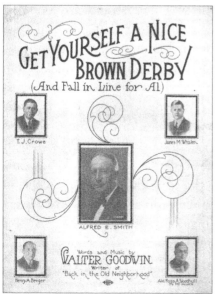

ued, Percy had no desire to replace it with a newer model. Because of its high recognition factor, the derby became an object of desire for collectors of movie memorabilia. One theater owner in Detroit even offered Percy a thousand dollars for it. He politely declined. One wonders: *Where* is that hat today?[20]

The publicity department seemed to work overtime in promoting *Go to Town*. The press kit sent out by the studio to theaters around the United States included gimmicks to bring in the customers. One idea involved a slogan contest. This is a natural tie-in, given that, in the story, Pa wins a slogan contest, the first prize for which is an all-expense-paid trip for two to New York.

Other publicity gimmicks suggest theaters hold "Ma and Pa Kettle Lookalike Contests," in which married couples are encouraged to dress up as their favorite movie duo. Another is to nominate parents with large families. The winning parents would be supplied with a "sitter for the night" (either the theater owner, a policeman, or a town dignitary, thus generating local newspaper coverage), allowing "Ma and Pa Kettle to Go to Town."

Due to the unexpected success of the series' debut film, *Go to Town* was given a bigger budget, allowing for the two sets of leads (Main and Kilbride, along with Richard Long and Meg Randall), director Charles Lamont, and a crew to travel to New York City for two weeks in August 1949. This was the first, and last, time that a Kettle film would be shot anywhere other than the Universal backlot. Despite the erratic nature of Manhattan, with its crowds, traffic, and *noise, noise, noise*, Lamont loved filming on location there. The world's largest city, he told the *New York Times* (August 28, 1949), affords "some wonderful opportunities for dramatic movie-making." Some of the locations used for the film included Grand Central Terminal, the Waldorf-Astoria and Plaza hotels, Columbus Circle, and the monkey house at the Central Park Zoo. The *Times* ran a story involving the preparation for one scene, in which Pa carelessly pours a paper cup full of water off the observation tower of the RCA building. Percy Kilbride rehearsed this action a half-dozen times before Lamont was satisfied. Finally,

---

20 Percy Kilbride kept meticulous records concerning his professional wardrobe for income-tax purposes. He listed four ordinary suits of clothes, one derby hat, six pairs of shoes, and thirty-two suits of long underwear, specifically the neck-to-ankle variety.

the director ordered "a take, with sound." The scene progressed smoothly until Kilbride overturned the cup. Suddenly, the sensitive microphone picked up a bellow of rage: *"Hey, you guys, cut that out up there!"* It seems that a couple of RCA engineers were chatting on a terrace two floors below the tower. According to Lamont, the crew was relieved to learn the unexpected voice had not come from the street, sixty-two floors below.

A more challenging scene involved something uniquely associated with Manhattan—a taxicab. The difficulty in shooting this scene involved not the actors but John Marley, the extra who played the cab driver. He had been cast just days before and seemed a natural for the part. According to the *Times*, "[H]e looked like a cabbie, he talked like one, he even argued like one." The only thing he could *not* do—and which he failed to mention to the casting director—was drive a car. No one knew about this until the scene was about to be shot. It took four burly crew members, just out of camera range, to push the cab to the front of the Waldorf-Astoria. Meanwhile, Marley rested his arm on the side of the window, trying to look at home behind the wheel.

Yet another scene that should have been a cinch to shoot offered some rather specific details. At one point in the story, Pa visits the Central Park Zoo, where he feeds a peanut to a caged monkey. For one thing, the monkeys in the Central Park Zoo were partial to bananas, not peanuts. To find one amenable to chewing on a peanut, a member of the crew had to contact a theatrical agency to hire a monkey specifically for that purpose. A smaller, yet still considerable, issue involved the paper bag Pa is holding in that scene. New York peanut vendors traditionally sold their product in brown paper bags, but movies dictate that the bags must be striped. Like the monkey, the bag had to be imported from elsewhere: in this case, Hollywood.

The Storyline

Before delving into the plot, the film opens with two of the best-remembered, and funniest, vignettes associated with the series. First, we have Ma preparing breakfast for her huge family in her still-new, still-immaculate, white, modern kitchen. Pancakes are on the menu today, and she is adept as can be as she smoothly pours the freshly made batter onto the griddle. At least, her *double* smoothly pours the batter.[21] The comic aspect of this sequence involves the unlikely placement of a box of whole-kernel popcorn on the counter, which spills into the batter. When the cakes begin to sizzle, they flip themselves!

The second vignette involves Pa, milking a cow. Seated on his stool, he bangs it on the floor of the barn, thus activating his trusty 1920s-era radio. And, as always, the tune it blares out is "Tiger Rag." But this clearly will not do. Banging the stool again, the radio changes to the correct station. We then hear the soothing tones of an announcer: "It's six fifteen, and KMAF, the farmer's station, presents 'Music to Milk By.' Science has proved that the relaxed cow gives more milk. And here's a musical medley to give your cow that 'contented feeling.'" The selection played is *The Blue Danube*. This gives way to the comical harmony of music and milking: "*Dum Da Da Da Bum/squirt squirt/squirt squirt.*" The director provides a close-up of Pa's expert hands, playing the udder like an instrument.[22]

Ma and Pa contemplate the idea of traveling to New York City.

Now to the plot. While standing together in the kitchen, Ma reads a letter to Pa from the Bubble-Ola Company. As you will no doubt recall, Pa received a telegram at the end of the previous film, announcing that he had won yet another contest, this one for praising a brand of soda pop. The grand prize is an all-expense-paid trip for two to New York City. The letter includes

21 Marjorie Main was an actress all her life, and like most professional women, she was not entirely at home in a kitchen, unless it was a set of a kitchen. When the camera cuts to a close-up of the person behind the perfectly formed pancakes, one can see they are the hands of a younger woman.

22 As in the scene of Marjorie scooping pancakes, a double had to be employed for Percy milking a cow. Another lifelong professional actor who lived in such big cities as San Francisco, New York, and Los Angeles, he had not the least bit of experience as a farmer. In fact, he was said to be terrified of the farm animals. He refused to even approach the cow until its feet and tail were properly secured.

two train tickets, plus confirmation of reservations at the Waldorf-Astoria. In closing, the vice-president of Bubble-Ola states, "Your entry on 'Why I Like Bubble-Ola,' was a sincere and magnificent tribute to our product. I'm looking forward to meeting you and your charming wife personally. Very truly yours, J. J. Schumacher, Vice-Pres. P. S. On re-reading your flattering letter, the stockholders voted to send you an additional prize: a ten-year supply of Bubble-Ola for each and every member of your family."

"*Ten-year supply?*" Pa says with a scowl. "I don't know what we're gonna do with the stuff. Taint fit for drinkin'."

"Wonder what it *is* good fer?" asks Ma.

"Don't rightly know. Was gonna write and tell 'em how *bad* it was, but I found out they don't give prizes for that."

Ma suddenly realizes that as much as they might want to, they could not possibly up and leave for New York: there is no one to watch the kids. Glancing at the newspaper, Ma says, "They haven't caught that bank robber, Shotgun Munger, who stole a hundred thousand dollars. They think he's headin' out this way. Got all the roads blocked."

And the plot, like the pancake batter, thickens.

A car is speeding down the highway. It is being driven by an unshaven young man, who looks so exhausted he can barely keep his eyes open. He has just entered the city limits of Cape Flattery when one of his tires has a blowout. Skidding out of control, he slams into a property of what appears to be a long-abandoned farmhouse. The Kettles' old place, naturally.

The man, wearing a suit that needs a good pressing, and a fedora, staggers out of the vehicle. He retrieves a small black bag, the type that bank robbers in 1930s crime-dramas use to carry stolen cash. On second thought, the farm is *not* abandoned, just severely run-down. Chickens run across the front lot, which has junk that is recognizable from the first two films. An old dog lounging on the front porch gives an obligatory bark before the stranger reaches the door.

"Anybody home?" he calls out in his gruff voice. Not a sound emanates from within. He knocks a few times on the front door, causing the torn screen to collapse altogether. Entering the house, he pushes away some cobwebs as he crosses the parlor to the outdoor bedroom. Perched on the old brass bedframe is a clucking chicken. Ignoring it, he climbs in and falls back onto the mattress. The mattress gives way, sending the intruder to the floor with a *bang*. He is soon fast asleep.

Pa Kettle shows up at his property. Just above the "Beware of the Childrun" sign is another hand-painted notice, this one reading "For Rent." The dog runs up to Pa to alert him that someone is there. The presence of a 1930s-style sedan parked on the property is another tipoff. He hurries in to welcome his guest, only to find him snoring loudly on the fallen-in bed. Ever solicitous, Pa goes to cover him with a blanket. The man wakes up with a start. Pa introduces himself to this welcome stranger. He says that he figured this nice young man saw the sign and wanted to rent the place. "Let me show you around," says Pa, affecting a salesman's tone. "It's very livable."

"Yeah," the man says under his breath. "If you happen to be a cockroach."

Pa finally gets around to asking the stranger his name.

It's uh, Jones, he says.

"What brings you up our way, Mr. Jones?"

"Well, you see, I'm a, uh—" Looking about for inspiration, his eyes lock on a wall calendar, featuring a short rhyming verse courtesy of Billy Reed. That's it, he says, he's a poet. "I came up here to get away from it all," he explains.

"A *poet?*" Pa says. "I thought you might be a traveling salesman. Lot of them visit farms, you know."[23]

When asked what kind of poetry he writes, Mr. Jones answers, "Jack and Jill went up the hill . . ."

Pa is amazed: "That's a pretty famous poem! *You* wrote that?"

"Well, to be honest with you," he says, moving in confidentially, "on that poem I had to cut another guy in."

---

23 This is the writers' nod to then-common off-color jokes about salesmen visiting a lonely country household, only to find the farmer has a shapely, sex-starved daughter. We would give you an example, but this is a family-oriented book.

"Oh, well, come on down to the new place and Ma'll fix somethin' for ya'."

"No, no time, I'm headin' up north," he says, turning to leave. "Someplace where I can hide out . . . and write. I need peace and quiet."

"Plenty of peace and quiet around here. Where you from?"

"New York."

"I won a free trip to New York, but I can't go. You see, I—"

"I got a tire that needs changin'," he says abruptly.

"Let me give ya' a hand."

Now in his shirtsleeves, Mr. Jones is struggling with the tire. Pa sits comfortably nearby, smoking his pipe.

"I got a son in New York. Tom Kettle? Maybe you've heard of him?"

"There's eight million people in New York, Pop."

"It's Pa. Sure would like to go to New York."

"Go ahead, I ain't stoppin' ya'."

"Can't. Got nobody to watch the kids."

"That's too bad." He pauses for a moment. "What's the name of this town, Pop?"

"It's Pa. This here's Cape Flattery."

"How far are ya' from the city?"

"Seattle? That's a hundred miles away."

"Not bad. I was thinkin' of writin' a poem about a small town. This might be the place. Tell me about the birds (pronounced *boids*, in a Damon Runyon–like depiction of a gangster), the trees, the grass, the police department—got much of a police department?"

"Just a sheriff. Course, he only works part time."

"I think I know how you can go to New York, Pop."

"It's Pa."

Mr. Jones tells Pa that *he* will stay at their house, write his poetry, and watch the kids. That way, Pa can "go to New York with Mom."

"It's Ma. Oh, the kids will bother you."

"*Nah*, I *love* kids. As far as I'm concerned, this is a perfect setup," he says, putting his arm familiarly around Pa's narrow shoulders. "Pa."

Pa shakes his hand and says warmly, "Thanks, son."

Mr. Jones sits in the Kettles' living room as Ma scrutinizes him at a distance. "It just don't seem right," she says. "How can we leave our kids in the hands of a stranger? Come to think of it, how can we leave a *stranger* in the hands of our *kids*?"

"It's him or nobody, Ma."

"We don't know a thing about this Mr. Jones."

"W-e-l-l, I'm a pretty good judge of character," Pa says, "and that boy has an honest face if ever I saw one. Take another look."

Ma stares a hole through their guest, his hard features and ragged appearance making him look like Robert Mitchum at his scummiest.

"All he needs is a shave," Pa says.

Ma is still skeptical: "Take a *lawn mower* to shave *him*. What's his business?"

"He's a poet."

"A *poet!*" Ma says, brightening considerably. "An honest-to-goodness poet stayin' at *my* house!" Turning on a dime, she looks at Pa and says sharply, "Why didn't ya' *say* so?" She walks into the living room to properly greet her guest—*and* the temporary guardian of her precious children.

The Kettles and Shotgun Munger—pardon us, *Mr. Jones*—have gathered at the Cape Flattery train depot to see Ma and Pa off on their very first vacation. Ma has some last-minute instructions, including sending the kids off to school following a good breakfast. Realizing the magnitude of responsibility being imposed on this unlikely sitter, she begins to say again that she and Pa should *not* go on the trip. Mr. Jones assures Ma that he will keep an eye on the kiddies. As he is saying this, Willie Kettle gives him a hot foot. Recovering from that momentary jolt, he takes this last-minute opportunity to ask Pa if he could drop off a black satchel to his brother in New York. Pa, naturally, is happy to oblige. Mr. Jones tells him that his brother will pick it up at their hotel. The train, with Ma, Pa, and their makeshift baggage safely aboard, begins its three thousand–mile journey across the country.

The Big Apple, 1949.

New York City—home in 1949 to eight million people, speaking two hundred different languages. New York City—the legendary place about which Sinatra songs have been written and countless movies (including this one) have been set. New York City—brimming with some of the nation's tallest buildings and historic landmarks, a place of constant drama, endless traffic, unparalleled spectacle, and the destination of untold numbers of tourists. Two tourists about to take their lives in their hands are Mr. and Mrs. Franklin Kettle of Cape Flattery, Washington.

Kim Kettle meets Ma and Pa at the Grand Central Terminal; Tom is still trying to get that boring incubator financed. Pa is already impressed with the Big Apple, opining what a nice-looking city it is. Kim explains that they are still in the station; the city is outside.

Attempting to hail down a cab, Ma is growing frustrated. One cab after another instantly fills up with people, making it impossible to get in. To make things even more cumbersome, Pa is carrying two large boxes. At one point, he sets down all such baggage, including Mr. Jones's black satchel. Just then, a limo pulls up and out steps Roberts, a chauffeur. He greets his boss, Harold Masterson, an expensive-looking gentleman, who tells him that he will be staying at his club tonight, but that the chauffeur may take the luggage. The chauffeur picks up the suitcases, and by accident, the black satchel, and loads everything into the limo.

When a fourth cab pulls up to the curb, Ma becomes downright aggressive. She grabs two large men by their lapels and shoves them away from the cab, into a wall. "C'mon, Kim. C'mon, Pa," she says, brazenly leading the way through the concrete jungle.

Arriving at the Waldorf-Astoria, the doorman has evidently never seen luggage like that being carried by Pa Kettle: an old basket and a good-sized orange crate. But when they get to their room, Pa notices that Mr. Jones's black bag is missing. The bellman promises to call the station to see if it had been turned in.

"Well, that's mighty nice of ya'," says Pa.

While approaching the door, the bellman is stopped by Kim, who hands him a tip. Pa is confused. Kim explains that, in New York, when someone does something for you, you give that individual some money.

"Don't seem right," Pa says. "Ma is always doin' things for me and I ain't never had to give her a cent."

The doorbell buzzes. Pa opens it and in steps Joseph "Little Joe" Rogers, a big man in a black suit, wearing a gangster-type fedora. He tersely announces that he is there to collect the bag. Pa explains that he hasn't got it, although the gruff visitor clearly has his doubts. As he makes his exit, he says he will keep in touch. After Rogers has left, Pa turns to Ma and says he didn't have the heart to tell the boy they had lost the black bag. Kim asks if there was anything valuable in it. Ma says that they were told by Mr. Jones that the bag was empty. She then says that, if it doesn't show up, they'll just have to buy him a new one. Pa calls that idea "a lulu." "Shouldn't be too hard to match," he adds. "Town this big should have a general store."

Little Joe calls Louie, the head of the gang, to inform him that the Kettles have arrived, but the bag has not. Louie is angry, saying he had warned Munger about this. He has no doubt that this

Kettle fellow is trying to cut himself in on the deal. They will go after him.

Another visitor shows up at the Kettles' room, this one decidedly more jovial, if completely insincere. He is the vice-president of Bubble-Ola, J. J. Schumacher. Another large man, Schumacher is wearing an expensive suit, a neatly trimmed black mustache, slicked-back hair, and a carnation on his lapel. Without taking a breath, he says: "Don't tell me! You're Ma and Pa Kettle! Guess who I am: J. J. Schumacher of the Bubble-Ola Company. How do you like New York? *Great* city! There's no place on earth like it. How'd you like your trip? I *knew* you'd like it! How do you like these accommodations? You can say *that* again! There isn't a finer suite in the Waldorf-Astoria. And is this *all* that Bubble-Ola is going to do for you? *No sirree.* Have *we* got a program planned for *you! And how!* You're going to the Rendezvous Room of the Plaza for dinner and back here to the Starlight Room for dancing. You'll shop in the best stores on Fifth Avenue—"

The doorbell buzzes.

"Excuse me," he says, interrupting himself to answer it. Standing there is a uniformed waiter holding a tray on which sits four empty glasses and a bottle of dark liquid. "Come in," Schumacher says abruptly. "Put it right down there. And pour it." Turning his attention back to the Kettles, he continues in the same avuncular manner: "You'll see the best shows on Broadway, the ball game, Coney Island. Are you gonna have *fun*? You *bet* you are. Now, here's your schedule and your tickets. How much is this gonna cost you? *Nothing.* It's *all* on Bubble-Ola. Know what *this* is?" he asks, gesturing to the glasses. "*Bubble-Ola.* I took the liberty of ordering a toast. *There* you are," he says, handing Ma, Pa, and Kim each a glassful of the soda pop. "To the Kettles! *Long may they wave!*" Everyone takes a taste, except for Pa, and no one seems to like it but Schumacher.

"*Ahh!*" he says after downing his. "You have *no idea* what this stuff does for your stomach. *What time is it?*" he asks himself, checking his wristwatch. "Oh, gotta go! *Busy* man! I'll see you later in the week. I want to hear some more about your trip!"

Ma and Pa go to say something but, in the background, we hear a door slam shut.

Tom shows up at the hotel suite and warmly greets his parents. But there is an oppressively chilly element in the room as well. Kim. She is clearly not happy with her new husband. Ma, ever astute, detects a problem immediately when Tom and Kim avoid making eye contact with each other.

"Back home, you couldn't *keep* a young, married couple from kissin'," she says.

Tom, looking at his unsmiling wife with utter distaste, moves toward her and barely gives her a peck on the forehead. Tom explains that the financing for his incubator is not coming through as hoped. Kim butts in, saying she knows a way for this to happen easily *if he wasn't so stubborn.* He shuts her up with a look that says, "*Not another word.*" Abruptly changing the tone of the conversation, Tom asks Ma about the kids.

"Oh, they're just fine. Only I hope they're not gettin' in that nice Mr. Jones's hair."

Cut to the Kettles' home, which is in a state of chaos. Mr. Jones has just received a face full of oatmeal, courtesy of Benjamin. This was the boy's less-than-subtle way of letting the sitter know that he and his siblings are sick of the stuff. Apparently, it's the only thing Mr. Jones can make.

When someone suggests a game of leapfrog, Mr. Jones immediately nixes the idea, saying, "Naw, you're too wild!" But when someone else suggests turning on the radio, he agrees to this lesser of two evils. A special bulletin announces that the escaped bank robber, Shotgun Munger, is believed to be hiding out in Oregon or Washington. Hearing this, the man in question changes the choice of media from radio to television. There is, however, no escaping his notoriety. His mug shot is on the large screen for all to see. Benjamin is looking a little too intently at that picture for Mr. Jones's comfort. To distract him, he encourages the kids to play leapfrog after all. While doing so, however, he knocks into the entertainment center's control panel, causing a chaos of television images, records being played, and the radio at full blast.

You know, *mayhem.*

Ma and Pa look a bit wilted as they are out walking in New York's summer heat. They are talked into taking a tour bus ride, which whisks them out of the area, only to be followed by a cab containing Little Joe. The tour bus is *so* crowded that Ma and Pa see nothing but the backs of other passengers' heads. Getting off at the nearest stop, they enter a shop that carries bags that are virtually indistinguishable from Mr. Jones's. Taking it to the register, the salesman informs them that the bag costs eight dollars. When Ma tells Pa that he had better keep his eye on this one, Pa agrees, saying, "Eight dollars is a lot of money to put into a bag."

Next, Ma and Pa decide to view New York's panoramic skyline from atop the RCA Observational Tower. As a guide points out the Empire State Building and the Statue of Liberty, Ma is transfixed by the size of everything down below.

"*Look, look!*" she says manically. "Look how *small* the people look! Look at those little *cars!* Look at the *buses!*"

"Well, if you wanted me to look at all the things *down there,*" Pa asks, "why'd you bring me *up here?*"

Pa sets the replacement satchel on the building's ledge as the guide states that they are 1,050 feet high. "I wonder how long it would take for this to get down there?" Pa asks, pouring a small paper cup of water over the edge. Ma scolds him for his childishness. As the two continue to take in the sights, Little Joe walks up unnoticed, picks up the bag, and makes his getaway.

"Stop! *Stop!*" Pa calls out when he realizes what has happened. "*Ma! He took the bag! He took it!*" They attempt to follow the culprit, but it is futile.

Just as they step outside at ground level, Pa says, "Yes, we'll just have to—" Suddenly, he is drenched by some falling water. "Hmm," he says, straight-faced. "Took longer than I expected."

A team of police detectives, Mike Eskow and Sam Boxer, are on to Louie and his gang. Shot in noirish silhouette, they are keeping watch from an obscured vantage point across the street from the rooming house where the bank robbers meet. Just then, Little Joe arrives at the building in a cab and hurries up the front steps. Seeing that he is carrying the type of black bag said to have been used during the bank robbery, they follow him.

Louie is about to open the bag to retrieve the hundred grand when undercover agents Eskow and Boxer burst into the room, their guns drawn. "Okay, Louie," one of them says, "drop the bag." He does. Detective Eskow unlocks it. To everyone's shock, the bag contains only cardboard and blank paper. Detective Boxer tries to make nice, saying with a smile, "Uh, fellas—excuse us. Accidents can, uh—well, so long!" The agents back out of the room, obviously embarrassed by their rush to judgment.

Dutch, the third member of the gang, breathes a sigh of relief and says, "Are we *lucky* there wasn't any money in that bag!"

Louie, however, is focused only on the missing 100K. "*That Kettle*," he says. "This is his way of tellin' us he wants a cut. *Nobody* does this to us. That's *our* dough and we don't have to make a deal. Little Joe, keep after Kettle. And from now on we meet at Tony's place. This joint is too hot."

Back at the hotel suite, Tom Kettle is troubled. "Why would anyone want to steal a bag, especially an *empty* bag?" he wonders aloud. "Pa, you're gonna have to watch yourself."

Pa, who is having his necktie straightened for him by his doting daughter-in-law, says, "Trouble ain't with watchin' myself. It's watchin' those black bags."

Tom and Kim are more concerned about getting a table at the swanky club they will all be dining in that evening. When Tom asks testily if purchasing yet another bag might be accomplished in the morning, Ma stands firm. If Mr. Jones's brother shows up tonight, she says, he will be disappointed if they don't have it for him. Kim and Tom agree to go buy a satchel together, but their expressions say they would rather be going with *anyone* else. Before leaving, Tom tells his parents to meet them downstairs in ten minutes, so "hurry up."

"All right, son," says Ma deferentially.

Ten minutes later, Ma and Pa, dressed in their Sunday best, meet Tom at the hotel entrance. He is holding the new bag.

"Got to put it in the room where it'll be safe," says Pa cautiously.

"Well, I'll just have to keep the cab waiting," whines Tom.

Pa saunters into the lobby, bag tucked securely under his arm, when he is stopped by Little Joe.

"Pardon me, buddy, do you have a match?" he asks, counting on the fact that Pa would not recognize him.

"Got one here, somewhere," says Pa, accommodating as always. His eyes cast down as he searches through his pants' pockets, he hands the bag to Little Joe. "Mind holdin' this?"

Little Joe grabs the bag and takes off, unbeknown to Pa.

"I'm *sure* I got one somewhere." Locating a match, he turns to offer it to the stranger. Seeing no one standing there, he calls out, "*Hey, you got my bag! You know it? You got my bag!*"

Pa returns to his family and says, "He didn't wait for the match. He took the bag instead."

"That makes *three* bags," says Tom, apparently believing he is the only one in the movie who can count. "You know, there's something rotten in Denmark."

"It ain't so good in *New York* either," adds Ma.

Ma, Pa, Tom, and Kim are at the nightclub, but no one is in a celebratory mood. They are stuck in the reception area, waiting endlessly for a table. The orchestra plays "I'll Remember April," a ballad about the death of a romance. Tom and Kim continue sniping at each other, while Ma and Pa exchange concerned glances. Tom's beseeching of the maître d' goes unanswered, and there will be at least an hour's wait before the next table is available. Just then, in walks a handsome devil wearing a white dinner jacket. He approaches Kim like the old flame she is. She is pleased to see him—*too* pleased, from Tom's perspective. Kim ignores her jealous husband and introduces her in-laws to George Donahue.

Mr. Donahue looks at Tom and says, "Those plans Kim showed me on the incubator are great! I thought you were going to bring it down for my partner and me to see."

"Uh—I've been tied up with the banks."

"Well, don't let the *bankers* cheat you. Come to *us*. Besides," he adds, looking at Kim, "I've already got money tied up in it: two martinis, three dollars—*seven*, counting the tip."

Ah, so *this* is what's causing a rift between Tom and Kim. Apparently, an old high society friend of Kim's had agreed to finance the invention, but when Tom learned *who* was behind the offer, his fragile male ego could not accept it.

"Do you still have that old influence with head waiters?" Kim asks George.

Tom interrupts: "There will be a *one hour's* wait."

"Well, there's nothing like finding out," George says smoothly. "I'll speak to Mr. Gigi."

Taking Kim by the arm, he approaches the same maître d' that Tom had only moments before.

"Good evening, Monsieur Donahue."

"How 'bout a table?" says George casually.

"For you and the young lady?" Mr. Gigi asks pleasantly.

"No," he says, looking back over his shoulder. "Tonight, we have three chaperons."

"This way, please. I just had a cancellation."

Looking like the weasel he is, Tom follows them into the dining room. "Come on, Ma and Pa," he says glumly.

In a seedier part of New York (a neon light reading POOL HALL can be seen in the background), Detectives Boxer and Eskow are in a parked car, doing surveillance, and second-guessing themselves. By choosing to follow Louie, they may very well be playing into the gangsters' hands—Louie might just be a decoy, after all. During this exchange, the detectives spot Little Joe again—and he's carrying a black bag. They exit the car in a flash and, seconds later, play out the same embarrassing scene as before, with another serving of egg on the detectives' faces. As for Louie, he is just steamed. He pledges to go after Kettle himself.

George Donahue, a good guy if a bit of a showboater, picks up the check for dinner for five. Kim thanks him with hearts in her eyes. Tom, still petulant as can be, turns to his host and demands to pay his family's share of the check. George refuses with a laugh, saying that when they invest in Tom's incubator, they will make a fortune off him. Well, that tears it. Tom lets his seams show by saying that Donahue is interested in *Kim*, not the incubator. Kim is humiliated, Ma and Pa are silent, and George remains his classy self: "You're a little mixed up, Tom," he says. "Good night, everyone."

"Good night," Pa calls weakly after him.

It's dark as the two couples step out of the club. Ma and Pa are tired; they announce that they'll be returning to the hotel (or *ho*-tel, as Ma pronounces it). Pa notices a horse and buggy parked at the curb. This is more their speed. They hire the driver to take them on a romantic jaunt around Central Park before returning to the Waldorf-Astoria.

The following morning, Ma and Pa are in their room, enjoying breakfast in front of the open window overlooking the New York skyline when the phone in the room rings.

"Howdy?" Pa says, answering it.

"Kettle, this is Louie. (*Pause*) Okay, Mr. Jones's brother. Kettle, let's not beat around the bush. I want the bag—the *right* bag."

"Glad to oblige," Pa says. "Want to pick it up *here*?"

"Oh, no, you don't. I'll meet you somewhere in the open. Like, uh, the zoo . . . how 'bout the Central Park Zoo? I'll meet ya' in front of the monkeys' cage at twelve o'clock."

"How'll I recognize you?" Pa asks.

"*I'll* recognize *you*. Just have the black bag."

"How'll I get there?"

"Take a cab. And Kettle, *be there* if ya' wanna stay healthy." He hangs up.

"Nice fella, Mr. Jones's brother," Pa tells Ma. "Worried about my health. We gotta meet him at the zoo."

"Well, you'll have to go by yourself, Pa, because this is the morning that Mr. Schumacher is sending me to the Lucien et Louise de Paris Beauty 'Saloon.'"

Pa is confused. "Uh-huh. Well, all right, Ma. I'll meet ya' back here." Looking slightly defeated, he says, "Well, I gotta stop and buy a bag."

We are at the Lucien et Louise de Paris Beauty Salon Consultation Room. The formally attired supervisor watches as two pompous-looking male beauticians are walking in circles around a seated, terrified-looking Ma. For this special case, they are calling in all the troops. To the beauticians, he commands, "There is no time to waste. Let's get started. She'll need a new face, new wardrobe, manners, speech lessons." He then walks to his desk and pushes a built-in button. A door opens and out walks four severe-looking women wearing starched uniforms. He claps his hands three times. "Come, come, come now. Right this way, madam."

The two beauticians each offer Ma an arm, helping her up and escorting her out of the reception room. She looks like she's being taken hostage by terrorists.

There follows a montage of shots worthy of a slapstick version of *Pygmalion*: Ma manically riding a stationary bike, being subjected to a steam bath, a painful massage, a manicure, a mud pack, and time under a hair dryer. She looks exhausted.

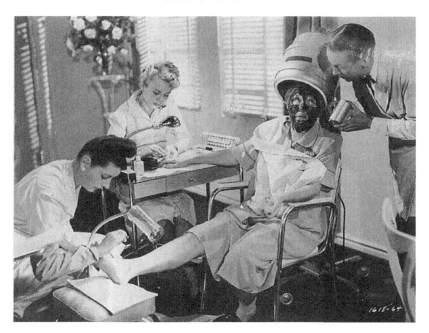

At New York City's Lucien et Louise de Paris Beauty Salon, Ma gets the full works. Olan Soule is at the far right.

The Central Park Zoo. A uniformed attendant is putting up a sign on the monkey cage. It reads: "Persons Feeding Animals Will Be Prosecuted to the Full Extent of the Law."

"How's it goin', Harvey?" a policeman asks the attendant.

"Terrible. Lost two more monks yesterday."

"Poisoned peanuts *again?*"

"Yeah. What kind of a guy goes around poisoning harmless animals?"

"A *fiend!*" the officer says. "And if I ever get my hands on him, I'll beat his brains in."

Who should enter the picture at that moment but Pa Kettle, holding the obligatory black bag number four. (See, we can count, too!) He stops to say "Howdy" to a caged monkey. "Have a peanut?" he asks sweetly.

The cop catches sight of him. "*Hey!*" he says sternly. "*Don't* feed the animals."

"Well, why not?" Pa answers. "I've been doin' it all my life."

"Try it again, wise guy, and I'll run ya' in!"

Louie shows up, his eye trained on the black bag. "Kettle?" he asks. "Mr. Louie?"

"Yeah. You alone?"

"Oh, sure. I can handle this myself."

"Okay, you're callin' the signals," Louie says brusquely. "What's the deal on the bag?"

"Your brother said to give it to you." Pa then looks closely at him and says, "Say, you know, you don't look much like your brother."

"Don't stall me." Sticking his pointed finger in his coat pocket, he says, tough-guy style, "Okay, Kettle, gimme the bag."

"With pleasure, Mr. Louie," says Pa, reaching into his inside jacket pocket. "I also want to give you this . . ."

"*Oh, no you don't!*" he says.

Pa takes out a key.

Louie grabs it and runs off until he reaches a bench, where he begins to fumble with the satchel's lock.

Pa smiles and shakes his head. "Nervous fella." He turns his head and notices that the monkey he just fed is standing close by him, behind the bars. "Not friendly like his brother," he confides to the simian.

Louie discovers that *this* bag, too, is empty. "Why, that dirty, double-crossin' rat!" he says under his breath.

Pa stands mindlessly by the cage. The monkey reaches into Pa's jacket pocket and removes the bag of peanuts.

The cop is back. "What'd I tell you about feeding the animals?" he says warningly.

"But I didn't!" Pa states. "He was, uh—"

"*Peanuts!*" the cop says accusingly. "Poisoned peanuts! *You!* You *murderer*, you!" He grabs Pa roughly by his coat collar.

Louie is back. "What's the matter?"

"This man is a *killer*," the cop tells him. And with that, he drags Pa off to the station.

The monkey chitters happily.

The police station interrogation room. Cutting through the darkness are two light sources, one just over the suspect's head, a

Pa is in the hot seat, suspected of having fed poisoned peanuts to a monkey in Central Park Zoo.

brighter one to his right, both casting harsh shadows on his face. Detectives Mike Eskow and Sam Rogers, along with two of their colleagues, are obviously weary from a long grilling session. This is one tough customer.

"You poisoned the animals. *Admit it,*" says Rogers.

"Come on, sign this confession," says Eskow.

"Like to oblige you," Pa says quietly, "but I'd be puttin' my name to a lie."

"Look, Pop—"

"It's *Pa.*"

"Sign that and we'll turn off the light."

"I wish you wouldn't—it feels *good!* If you'd move it over *here,*" he says, indicating his left shoulder, "it'd take the dampness outta my bones."

"Look, Kettle, we let you call your wife at the beauty parlor. But if you don't talk, you won't see her."

"*Talk!*" demands Eskow.

"*Talk!*" demands Rogers.

"*Talk! Talk!*" say the nameless colleagues.

"All right," Pa says agreeably. "What'll we talk about?"

Tom is in the office of one Police Lieutenant Klein. In the lieutenant's hand is a candid shot of the man currently looking after the Kettle brood in Cape Flattery.

"So, you think Munger and Jones are the same?" Tom asks.

"What you've told me about the black bags and what we already know, I'd say yes. But we've got to have positive identification. Where can I get ahold of your father?"

"He's at the Waldorf. And if he's not there, he's probably out seeing the sights."

We are back in the interrogation room, with the even-more defeated detectives. They desperately want the suspect to admit that he fed the monkey. "Sure," Pa says. "But they gotta eat, too, ya' know. Funny town. Get arrested for feedin' animals. But people take my black bags, and no one does nothin'. New Yorkers are the finest people ever I see, but they got a weakness for little black bags."

"Now look, Kettle," says Eskow. "Wait—*black bags*?" He looks at his colleagues. "*Black bags*! I'll be right back."

Tom asks Police Lieutenant Klein if there is a chance the bag containing the money could be returned to Pa. Klein answers that it is most unlikely, but without it, there is no evidence to convict Louie's mob. They are interrupted by the arrival of a breathless Detective Eskow, who says that the suspected animal poisoner just mentioned that he had been robbed of black bags. Tom asks Eskow if that suspect is a thin little man who wears a derby with badges on it, and you know the answer to that. Police Lieutenant Klein immediately formulates a plan. They walk into the admittance room, where Klein asks Officer Hackshaw at the front desk to give him the keys to the Rogues Gallery file. They take it and go.

Just then, Hackshaw hears a dignified, ladylike voice say, "I'd like to see Mr. Kettle."

Hackshaw looks up and, liking what he sees, adjusts his necktie and gives out with a wolf whistle. Cut to a shot of an all-but-

A dolled-up Ma Kettle seems to be channeling Mae West in this publicity photo for Ma and Pa Kettle Go to Town.

unrecognizable Ma, stylishly dressed, her hair coiffed beneath a fashionable hat, flawlessly made up, and wearing false eyelashes. With a honky-tonk rendition of "Frankie and Johnny" setting the scene, she saunters up to the desk, looking and acting like Mae West. "I *said*, 'I'd like to see *Mr. Kettle*.'" At first, Hackshaw, obviously gaga over this ravishing creature, explains that such information is confidential. But Ma really lays it on thick, telling this homely fellow that her weakness is a man in uniform. That does the trick: he tells her where the suspect is being held and that he is being grilled—that is, being questioned.

Now in the room with Pa and his interrogators, Ma is back to her old self. "I come after ya', Pa," she says roughly. "What's goin' on in here?"

Pa takes a gander at his newly gorgeous wife and says, "Ya' *sure* look pretty, Ma." He sniffs the air. "Ya' *smell* pretty, too!"

"Never mind the sweet talk! What've they been doin' to ya'?"

"Nothin'," Pa answers pleasantly. "It's been right sociable."

Ma, taking control as usual, grabs her husband by the arm and heads for the door. Outside the interrogation room, Klein stops them and apologizes for the misunderstanding; they merely wanted to speak to Mr. Kettle about the black bags. Ma, suspicious as always, asks how they knew about that. Klein explains that their son had phoned the department. He then takes out the binder of mug shots and asks if they recognize the man in the photo. Why, yes, it's that absent-minded fellow who wouldn't wait for the match. "How about this guy?" Klein asks, showing them a candid photo of Shotgun Munger. Certainly, that's Mr. Jones, the poet;

he's the one who gave the bag to Pa in the first place. Klein, a sharp cookie, plays along, saying, "Of *course*! How did *this* get in there? He's a great poet! I'm one of his greatest fans!" Turning back to the Kettles, he says, "We'll get to work right away. You're free to go."

Ma begins to tell Pa about taking the subway back to the Waldorf, but he isn't listening. He's circling his wife, admiring everything there is to see. "C'mon, Ma," he says.

"Where're we goin', Pa?"

"For another ride through the park," he smiles.

We are now in the wealthy home of Mr. and Mrs. Masterson. You may recall that Masterson was the man whose chauffeur loaded the wrong bag into the limousine. At this moment, the butler is standing at the entrance of the living room, holding the infamous black bag. He hands it to Mr. Masterson, saying that the chauffeur had brought it along with the luggage. Masterson surmises that he must have inadvertently picked it up at the station. The attached tag indicates that it belongs to a Mr. Kettle at the Waldorf-Astoria.

"*Kettle*?" Masterson muses. Could that be *C.P.* Kettle, "the underwear king"? He had been trying for ten years to do business with him, but he rarely, if ever, comes to New York. This could be Masterson's chance to finally meet the elusive tycoon. Against his wife's protestations, he opens the satchel and finds money—lots of it. Excellent. He will phone Kettle immediately and let him know that he has located his missing bag. This will really put him in solidly with the old gentleman, he says.

The phone is ringing in the hotel suite. Ma looks like her makeover has expired. She is seated, exhausted, on a divan, her feet soaking in a tub of water. Pa enters the room, wearing his Long Johns and derby. The phone rings.

"Howdy?" he says into the receiver.

"Mr. Kettle, I don't know if you'll remember me. I'm Harold Masterson, investment broker. I've written you several letters?"

"Never got 'em."

The Kettle in underwear tends to his wife's perpetually sore feet.

"Well, are *you* the Kettle in underwear?"

Pa, completely mystified, looks down at his Long Johns. "Well, yeah, but how did ya' know?"

"Why, *everybody* knows."

"Wait a minute," Pa says. He puts down the receiver and walks to the window, where he pulls the shade. Returning to the phone, he says, "Go ahead, I'm back."[24]

"Mr. Kettle, get ready for a big surprise. I have your black bag. It got mixed up with my luggage at the station."

"So, *that's* what happened," says Pa, smiling.

"Look, Mr. Kettle, we're having a little party tonight," Masterson says, much to his wife's apparent consternation. "Why don't you come out and pick up the bag? You can kill two birds with one stone."

"Well, what do they do to ya' for killin''em?" Pa asks innocently. "I got arrested for feedin''em."

Masterson laughs indulgently. "Oh, what a sense of humor! I won't take 'no' for an answer. My car'll pick you up at eight o'clock. If there's anyone you want to bring, don't hesitate."

"Well, that's right neighborly of ya'," says the gracious Pa.

"Glad to oblige," we hear through Pa's receiver. "Good-bye."

"Oh, Ma! Man found Mr. Jones's bag. We'd better find his brother Louie and tell him what happened. Might as well give him the right bag, long as we found it."

---

24 At one point, someone with far too much time on his hands gave an accounting of the exact amount of footage devoted to Pa in his signature Long Johns: 270 feet in *The Egg and I*; 450 feet in *Ma and Pa Kettle*; and over 600 feet in *Go to Town*. Percy Kilbride even used this look to get laughs from his fellow actors and crew members. He was known to show up for lunch at the studio commissary in his skivvies. Casually ordering lunch, he would sit down for his meal, all the while employing the deadpan expression that made him a star.

Back at the precinct. Eskow, Boxer, Tom, and a few assorted plainclothes men are in Klein's office, listening to his newest tactic for catching the bank robbers. If, and when, this bag shows up, Klein explains, we've got to be prepared to swing into action. Tom, however, feels his parents' safety might be at risk in their unwitting roles as decoys. Klein counters that there is no other way; if Ma and Pa were told about the hundred grand, they would get nervous and unconsciously tip off Louie. Eskow also assures Tom that this is the only way to go. And as soon as Pa gets the *real* bag, the mob will move in. That's what we need, Klein adds: to nail them with the evidence. Finally, Tom expresses genuine concern for the safety of his younger brothers and sisters. They are, after all, living with a killer. That's already been addressed, says Klein. He has notified the Washington State police. Tom reluctantly agrees to go along with the plan.

Speaking of the kids, they aren't the ones who need help. Mr. Jones—that is, Munger—does. He is hanging upside-down in the kitchen, the other end of the rope firmly tethered to the washing machine's agitator. When Benjamin turns on the washer, Munger begins to bob up and down, while the kids drown out his screams with their childish laughter.

The sheriff and a car full of uniformed police show up at the entrance to the house just in time to hear the plaintive cries for help. "He's got one of the kids," the sheriff says, deeply concerned. "We're going around the back. Come on." Charging in through the kitchen door, the feds quickly assess the situation. Shutting off the washing machine, the sheriff says, "Nice going, Benjamin! But how did you *know* he was Shotgun Munger?" Danny pipes up, saying that they had no idea he was Munger; they were just playing "cops and robbers." The sheriff approaches Munger, who has been cut down from his punishing position. He is thrilled to be arrested; at least, this way, he'll be safe.

"Murphy," the sheriff says, "stay here and protect the kids." Approaching another agent, he says, "Brodney, *you* stay here and protect Murphy."

The garden party is in full swing in the Mastersons' lovely back yard. An orchestra is playing, champagne is flowing, and a magnificent buffet, ornamented by a large swan-shaped ice sculpture, is being tended to by the caterers. The tuxedo-clad Mr. Masterson is just reaching the punchline of a joke when we come in.

". . . so, the salesman says to the farmer, 'If you find me in the barn, I *deserve* to get shot!'" This is followed by raucous laughter, much of it from the joke teller. The moment is interrupted by Mrs. Masterson, who informs her husband that their guests of honor have just pulled into the driveway. He excuses himself and joins his wife to meet the Kettles at the door. Mr. Masterson tells Victoria to pour on the charm with these guests. He could make a million out of this, after all.

Pa is made to feel protective of his derby when the Mastersons' butler (Charles Coleman) seems intent on taking it.

The pompous butler, Charles by name, opens the door, revealing two country bumpkins and their younger, better-dressed son and daughter-in-law. He frowns in disapproval.

Removing his derby, Pa says, "Mr. Masterson, howdy."

"Mr. Masterson is inside, sir. Whom shall I say is calling?"

"Uh, Kettles calling."

Charles, reaching out his hand in a servile manner, asks, "Your hat, sir?"

Pa is a tad defensive. Of *course* it's *his* hat.

"Haven't the Kettles come yet?" asks Mr. Masterson, freshly arrived.

"*These* . . . are the Kettles, sir," Charles sniffs.

Masterson graciously introduces his wife and himself to these fish out of water. He then asks the missus to take the Kettles into the garden. After these special guests are escorted out of the foyer, the doorbell buzzes again. It's Louie, looking, as always, like your garden-variety gangster, complete with pinstripe suit and fedora. "I'm a friend of the Kettles," he tersely informs the butler.

"Your hat?" says Charles, quickly thinking better of it.

Louie hurries off, hat still in place. Another buzz. "Friend of the Kettles," announces Detective Boxer. While these motley party crashers disappear into the gathering, Ma and Pa enjoy the music from the live orchestra as well as some caviar (that is, Ma does; Pa makes a face and returns his canopy to the serving tray). As the music ends, Tom and Kim come face to face with George, Kim's old flame. Showing not the slightest evidence of hard feelings, he says, "Hello, Kim. Hello, Tom."

Tom, to his credit, accepts George's hand in greeting. "I'd like to apologize for being so stupid the other night," he says sheepishly.

"Oh, forget it; *I* have," George responds. "I didn't know you knew the Mastersons."

"Well, we didn't until tonight," says Kim.

George explains that Masterson is his partner; *he's* the one who's interested in backing Tom's incubator. (Now *there* is a happy coincidence for you.)

"Oh, really?" Tom says, smiling pleasantly. Just then, he catches a glimpse of Detectives Boxer and Eskow standing behind some shrubbery. "George," he says with some urgency, "I need to talk with you about something. Where can we talk?"

"Let's go right over here," he says.

Behind another set of bushes lurk Louie, Little Joe, and Dutch. "The place is loaded with cops," Little Joe says.

"So *what* if the place is crawling with cops? What are they gonna arrest us for? Crashin' a party?"

"Maybe it's a trap."

Louie pays him no mind. "We gotta get to that bag before they do or it's good-bye to a hundred Gs. Havin' to steal the same dough *twice*! It's a crime."

The Mastersons are plotting in the library.

"What are you going to do?" Victoria asks.

"Sell Kettle a million dollars' worth of bonds."

"You're going to sell Kettle a million dollars' worth of bonds when he doesn't even spend twenty dollars on a *suit*? And did you see those 'friends' that followed them in?"

"Maybe they're bodyguards. I'm sure they're enjoying themselves."

Back outside, Tom spots Lieutenant Klein and tells him he has seen his agents in the crowd. He then relays the news that Masterson claims to have located the original bag. Klein is pleased: this means that, if the dough's in it, they can pinch the whole bunch.

Ma and Pa are approached by Mrs. Masterson, who asks if they enjoy dancing. Sure do, they say, but they're more accustomed to square dancing. This gives the hostess an idea. Why not ask the orchestra to play for a square dance? When she approaches the conductor, he readily agrees, but says they need someone "to call." Pa, who is apparently well versed at this practice, is introduced to those in attendance by Mrs. Masterson. When the upper-crust guests seem a bit perplexed as to how to go about a square dance, Pa asks Ma to help them out, which she does dutifully. "Excuse me, folks," she says to the prospective dancers, "make a square here now. Come on, make a square . . ." And then, at full volume, 'ALL RIGHT, PA! START THE MUSIC!'"

Tom (left) and Pa (right) watch in astonishment as Ma and the plainclothes detectives capture the bank robbers while keeping perfect time with the square dance.

"Let's have a little quiet, folks," Pa announces. "This is going to be ladies' choice. I'll call my version of a square dance twister." Clapping his hands together to set the beat, he says, "*Music!*" This is the lead-in to a cleverly written and well-staged climax. It starts when Masterson approaches Pa to return the bag, right in the middle of the song. Like a football game, Louie's boys intercept it, followed by the undercover detectives. Between choruses, Tom reveals to Pa that the bag is full of money stolen by Louie and his men during a bank robbery. Comprehending the situation immediately, Pa begins to ad-lib, telling Ma (in square dance lingo) to get that bag from the gangsters. She, too, is quick to comprehend a rather complicated situation and goes into action. By the final stanza, Louie has caught the bag in both hands (again, like a football game) and is tripped by Pa. The bag, and the money, are now in the hands of the law.

The Payoff

The box-office take—$2,125,000 (or $28 million in 2021 money)—reflected the extra effort put into this latest entry. *Go to Town* was such a success, in fact, that U-I was at last convinced to release one Kettle film every year until further notice. Even the critics grudgingly gave this one a passing nod. The *New York Times*, which had taken a special interest during its location shooting in August 1949, featured a lengthy review by the paper's resident film critic, Bosley Crowther. A bit of a snob, Crowther nevertheless concedes that he likes *Go to Town*, believing it is, "well, a fair descriptive might be a bushel of prize American corn, plucked from the rich, productive areas of uncomplicated rural jokes." He goes on to say that the film "was meekly launched in the neighborhood theaters here and has been frankly aimed at an audience of modest tastes and small-town attitudes." Despite that condescending statement, he has nothing but praise for the leads: "[N]o one can say that Percy Kilbride as Pa Kettle lacks insight or style in his ponderous and dead-panned performance of a solid American country type or that Marjorie Main is not ingenious as the boisterous and wildly uncouth Ma. These two are experienced actors in native character roles, and the stuff that they do in this picture may be obvious but it's adroit."

Ma and Pa Kettle Go to Town remains as fresh and funny as it was on that day in 1950 when it was "meekly launched." Its popularity warranted theatrical reissues through the fifties and would go on to be shown and reshown on television from the sixties to the eighties. In the nineties it had another renaissance, this time on video tape and DVDs. It continues to be seen and enjoyed in the age of YouTube and streaming. And those of us with modest tastes and small-town attitudes absolutely love it.

Chapter 5
Ma and Pa Kettle Back on the Farm (1951)

Released on May 10, 1951. 80 minutes. Directed by Edward Sedgwick. Produced by Leonard Goldstein. Associate Producer: Billy Grady Jr. Story and Screenplay by Jack Henley. Director of Photography: Charles Van Enger. Film Editor: Russell F. Schoengarth. Special Photography: David S. Horsley. Art Direction: Bernard Herzbrun and Emrich Nicholson. Music: Joseph Gershenson. Set Decorations: Russell A. Gausman and Oliver Emert. Make-Up: Bud Westmore. Hair Stylist: Joan St. Oegger. Sound: Leslie I. Carey and Robert Pritchard. Wardrobe: Rosemary Odell.

Cast: Marjorie Main (*Ma Kettle*); Percy Kilbride (*Pa Kettle*); Richard Long (*Tom Kettle*); Meg Randall (*Kim Parker Kettle*); Ray Collins (*Jonathan Parker*); Barbara Brown (*Elizabeth Parker*); Emory Parnell (*Billy Reed*); Peter Leeds (*Manson*); Teddy Hart (*Crowbar*); Oliver Blake (*Geoduck*); Dale Belding (*Danny Kettle*); Edward Clark (*Dr. Bagley*); Edmund Cobb (*Jerry*); Harold Goodwin (*Train Conductor*); Jerry Hausner (*Steve*); Joyce Holden (*Hospital Receptionist*); Teddy Infuhr (*Benjamin Kettle*); Jack Ingram (*Uniformed Deputy*); Sherry Jackson (*Susie Kettle*); Rex Lease (*Clallan County Sheriff*); Anne O'Neal (*Miss Quimby*); J. P. Sloane (*Billy Kettle*); Harry von Zell (*Mr. Chadwick*)

The reality of working on a set that was intentionally run-down was not without its (literal) pitfalls. While filming her first scene in this third series offering, *Ma and Pa Kettle Back on the Farm*, Marjorie Main had an accident on the set of the old place. Stepping outside to inhale the crisp, country air, she fell right through the rickety porch, a moment not included in the script. Four set workers were required to assist Marjorie up through the rotted planking. Fortunately, the actress was not injured. In fact, she even had the presence of mind to make a joke: "I'm gonna have to get Pa to fix that one of these days."

Percy Kilbride had his own travails, appearing in a scene inside a collapsing chicken coop. Although a bit shaken by the experience, he managed to escape injury as well.

Ma and Pa's three eldest children—Tom (*The Egg and I, Ma and Pa Kettle, Go to Town, Back on the Farm*), Rosie (*At the Fair,*

*A family portrait, 1951. The fifteen Kettle kids, from the youngest, Suzie
(Sherry Jackson, far left), to the eldest, Tom (Richard Long, far right),
flank their proud parents, Ma and Pa (Marjorie Main, center, and Percy
Kilbride, seated). Billy Kettle (J. P. Sloane) is seated on the arm of the chair.*

At Waikiki), and Elwin (*At Home*)—are well-spoken, intelligent,
upwardly mobile adults, which is remarkable given their parents'
lack of formal education. The other thirteen? Well, they are a mixed
bag at best. The Kettle kids are an important element of the films,
but most of them are basically extras. Supposedly, there are fifteen
children in all: eight boys and seven girls. In alphabetical order,
their names are: Albert, Benjamin, Betty, Billy, Danny (occasionally called Donny, and even Donnie), Elwin, Eve, George, Henry,
Nancy, Rosie, Ruthie, Sally, Sara, Susie, Teddy, Tom, and Willie.
This comes to eighteen kids, not fifteen, but then who's counting?
A running gag is that Ma can barely remember her own children's
names, due to their sheer number. This seems to have reflected
Marjorie Main and Percy Kilbride's perception of their youthful
co-stars. Main, as mentioned previously, was concerned that the
youngsters might be contagious, causing her to keep her distance
from them when not filming. And Percy Kilbride was quoted as
saying, "Darned kids grow like wildflowers. Ma and I stay jes' the
same, then all of a sudden the brats are bigger than we are. You
know, I don't know a single one of my kids by their real names."
The job of keeping Ma and Pa knee deep in young'uns must have

kept several casting directors busy sorting through the latest stack of head shots provided by the U-I front office. The unofficial rule on the set became this: when a child actor can stand face to face with the five-foot-seven-inch Percy, they receive their walking papers.

Back on the Farm features only three of the original fifteen kids introduced in *The Egg and I.* Teddy Infuhr, Eugene Persson, and Diane Florentine were the youngest of the bunch in 1947; by 1950, they were the oldest. Making his third, and final, appearance as a Kettle kid is Paul Dunn. He began his career as a child actor at U-I by playing one of Marjorie Main's brood in *The Wistful Widow of Wagon Gap* (1947). He would be cast as one of her offspring twice more, as George Kettle in the series' first entry and its immediate follow-up.

Percy Kilbride poses for a publicity picture with Edward Sedgwick's young protégé J. P. Sloane.

A promotional campaign for *Back on the Farm* focused on J. P. Sloane, born September 6, 1942. J. P. comes from a show business family. His father was Jimmie Jackson, who hosted his own radio show that was broadcast on WHN from atop the Lowe's State Building in New York City's Times Square, and on KFWB (Warner Bros.) in Hollywood. At age five, J. P. made his national radio debut when he appeared on "Kids Say the Darndest Things," a regular segment of *Art Linkletter's House Party*, broadcast over the CBS network. While dining with his parents in the Blue Room, a restaurant on Ventura Boulevard in Sherman Oaks, nine-year-old J. P. was introduced to Edward Sedgwick. The boy's sassy manner appealed to the director so much that he immediately offered him a role in his latest project, a Ma and Pa Kettle picture. When J. P.'s mother demurred, Sedgwick insisted, saying that a limo would be in the family's driveway the following morning, waiting to take the boy to Universal. That did it. J. P. Sloane became one of the youngest actors ever to be given a studio contract. During the authors' interview with J. P. in 2020, he recalled with pleasure his experience of playing Billy Kettle in *Back on the Farm*, saying that both Marjorie Main and Percy Kilbride were especially nice to him. At one point, J. P. accidentally stepped on Main's foot. "You stepped on my *foot!*" she said with tears in her eyes. "That is so *mean!*" J. P. apologized profusely to the actress, who eventually dropped the "injured" act and began to laugh. She was only teasing the well-mannered child. At this writing, seventy-eight-year-old J. P. is an award-winning television and radio producer, recording artist/actor, writer, and Biblical scholar. As Pa might say, "Not bad for a Kettle kid."

Another of the Kettle offspring who went on to bigger and better things is Sherry Jackson, who plays Susie Kettle in the second, third, fourth, and fifth installments. Born in Idaho on February 15, 1942, she and her brother Robert were the stepchildren of television writer Montgomery Pittman. Sherry was a natural screen presence who took direction well. As a result, her roles became more prominent, especially in *Trouble Along the Way* (1953), in which she played John Wayne's daughter. She is also impressive as a Portuguese child who witnesses a vision in *The Miracle of Our Lady of Fatima* (1952). *Come Next Spring* (1956) was a vehicle written especially for her by her stepfather. (Her younger brother in that film was Richard Eyer, another Kettle kid.) Sherry was a standout as Terry Williams on television's *The Danny Thomas Show*, beginning when she was eleven. It was during the run of that popular show that she blossomed into a stunning teenager, with a figure to match. Upon leaving the sitcom, her career slowed precipitously. The parts she ultimately landed were due to her vixen-like appearance. She developed a cult following for her work in such low-budget films as *Wild on the Beach* (1965), *Gunn* (1967), and *The Mini-Skirt Mob* (1968). Equally memorable were her guest appearances on the television series *Lost in Space, Batman,*

The Wild Wild West, and *Star Trek*. In 2020, Sherry is living a quiet life in Happy Valley, Oregon, with her beloved Yorkshire Terrier Bella. She was kind enough to grant the authors a brief telephone interview, during which she was asked to relay her memories of working in the Kettle films. Only seven or so at the time, Jackson recalls little of the experience, although one negative incident remains vivid seventy years later. Apparently, a small boy in the cast had the temerity to sneeze on Marjorie Main. She promptly had him fired and removed from the set.

Reprising their roles as Tom and Kim Kettle are Richard Long and Meg Randall. The U-I contract players had become something of a screen duo, appearing as husband and wife in five films within an eighteen-month period. There are the three Kettle pictures, of course, as well as *Criss Cross* (1948), starring Burt Lancaster, and *The Life of Riley* (1949), based on the popular radio comedy. *Back on the Farm* marks this oddly querulous couple's final appearance together. Meg Randall walked away from the industry a few short years later. She died in 2018 at the age of ninety-one.

Richard Long.

Richard Long may have gone on appearing as Tom Kettle in picture after picture had it not been for the war in Korea. He was drafted in 1951 and served his time in uniform while stationed at Fort Ord, in Monterey, California. Resuming his career following his stint in the military, Long was frequently cast in western television programs, the latest craze of the advancing decade. Much less successful was his personal life, which was fraught with tragedy. His first wife, actress Susan Ball, whom he married in April 1954, was stricken with cancer, forcing the amputation of one of her legs; she died, aged twenty-five, in August 1955, following a two-year battle with the disease. His second marriage, to Playboy

Playmate Mara Corday, produced three children. This marriage was also troubled, but for an entirely different reason. Long was drinking heavily and allegedly became abusive when under the influence. He was arrested more than once on suspicion of battery while drunk. Inevitably, this lifestyle began to tell on him. "I'm rotting from the inside-out and it's just gotten to my face," he told a reporter. "A man doesn't get interesting on the screen until he's in his forties." More than anything, he desired to be a character actor. His best-remembered television role may be that of Jarrod Barkley, the eldest of three telegenic sons of the tough-as-nails rancher Victoria Barkley (Barbara Stanwyck) on the western series *The Big Valley* (1965–1970). This was followed by the supernatural sitcom *Nanny and the Professor* (1970–1971), co-starring British actress Juliet Mills. His final series, *Thicker Than Water* (1973), in which he starred with the legendary Broadway actress Julie Harris as his needling sister, was based on the British sitcom *Nearest and Dearest*. Sadly, Richard Long was plagued by heart disease from a relatively young age; this, no doubt, was exacerbated by his frequent use of cigarettes and his chronic alcoholism. On December 21, 1974, he died at the Tarzana Medical Center, just four days following his forty-seventh birthday.

Other Supporting Cast Members
Barbara Brown as Elizabeth Parker ...

When young Tom Kettle married Kim Parker, the daughter of New York socialites Jonathan and Elizabeth Parker, Ma and Pa not only gained another daughter—they gained two in-laws. Originally, the Parkers were to have made their first appearance in *Go to Town*, but that film has so many story threads that their scenes were cut. Elizabeth Parker is portrayed by a veteran of the Broadway stage, Barbara Brown (1901–1975). Her specialty, playing upper-crust matrons, is used to excellent effect in George Cukor's

Barbara Brown.

film adaptation of the Garson Kanin/Albert Mannheimer play *Born Yesterday*, in which she gives an especially memorable performance as the wife of Congressman Norval Hedges. At one point, when the gum-chomping former chorus girl Billie Dawn (Judy Holliday) asks Mrs. Hedges, "Ya' wanna go powder your nose, honey?" the utterly refined lady smiles sweetly and simply mouths, "No, thank you." It is a subtle, yet sublime, comic moment.

Ray Collins as Jonathan Parker . . .

Ray Collins.

Like Percy Kilbride, Ray Collins (1889–1965) had his first role onstage when he was just a boy. He gained additional experience in the 1930s by making some guest appearances as Commissioner Westin on *The Shadow* radio program, starring the bigger-than-life Orson Welles. Welles knew quality when he saw it, calling Collins "the finest actor I've ever worked with." He asked him to join the cast of his program, *The Mercury Theatre on the Air*, featuring a company of talented writers and actors performing some timeless presentations of classic novels. Collins's best-known work on this series is the infamous "War of the Worlds" broadcast of 1938, in which he essayed multiple roles, including Mr. Wilmuth (on whose farm the Martian craft lands), and the newscaster who describes the destruction of New York. Along with other Mercury Theatre players, Collins made his first notable screen appearance in *Citizen Kane* (1941) as the ruthless Boss Jim Gettys. Although Collins appeared in more than ninety films and on countless radio broadcasts, he found lasting fame on television, playing the world-weary detective Lt. Arthur Tragg on *Perry Mason* (1957–1966).

And Oliver Blake and Teddy Hart as Geoduck and Crowbar.

Geoduck and Crowbar were once again recast, and this time the actors and the characters meshed so well that they would become

Pa (center) strikes a pose with Geoduck (Oliver Blake, left) and Crowbar (Teddy Hart, right), his loyal, long-suffering sidekicks.

the ones most associated with the roles. Geoduck was now played by Oliver Blake (1905–1971). A classically trained actor, he was billed by his real name, Oliver Prickett, in his stage work, especially when appearing at the Pasadena Playhouse, where he taught acting classes. As Oliver Blake, he portrayed Geoduck (said to be pronounced *Gooey-Duck*, but Pa always says the name the way it is written: *Gee-a-duck*) in five films. As the character was developed by the screenwriters, he became the witty spokesman for the team. Playing the mostly silent Crowbar in four of the series entries is Teddy Hart (1897–1971), the younger brother of Broadway lyricist Lorenz Hart.

Edward Sedgwick.

Charles Lamont may have been the regular director of the Kettle films, but a few others took their turn when he was unavailable.
In this instance, the man with the megaphone was Eddie Sedgwick (1892–1953), for what would prove to be his final completed
film. His career in entertainment had begun in vaudeville as part
of his family's acrobatic comedy act, led by his parents, Edward
senior and Eileen Sedgwick. He would later be associated with
the brilliant silent film comedian Buster Keaton (1895–1966),
whose early background in vaudeville was virtually identical to his
own. Eddie first acted on the screen in 1915, primarily in short
comedies for Vogue Films, as well as Carl Laemmle's Independent Moving Pictures Company (Imp). He worked as a director
for Fox (1920–1922), Universal (1922–1926), and finally, MGM
(1926–1932), although he is best known for co-directing (with
Keaton, the films' star) *The Cameraman* (1928) and *Spite Marriage*
(1929). He continued to turn out comedies during the thirties and
forties, but hardly at that level of success. For a time, he and Buster
collaborated as $300-a-week gag men at MGM, working on some
Keaton remakes starring Red Skelton. Certainly, the greatest discovery of Eddie Sedgwick's career was a former Goldwyn Girl by
the name of Lucille Ball. This led to the director becoming the head
of Desilu Studios, the home of *I Love Lucy*. Sedgwick's silent film
roots are readily apparent in *Ma and Pa Kettle Back on the Farm*;
its climactic car chase, for instance, evokes cheerful memories of
the Keystone Cops. His long collaboration with Buster Keaton
can also be detected in the shot when the train rapidly approaches
the camera. Incidentally, Harold Goodwin (1902–1987), the actor
playing the conductor, had supporting roles in several of Keaton's
late-silent and early-sound films. He also scored small roles in two
other Kettle comedies, *On Vacation* and *At Waikiki*.

Another silent film veteran gracing this project is Helen Gibson
(1892–1977), the former star of the Kalem Company's famed thrill
series *The Hazards of Helen* (1915–1917). It is that sturdily built lady,
the widow of cowboy actor Hoot Gibson, who doubles for Marjorie Main in all nine Kettle films, as well as the 1942 Main-Beery
oater *Jackass Mail*. Helen Gibson recalled that she was filmed in
long shots while driving a team of horses and fighting with other

Helen Gibson, Hollywood stunt woman, doubled for Marjorie Main in all the Kettle films. Photo courtesy of Larry Telles.

women. "It wasn't very dangerous, but she [Main] couldn't do it, and I didn't care," Gibson said. When asked what the actress was like, she described her as a rather quiet woman who "stayed by herself" all the time and was "afraid of germs. She was also allergic to dust and wouldn't allow the studio to turn on the air conditioning when she was on the set."

The story and screenplay for *Back on the Farm* are the brain children of Ireland-born Jack Henley (1896–1958). The diminutive writer (he stood just five-one) had some rather notorious films to his credit, including the East Side Kids cheapies, *Spooks Run Wild* (1941) and *Mr. Wise Guy* (1942), for Sam Katzman's poverty-row Banner Productions; *Bonzo Goes to College* (1952), the highly unanticipated sequel to *Bedtime for Bonzo* (1951) for Warner Bros., and a handful of Blondie and Dagwood pictures at Columbia. At U-I, he contributed either stories or screenplays for the Kettle pictures *At the Fair*, *On Vacation*, and *At Waikiki*. In *Back on the Farm*, he tackles such diverse topics as child rearing, marital discord due to in-law interference, the U.S. uranium craze, racism against Native Americans, and unpaid property taxes. Having spent the majority of *Go to Town* in the hubbub of New York City, this latest installment has the Kettles getting back to their roots. Yes, they still live in the world's most modern house with the most up-to-date amenities, but their hearts will always remain with their old, broken-down farm. Audiences found this somehow endearing.

The Storyline

Jonathan and Elizabeth Parker, the Kettles' wealthy in-laws, arrive at the model home, unannounced and insufferable. They are there to be with their daughter, Kim, and her newborn baby. Yes, apparently Tom and Kim Kettle stopped arguing long enough to, shall we say, *collaborate* on starting a family. But combining this wealthy couple from Boston and the rustic Kettles under the same roof for an indefinite period is surely a recipe for disaster, not to mention an ideal premise for a Ma and Pa Kettle movie.

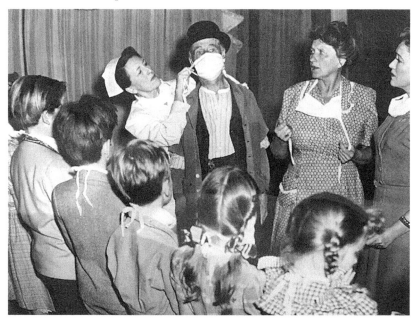

A hired nurse (Anne O'Neal, left) insists that the Kettles wear surgical masks to protect the health of Tom and Kim's newborn baby. Elizabeth Parker (Barbara Brown, far right) looks on approvingly.

The Kettle kids are the first to make an impression—a *bad* one—on the nervous Mrs. Parker. While fighting over just who gets to take in her luggage, one of her brand-new designer suitcases is torn in two. Ma is furious, saying that she is mighty glad that school starts tomorrow. Mrs. Parker responds icily, "I didn't realize that *reform* schools *ever* closed." Ma shoots her a dirty look. These two are not off to a good start. They later clash over a name

Pa attempts to calm down Ma when Mrs. Parker makes one too many demands concerning their grandchild.

for the baby. Kim favors Tom, after his father, but Mrs. Parker prefers Jonathan, after Kim's father. The next bone of contention is the presence of Miss Quimby, the private nurse Mrs. Parker has hired for the baby. She insists that every member of the family must wear a face mask when in the presence of the child. Mrs. Parker informs Ma in no uncertain terms that what Miss Quimby and she are doing is helping the child "hygienically." This galls Ma almost to the point of madness. All fifteen of *her* kids were born at home, nobody wore masks, "and there ain't nothin' wrong with any of 'em!"

Privately, Mrs. Parker has a plan: When the time is right, she, her husband, and daughter will leave these dreadful Kettles and live together in their home state of Massachusetts. No grandchild of hers is going to be brought up in this questionable environment. Meanwhile, Pa, ever the peacemaker, recommends that he and "the boy kids" stay at the old place until Kim's folks leave. Just then, Mr. Parker comes downstairs and asks if his wife's breakfast could be sent up to her. She wants coddled eggs, something Ma has never heard of. She will *boil* her some eggs, though. Jonathan asks to try Ma's grits, a pot of which are on the stove. She sets him up at the

Jonathan Parker (Ray Collins, left)—acting as an emissary for his imperious wife—tries to explain to Ma and Pa what coddled eggs are.

kitchen table with cream and sugar. He is in heaven. When Ma says she'll get to those eggs, he says, "Oh, let the old buzzard *wait!*" Ma decides, then and there, that Jonathan is all right.

Following a particularly ugly spat, during which Mrs. Parker excoriates Geoduck, Crowbar, and members of their tribe for daring to want to see the baby, Ma announces that it would calm the situation if she and her daughters were to join Pa and the rest of the kids at the old place. Tom objects, saying his parents should not be run out of their own house. If *anyone* should leave, he adds, it should be his dragon lady of a mother-in-law. This sets off his unstable wife, who informs him that she will not stand idly by while he impugns her mother. This still-recent marriage is in even worse shape than it was in New York! To help heal the latest rift, Ma now insists on temporarily relocating, a decision heartily seconded by Pa and the kids.

There are strangers at the old place: two men with a Geiger counter—and they think they have detected something.[25] When Pa shows up, he welcomes the interlopers, who are clearly opportunists, although he fails to see it. The men say they are hoping to form a hunting club and that *this* would be an ideal spot. Would Pa consider selling the place? Always honest to a fault, he tells the prospective buyers that there's "nothin' out here but a few chipmunks." No problem, one of the men responds, they will stock it. So, how much does he want for the place? Pa has the wherewithal to say that he would have to take up the matter with his wife and, within a few days, he would let them know their decision.

Later that morning, Jonathan takes a walk around the property. Pa, who is there to gather some eggs from the chicken house, becomes more familiar with his affable in-law. When Jonathan volunteers that he is a retired mining engineer, Pa asks if he has ever "come across any of this atom stuff he's heard so much about?" Jonathan says that he wishes he would. He then goes on to explain to his host (and to the viewer) that uranium is a white, lustrous, radioactive, metallic element having compounds that are used in photography and coloring glass. It is also used in the atomic bomb.

Making good on their promise to temporarily relocate, the Kettles, all piled into Pa's horse-and-mule-drawn wagon, arrive at the old place. Not much has changed since they won the model home. Chickens are still everywhere,

Ma and Pa Kettle, back on the farm.

---

25 When this film made its debut in 1951, atomic energy was on the mind of every American. This national obsession led to what has since been called the Great Uranium Rush. Geiger counters became hot commodities when hobbyists learned there was atomic ore in them thar hills.

as is the junk on the property. But Ma, Pa, and the kids are truly home again.

Awaiting Ma in the kitchen are a goat, a sow and her piglets, and more squawking chickens. Cut to a shot of the house's front door and out they come—the goat, the sow and her piglets, and the chickens—with Ma holding two brooms and yelling, "*Git outta here, you!*"

Pa is near the front porch, just taking it all in. "How *peaceful*," he says.

Ma is hardly as sanguine: "Pa, this ain't healthy! Havin' these chickens and pigs and that sow in the house."

"How can you say that, Ma? That sow ain't been sick a day since we had her."

"Oh, I meant it ain't healthy for *us*. And fix that screen door 'fore the flies swarm in."

Ma, who has grown accustomed to a house with every possible convenience, finds herself frustrated by the primitive features of the old place. One such example is the dry well. "You need to go blast a new one," she says firmly. One would think that after his last attempt at blasting a well during the series' first entry, Ma might suggest another avenue. But Pa is more than willing to do it . . . one of these days.

The following morning finds Ma, as usual, making breakfast. Even Pa is up early, saying that he's turned over a new leaf. Right after breakfast, he's going to round up Geoduck and Crowbar and dig that well. True to his word, he and the faithful Indian pair are out back, preparing to blast. Two sticks of dynamite are protruding out of Pa's back pocket. When his back is turned, a goat, Julius by name, begins to gnaw on them.

Despite turning over that new leaf, nothing has really changed. Pa snoozes while Geoduck and Crowbar work. They light a stick, throw it into the well, and run for cover. Julius jumps into the hole after it. A moment later, he climbs out, the still-active dynamite in his mouth. He goes over to Pa, whose eyes are shut. "Geoduck," he says sleepily, "that tobacco you're smoking smells *terrible!*" At this point, he opens his eyes, only to learn that he and the goat are about to be blown to smithereens. He calls out for Geoduck, but he and Crowbar have taken off like a shot. Pa takes the dynamite and throws it into the hole and turns to run away. But he slides backward into the hole just in time for a huge explosion that rocks the house, turning on Pa's battery-operated radio. Geoduck and Crowbar pull Pa out of a pile of dirt. He has been spared any injuries, but, he says, "It was more work than I expected."

Billy Reed shows up, complaining of how hot it is. Too bad the old place doesn't have electricity, or he would sell Pa a little fan with rubber blades. Pa holds the plug in his hand, causing the fan to start up mysteriously. Concerned, Billy offers to take Pa to the hospital, but before they can leave, Jonathan shows up. Billy explains to him that Pa has turned into a human battery; he is loaded with electricity. Reed helps to demonstrate Pa's new superpower, to Jonathan's astonishment. Pa, he insists, is radioactive. This, Jonathan says, means that the property must be rich in uranium. The government will purchase all the uranium on the property and give Pa a ten-thousand-dollar bonus!

In a rather surreal gag sequence, Ma has Pa acting as a power source. Holding the plugs to a vacuum cleaner, an ice cream maker, a clothes washer and dryer, a mix-master, and other household appliances brought in by Billy Reed, Ma sets to work, cleaning up the old place.

Tom drops in on his parents late at night, depressed over his failing marriage. As soon as the baby is released from the hospital (where he is being treated for a cold), Ma and Kim will take him and return to Boston. Tom asks to stay with Ma and Pa; they are incredibly sweet to him, especially Ma.

Late at night, Billy Reed shows up with a baby. He says he just snuck in the back way of the hospital and grabbed it. When Ma goes to change the infant, she makes a startling discovery: the baby is a girl! Geoduck and Crowbar then show up with *two* babies.

"You pick one you want; we take other one back," Geoduck says. "We your friends, Pa. Plus, we don't like Eastern squaw."

"Sorry about Mrs. Parker," Pa says. "She's from 'society.' Says that her ancestors came over on the *Mayflower*."

"When they did," Geoduck responds, "*my* ancestors were there to greet them."

As it turns out, *these* babies are girls as well. And to make matters worse, the sheriff shows up. Three newborns have been stolen from the hospital, they tell Ma and Pa, both of whom are attempting to act natural. One of the newborns can be heard crying, and then another, and another. Have the kidnappers been caught red-handed? No— the babies are lined up on the back seat of the squad car.

Ma and Pa visit the baby at the hospital the following day. Upon their return to the old place, the two con men with the Geiger counter are there with a new sign, reading, "PRIVATE PROP- ERTY—KEEP OUT."

Ma is incensed. "We been livin here for twenty-five years!" she says.

"And for twenty-five years you didn't pay your property taxes," says one of the cons smugly. "*We did*—and now the property is *ours*."

Jonathan shows up and asks the men just how much the taxes were. Two hundred and seventy-five dollars, they answer. Jonathan asks to buy the place from the new owners, first for $500; when that offer is met with indifference, he raises the amount to $750. Jonathan then introduces an esteemed mining engineer he had hired to investigate the property. His verdict: "There's nothing on it." Now the guys want to sell the worthless property back to Ma and Pa.

No deal, Jonathan says, suddenly sounding like an attorney. For one thing, they are *not* the legal owners. To obtain ownership after paying the delinquent taxes, they must inform the actual owners within three days by registered letter. No such letter had been sent. The cons offer to *give* Pa the receipt for the back taxes. But Jona- than wants blood. These men are guilty of defamation of character, among other charges. Pa, he says, is entitled to a cash settlement.

"Would four dollars be too much?" Pa asks.

"Here's ten—and the deed," one of the men says abruptly. "Now, let's get outta here before they change their minds."

Even though there is no uranium on the property, Pa is thrilled: the back taxes are paid, plus he has ten dollars that he did not have yesterday.

Ma believes she may have made a discovery with a Geiger counter.

The engineer begs off, leaving his Geiger counter with Jonathan, who immediately picks up a signal. The uranium *must* be in the house . . . why, it's in the bedroom, under the bed! He kneels down and pulls out a knapsack marked "U.S. Navy." Inside are Pa's coveralls, given to him by his nephew, who got them when he was in the service. This nephew, it turns out, had been involved in the testing of the atomic bomb. The coveralls are the only radioactive item in the area for at least twenty miles.[26]

Tom shows up again, even more desperate than before. Kim and her mother are leaving with the baby on the twelve-fifteen train. Ma and Pa are determined to stop them. Pa, driving a neighbor's open-topped Ford, takes Ma, Jonathan, and Tom for a ride to the depot.[27] Meanwhile, Mrs. Parker and Kim are boarding the train. *Will* the Kettles make it on time? Before reaching the obvious conclusion, we are treated to an old-fashioned chase sequence. Many familiar tropes are employed, including driving through haystacks and fences, barely missing boulders, running

---

26 For those readers who have not been subjected to pretentious film books, this is what is known as the *deus ex machina*, a plot device whereby a seemingly unsolvable problem in a story is suddenly and abruptly resolved by an unexpected and unlikely occurrence.

27 Percy Kilbride could no more drive an automobile than he could milk a cow. This necessitated another use of a double. Game trouper that he was, in a later scene, Percy, *without* the aid of a double, starts the car and backs it up a few yards.

through a clothesline (covering every passenger with someone else's laundry), and a chicken coop (feathers everywhere). They miss the train, but Pa says he will meet them at the next station—and he knows a shortcut. Driving onto the railroad tracks, Pa stops the car. Everyone piles out ("Come *on*, Pa!" says Tom. "This is *crazy!*") as the train comes directly toward the camera, stopping just before it mows down the car. Pa stands (or sits) his ground, ignoring the verbal threats of the conductor and engineer. Tom, Ma, and Jonathan board the train and confront Kim and Mrs. Parker, as the latter becomes combative. Looking for support from her husband, he tells her firmly to "dry up!" Perhaps inspired by a fellow worm's turning, Tom tells his wife, "Ah, go to—*Boston* with your old lady!"

Jonathan concurs: "*Yes*—go back to Boston and take this spoiled brat of a daughter with you. *I'm* staying *here*; I *like* these people."

Tom, now holding his child, goes to leave the private car. Kim, suddenly (and unconvincingly) sweet, tells her husband that she doesn't *really* want to go to Boston; she wants to stay here, with him. Tom agrees to let her stay *if* she agrees to behave herself. She does, setting feminism back a few hundred years.

"*Hurry up!*" Ma says. "Kiss her and get it over with. Pa can't keep this train waitin' forever!"

Mrs. Parker is all alone. Ma, a tough lady with a soft heart, goes back to see this pitiful woman, now dissolved in tears. Tom, Jonathan, and Kim get into the car and Pa finally agrees to move the car off the tracks. Ma is still with Elizabeth, and now *she* is crying as well. Apologizing for her regrettable behavior, Elizabeth says that she hopes "you can forgive me, Mrs. Kettle."

"Ma's the name," she says kindly.

"You can call me 'Lizzie,'" she responds.

The train leaves, with Ma and Mrs. Parker on board. Seeing the others through the closed windows, they signal for them to go on ahead. Ma then pulls the emergency break, exciting the ire of the conductor once again. But it works. The two stowaways are permitted to disembark. Now on their own, Mrs. Parker wonders aloud if it would be possible to find a taxi in this remote area. The only "taxi" they are liable to find, Ma says, is an old-fashioned handcar. Mrs. Parker—Lizzie—makes a point of saying that this is the first time she and Ma have "pulled together."

"Well, let's *keep* pullin' together," Ma says, signaling a new beginning.

Meanwhile, the car's battery has died, stranding Pa and his group. Cut to a shot of Ma and Elizabeth (their doubles anyway), pumping furiously as they are chased by an oncoming train. To prevent this from being a grizzly tragedy, the ladies manage to change tracks just in time. The others receive assistance from a fellow motorist and are finally returning home. We overhear them speaking about Ma and Elizabeth. "Too bad the two of 'em can't get along," is one of the comments. As they enter the old house, they hear Ma's familiar voice saying, "Sit down, folks. Lizzie's fixin' us some coddled eggs!" And, sure enough, there she is at the stove, dressed and acting like Ma, as she yells out, "COME AND GET IT!"

At first startled, the onlookers have a good laugh before the fade-out.

The Payoff

Ma and Pa Kettle Back on the Farm, one of the lesser series entries, still banked an astonishing $2,350,000 for U-I. And although it played in small, neighborhood theaters everywhere, it had a big-city debut at Manhattan's Capitol Theatre, which included a live stage show featuring Percy Kilbride. It is mentioned in the May 11, 1951 issue of the *New York Times*.

> Ma and Pa Kettle and their brood, plus their son's in-laws and a brand-new grandchild, are crowding the screen of the Capitol. They are a noisy, good-natured family given to the simple things in life, which, of course, embraces the most obvious sort of humor. The Kettles and their shenanigans have been very profitable for Universal-International and most likely this new chapter of their adventures, called "Ma and Pa Kettle Back on the Farm," will be another bonanza . . . Percy Kilbride is featured on the stage of the Capitol doing a comedy mind-reading act. Also on the bill are Kitty Kallen and Frankie Carle and his orchestra.

Chapter 6
Ma and Pa Kettle at the Fair
(1952)

Released by Universal-International, July 11, 1952. 78 minutes. Directed by Charles Barton. Produced by Leonard Goldstein. Story by Martin Ragaway, Leonard Stern, and Jack Henley. Screenplay by Richard Morris and John Grant. Director of Photography: Maury Gertsman, A.S.C. Film Editor: Ted J. Kent. Second Unit Director: B. Reeves Eason. Special Photography: David S. Horsley. Musical Direction: Joseph Gershenson. Art Direction: Bernard Herzbrun and Eric Orbom. Set Decorations: Russell A. Gausman and Ruby Levitt. Make-Up: Bud Westmore. Hair Stylist: Joan St. Oegger. Costume Design: Rosemary Odell.

Cast: Marjorie Main (*Ma Kettle*); Percy Kilbride *(Pa Kettle)*; Lori Nelson (*Rosie Kettle*); James Best (*Marvin Johnson*); Esther Dale (*Birdie Hicks*); Emory Parnell (*Billy Reed*); Oliver Blake (*Geoduck*); Russell Simpson (*Clem Johnson*); Rex Lease (*Sheriff*); George Arglen (*Willie Kettle*); Lois Austin (*Elsie Baker*); Frank Baker (*Jam Judge*); Alex Ball (*Townsman*); John Barton (*Vendor*); John Breen (*Fair Worker*); Margaret Brown (*Ruth Kettle*); Douglas Carter (*Ticket Seller*); Wheaton Chambers (*Injured Man*); Zachary Charles (*Crowbar*); Harry Cheshire (*Pastor*); Billy Clark (*George Kettle*); Juanita Close (*Minor Role*); Edmund Cobb (*Fairgoer*); James Conaty (*Sulky Race Spectator*); Harry Cording (*Ed*); Russell Custer (*Townsman*); Harold DeGarro (*Stilt Walker*); Bob Donnelly (*Clown*); Lester Dorr (*Heckler at Fair*); George Eldredge (*Man at Accident*); Frank Ferguson (*Sam*); Helen Gibson (*Ma's stunt double*); William Gould (*Baking Judge*); Billy Gray (*Kettle Boy*); James Griffith (*Medicine Man*); James Guilfoyle (*Birdie's Trainer*); Robert Haines (*Townsman*); Harry Harvey (*Jam-Judging Committee Chairman*); Hallene Hill (*Birdie Hicks's Mother*); Teddy Infuhr (*Benjamin Kettle*); Gary Lee Jackson (*Billy Kettle*); Jackie Jackson (*Henry Kettle*); Sherry Jackson (*Susie Kettle*); Kenner G. Kemp (*Sulky Race Spectator*); Donald Kerr (*Man on Street*); Donna Leary (*Sally Kettle*); Nolan Leary (*Church Usher*); Jenny Linder (*Sara Kettle*); Frank Marlowe (*Man at Accident*); Sydney Mason (*Philo McCullough*); Frank McFarland (*Judge*); Claire Meade (*Sarah*); Beverly Mook (*Eve Kettle*); William H. O'Brien (*Fairgoer*); Frank O'Connor (*Jam Judge*); Eugene Persson (*Teddy Kettle*); Rose Plumer (*Townswoman*); Mel Pogue (*Delivery Boy*); Roy Regnier (*Fairgoer*); Robert Robinson (*Fairgoer*); Edwin Rochelle (*Balloon Salesman*); Ronnie Rondell Jr. (*Dannie Kettle*); Dick Ryan (*Carnival Barker*); Syd Saylor (*Postman*); Elana Schreiner (*Nancy Kettle*); George Sowards (*Townsman*); Brick Sullivan (*Fairgoer*); Charles Sullivan (*Fairgoer*); Sara Taft (*Gossip*); Forrest Taylor (*Horse-Owner with Sheriff*).

Ma and Pa Kettle at the Fair has much to recommend it to fans of the series. The story is solid, the characterizations are well defined, and the leads are in their element. As for the story, it has heart, drama, and comedy, delivered in equal measure. The results are not unlike a prize-winning jam: delicious, without being overly sweet.

The director this time around was the affable Charlie Barton (1902–1981). Beginning his career at age fifteen during the silent era, he was an extra and bit player. In *Wings* (1927), the World War I aviation film that won the first Academy Award as Best Picture,

Charles Barton.

he was both an assistant to director William Wellman and appears unbilled as a Foreign Legionnaire who feigns an injury to elicit the sympathy of a beautiful nurse, played by "IT Girl" Clara Bow. In the capacity of assistant director, Barton was awarded an Oscar in 1934. In that same year, he directed his first feature, a western called *Wagon Wheels* for Paramount. Another assignment, working with the autocratic Cecil B. DeMille on *Union Pacific* (1939), proved so unpleasant that Charlie left the studio altogether. He was put under contract to Columbia, where he turned out a steady stream of seven or eight

Bud Abbott (left) and Lou Costello (right) look positively natty in The Naughty Nineties *(1945).*

B-pictures a year. Another studio change occurred when he moved to Universal. It was on that unpretentious lot that Charlie found his true calling as a comedy director. Charles Barton would soon become the name moviegoers associated most with the numerous Abbott and Costello pictures flooding the neighborhood theaters. Barton was responsible for some of the team's best vehicles, including *The Time of Their Lives* (1946), as well as their absolute worst, *Dance with Me, Henry* (1956), which also happened to be their absolute last. Although Bud and Lou were infamous for not getting along with their directors, Barton had no such trouble with them. He and Lou were kindred spirits, both men being short, pudgy, and always ready for a laugh. The contributions of the duo's regular director and their regular writer, John Grant (who specialized in verbal routines involving puns and misunderstandings, the ultimate example being the brilliantly constructed "Who's on First?") and the returning team of Leonard Stern and Martin Ragaway, who provided scripts for the duo's radio show, can at times make *Ma and Pa Kettle at the Fair* seem like an Abbott and Costello comedy without Abbott and Costello.

The Supporting Cast[28]

Lori Nelson as Rosie Kettle . . .

Lori Nelson.

This film introduces the lovely ingénue and former model Lori Nelson (1933–2020) in the first of her two turns as Rosie Kettle, Ma and Pa's eldest daughter. Like Richard Long's depiction of Tom Kettle, Rosie is the antithesis of her raucous mother. Nelson was just seventeen years old when she was cast in the Kettle film, and was a rather shy, retiring girl. When asked by an interviewer for *The Astounding B-Monster Archive* what Marjorie Main and Percy Kilbride were

---

28 A casting change was made in the case of Crowbar, played this time out by Zachary Charles (b. 1918). Another involved Birdie Hicks's mother. Isabel O'Madigan, who had essayed the role in *The Egg and I* and *Ma and Pa Kettle*, died in 1951 at the age of seventy-nine. She was replaced by the more cheerful Hallene Hill (1876–1966).

like, she recalled, "They were pretty much the same characters they portrayed on the screen. Percy was a very intelligent man, however. On the set one day was a huge cake, a tribute to Percy, celebrating his fiftieth year in show business. What a wonderful man—very quiet and sweet. Marjorie, by contrast, was rough and gruff and boisterous." In fact, Lori admitted that she was quite intimidated by her veteran co-star. In an early scene in the film, Ma and Rosie are in the living room, having a conversation; Pa is in the kitchen, slightly out of earshot. Ma would talk in a normal tone when speaking to her daughter but, when her husband has a question (which he frequently does), Ma yells the answers in her harshest, loudest tones. One can almost see Lori Nelson wince each time the older actress raises her voice.

To earn her contract at U-I, Lori Nelson trained with the studio's dramatic coach, enacted a scene for the front office, and was ultimately offered a seven-year contract, which was approved in court on her seventeenth birthday. She soon became one of the studio's most popular stars. Born Dixie Kay Nelson in Santa Fe, New Mexico, on August 15, 1933, she had the stereotypical stage mother, someone who lived out her own show business fantasies through her talented child. When she was just four years old, her family moved to Hollywood, where she soon won the title "Little Miss America." She worked as a fashion photographer's model, then (in the early forties) made her first bid for a movie career, testing (unsuccessfully) for a role in the acclaimed Warner Bros. drama *Kings Row* (1942). It was agent Milo O. Frank Jr. who helped Nelson get into the movies, taking her to Universal to meet with members of the casting department. Being a contract player, however, meant that she did not have any say over which projects she was assigned. "The one I *didn't* want to do was *Revenge of the Creature*," she once admitted. "Science-fiction was considered bottom of the barrel in those days. Of course, *that's* the picture I am most remembered for," she said, laughing.

James Best as Marvin Johnson . . .

Nelson's leading man in *At the Fair* is James Best (1926–2015). A likable actor, his background story is particularly inspiring.

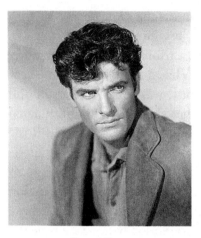

James Best.

Born Jewel Franklin Guy in Powderly, Kentucky, he was taken to an orphanage at age three in 1929. His adoptive parents, Armen and Essa Best, renamed him James K. Best and raised him in Corydon, Indiana. Following a stint in the U.S. Army, stationed in Germany during (and just after) World War II, he was transferred to Special Services and began his acting career. According to Best, he first acted in a European tour of *My Sister Eileen*, directed by Arthur Penn. Upon his return to the States, he toured in road and stock companies in plays and musicals and was spotted by a scout from U-I, who put him under contract. During the fifties and sixties, he was a familiar face in movies and on television in a wide range of roles, from western bad guys to contemptible cowards to country bumpkins. Physical ailments curtailed his work for a long period late in his career, and he later established a well-respected acting workshop in Los Angeles. He also served as artist-in-residence at the University of Mississippi, teaching and directing dramatic arts. Although his role as Sheriff Roscoe Coltrane on the ABC series *The Dukes of Hazzard* (1979–1985) was considered beneath his abilities, it is the part that gave him his greatest fame.

Russell Simpson as Clem Johnson ...

Russell Simpson.

Russell Simpson (1877–1959), whose hawklike appearance became a familiar one to fans of John Ford westerns, had made his debut decades earlier with an unbilled role in Cecil B. DeMille's *The Virginian* (1914). His finest role, however, must surely be that of Pa Joad in the film adaptation of Steinbeck's *The Grapes of Wrath* (1940).

Rex Lease as Sheriff John . . .

Rex Lease during his days as a silent film idol.

Rex Lease (1903–1966) set his sights on Hollywood in 1922 and broke into films as an extra and bit player. Within a few years, he had advanced to the co-starring ranks and made an easy transition to talking films as a minor-league hero in Saturday matinee cliffhangers. His star soon descended, and he found his name lower on the crawl sheet in musical westerns starring up-and-comers Gene Autry and Roy Rogers. Twenty years later, Rex Lease was lucky to get *any* billing of any kind. He had a durable career, nevertheless, appearing in well over three hundred films.

Frank Ferguson as Deputy Sam . . .

Frank Ferguson in one of his countless character roles.

Frank Ferguson (1906–1978) broke into films in the early forties and had a long career playing self-important ranchers, bankers, and police detectives, in films and on television, throughout the sixties. He is perhaps best known to film buffs as the exasperated owner of "McDougal's House of Horrors" in *Abbott and Costello Meet Frankenstein* (1948).

And Teddy Infuhr as Benjamin Kettle.

At the Fair was the final Kettle film for this child star of the forties and fifties. Teddy Infurh (1936–2007) became a Kettle kid as early as *The Egg and I*, in which he plays Henry, who is mistaken by Ma for his brother Albert. In his four other films in the series,

Despite being typecast as a brat, Teddy Infuhr was said to be a sweet, well-mannered boy. Natalie Wood enjoys an ice-cream soda with her smiling contemporary.

Infuhr was firmly established as Benjamin. He even has the distinction of being the only Kettle kid to be featured in a freeze-frame in the title sequence, seated next to Pa in the wagon. Born in St. Louis, Missouri, Teddy was three years old when his parents decided to move to Southern California. Once in the movie capital, the boy's mother prodded him to become an actor. His career took off after a talent scout spotted him while he was attending school at the Rainbow Studios. Working as a freelancer, he landed his first movie acting job as one of Charles Laughton's children in *The Tuttles of Tahiti* (1942). Another role that brought him some unexpected acclaim was that of a mute, semi-autistic, fly-swallowing pygmy in Universal's *Sherlock Holmes and the Spider Woman* (1944). This was followed by small roles in several A-pictures, including *A Tree Grows in Brooklyn* (1945), Alfred Hitchcock's *Spellbound* (1945), and William Wyler's *The Best Years of Our Lives*, which won the Academy Award for Best Picture of 1946. When Hollywood was done with him, he became a chiropractor.

The Storyline

While posing as a dressmaker's model for Ma, Pa takes a break to retrieve that day's mail, generating looks from passersby.

Ma is in the living room, putting the final touches on a dress for Rosie's high school graduation party. Only Rosie isn't there at the moment. Fortunately, Pa is, and *he* is stuck with the job of modeling the dress. When told by Ma to "walk over to me," he does so, schlumping all the way.

"Aw, land sakes, Pa, walk like a *girl*!"

"That's asking a bit too much," objects Pa.

"You're doin' it for your daughter, ain't ya'?" Ma counters. "Now, *walk like Rosie.*"

Pa sashays a bit, his hands delicately poised in the air.

"If Rosie walked like *that*, I'd disown her," Ma says.

"Oh, Ma, I never watch how girls walk nowadays."

"Well, they walk nowadays like they did in *your* days. You've seen *me* walk, ain't ya'?"

He nods.

"Well then, walk like *me*."

Pa struts, taking long, decisive steps with his arms poised like a stevedore.

Ma scowls and says, "If I wasn't afraid of my bread in the oven fallin', I'd lambast ya'!"

Pa insists he was only joking. He then saunters outside to the mailbox, still wearing Rosie's dress and his derby. Two ladies pass by. "Howdy," he says, not in the least self-conscious. Geoduck and Crowbar see what appears to be a woman bending over the mailbox. "Must be Pa's sister from Portland," Geoduck says.

Along comes a horse-drawn carriage, with Birdie Hicks at the reins, and accompanied by her aged mother. "I see Ma's still wearin' the pants in the family," Birdie says with heavy sarcasm. Of course, just mentioning Birdie by name can get Ma boiling mad. The county fair is coming up and that Hicks woman takes home the honors every year. Not *this* year, though, Ma believes. She is working on a new recipe for fresh-baked bread and she is hoping against hope that she will be, at long last, the victor. Placing the first new loaf on the spotless counter with care, Pa enters the kitchen through the back door, slamming it behind him.

"Here's the—" The bread falls, a slide-whistle being employed as the sound effect. Ma is incensed. "*Now* look what ya' did! When ya' went out the front door, didn't I tell ya' *not* to slam it?"

"Well, yes," Pa answers, "but you didn't say anything about the *back* door."

Fortunately for Pa, Ma is distracted by the mail, specifically the envelope from Sheridan College, where their eldest daughter, Rosie, so desperately wants to attend. Ma, ever practical, wonders where they will get the money to pay her tuition. Pa, ever the dreamer, believes their money worries will be in the past once Ma wins the bread-and-jam contest at the fair.

"Why, with Billy Reed sellin' the prize jam all over these parts like he promised," he says optimistically, "we'll have the money for Rosie in no time."

Just then, Rosie can be heard entering the house, asking Ma if the mail has arrived. Ma tells Pa to get that dress off before the girl sees it. She waylays her in the living room, envelope in hand. "Look what just come for ya'! It's from the college."

"Oh, it must be the catalogue," she says. "It *is!*" Suddenly downcast, she adds that it would be a waste of time to even read it.

"Why is that?" Ma asks softly.

Cut to a shot of Pa in the kitchen, holding a sack marked *Porcelain Cement*. He yells to Ma that he is looking for "a tin to put something in." Ma yells back that he should use something on the shelf. Reducing her volume, she asks Rosie, "If you're not goin' to school anymore, what *do* you want to do?"

"I'm going to get a job."

"Graduate from high school one week and go to work the next. Ain't ya' ever gonna take a *vacation?*"

"Oh, *Ma*. How many times do I have to tell you about *ain't?* Now, listen. I *am not* going to take a vacation. You *are not* going to take a vacation. We *are not* going to take a vacation. Understand, Ma?"

"Oh, *sure*, honey," says Ma, missing the point entirely. "Ain't *nobody* gonna take a vacation. 'Cept maybe your pa."

Pa calls out from the kitchen again. "Oh, *Ma?* What about usin' the *checkered* tin?"

"ANY ONE THAT'S EMPTY!" she shouts.

Rosie, believing that Pa is out of earshot, explains that it is impossible for her to find a job anywhere in Cape Flattery, with Pa having run up credit all over town. The store owners let the girl know up front that she would be paying off Pa's debts before she ever expects to receive a dime. Besides, she adds selflessly, she has had enough schooling. And Ma *does* depend on her around the house. "Oh, Ma," she asks suddenly, "*why* is Pa such a *failure?*"

Cut to a shot of Pa pouring the porcelain cement into one of Ma's checkered tins. Overhearing the conversation, his expression is one of sadness.

Ma hesitates. "Well, Rosie, uh . . . I wouldn't say your pa's such a *failure.*"

"He certainly isn't a *success.*"

"Well . . . maybe we can call him a '*successful* failure.' It ain't been easy for Pa. He's had fifteen mouths to feed. Most men work night and day, barely makin' ends meet with only three or four in the family. Your pa don't work at all—*he's* got fifteen, and our ends meet. He's a remarkable man."

Ma (left), Rosie (center), and Pa (right) have a congenial meeting in their kitchen.

Ma and Rosie walk into the kitchen, where Pa is putting the now-full tin into a cupboard. Rosie goes up to him and plants a kiss on his cheek, saying, "How's my remarkable pa?"

Grateful for his daughter's acceptance, he tells her that, in addition to the bread-and-jam contest, he has another plan in mind to make money. Rosie is greatly encouraged by this unspecific news. She leaves the kitchen, college catalogue in hand, feeling more hopeful than she has in quite some time.

Ma asks Pa what exactly he has in mind. He tells her that he plans to borrow money on the house. Ma reminds him that he has already borrowed as much as he can on this house. Well, he reasons, he will borrow money on the *old* house. Ma asks if he remembers that he already borrowed money on the old house to make the money he borrowed on *this* house. Oh, well, then, he will borrow money on his insurance. Ma reminds him that he already borrowed all he could on his insurance to pay the money he borrowed on the old house to make the payments on the money he borrowed on *this* house. *See?* Nevertheless, Pa insists that, somehow, they will find a way.

Geoduck (seated, left), Crowbar (center), and Pa (right) infuriate Billy Reed (Emory Parnell, standing) by loitering at his store.

Ma asks Pa to go to Billy Reed's store to pick up some groceries. Pa is reticent to do so. It seems Billy has banned Pa from the store until he has paid for the groceries credited to his account. Ma begins to think of *anything* that can be used for bartering, like a basket of eggs. She then adds, "If we could just find a plow horse like old Nellie, there might be some farmin' goin' on around here and a little money comin' in."

"Yeah, it's too bad Nellie died," Pa says. "Sure would like to find another horse to take her place. Taint easy pullin' that plow across the field," he adds as he leaves through the kitchen door. "You're not as young as you used to be, Ma."

Ma goes to throw a pan at her husband, but he has already gone.

Pa, a basket of eggs in tow, is downtown, approaching Billy Reed's store. He witnesses a minor traffic accident, in which the elderly man who is hit by a car collects a quick five hundred dollars from the driver. (The man's blonde passenger is someone other than his wife, and he does not wish to involve his insurance company and their nosy questions.) Hoping to make a fast five hundred bucks for Rosie's college fund, Pa decides to cross the town's Main Street blindly at the height of early-morning traffic. But first, he takes his basket of eggs and walks into Billy Reed's store, where he is greeted affably. When Pa asks for the total on his account, Billy says, "Twenty-four, ninety-five." He then asks Billy if he can borrow his phone for a minute; he needs to make a call. Billy consents, but he reminds Pa (probably for the umpteenth time) that he must settle his account. Waiting for his call to go through, Pa says he is working on a plan to finance his daughter's college education; he'll have enough to pay Billy as well—"quicker than an auto horn can let out a peep." He asks the operator to connect him with Ben Simpson, the attorney.

"Ben, do you handle accident cases? . . . *Good*. Well, come down in front of Billy Reed's store. There'll be a case for you." Pa hangs up the receiver and rings for the operator again. This time he wants to reach Cape Flattery Community Hospital. "Hello, hospital? Send an ambulance down in front of Billy Reed's store. Auto accident."

"When did it happen?" a voice on the phone asks.

"Any minute now," Pa says.

Leaving the store, Pa places his right hand over his eyes and begins to walk slowly across the busy street. A bus approaches, the driver honking his horn loudly. Pa, taking his hand away from his eyes, looks terrified and jumps back to the sidewalk. Bravely (or stupidly), he covers his eyes again and makes another slow trek across the street. Horns honk, tires skid, and metal hits metal. When he reaches the other side of the street, he uncovers his eyes, only to see the devastation in his wake.

"Well, good thing I ordered an ambulance," he says with a shrug. A siren can be heard approaching.

The scene switches to the blacksmith's shop, where an old trotter horse named Emma, belonging to Pa's neighbor Clem Johnson, is tethered to a post out front. Emma, bless her heart, has seen better days, but Johnson claims she could still be useful enough for some sucker. What Johnson is currently excited about is his *new* horse, Peter J., whom the town blacksmith, Ed, agrees is "as pretty a piece of horse flesh as I've seen in many a year." He also believes, unquestionably, that Peter J. will give Birdie's horse, Dixie, a run for the harness-racing prize.

"Birdie's got a fine horse in Dixie, but with my boy here running, she'll stand as much chance of winning as old Emma," Clem replies. "Say, that's something we gotta keep under our hats, on account of the betting odds."

"That's *right*," Ed agrees. "Let 'em make Dixie the favorite, and we can win some money."

Just outside the shop, Clem's sucker shows up.

"Ed, *look*, it's Pa Kettle," Clem says quietly. "Seems mighty interested in old Emma." Greeting Pa, Clem gets into the conversation by offering his condolences to Pa on the loss of Nellie.

"Nellie was a good horse," says Pa.

"You'll be needing another horse now."

"I haven't given it much thought."

"Well, I sorta half-decided to sell that horse outside," Clem says. "Did you see it as you came in?"

"Can't say as I did."

"Well, it's standin' right in front."

"Oh, you mean that old, tired bag of bones out there? He's too old to be standin'. He's ready for a rocking chair."

"*He* is a *she*."

"You don't say," Pa says, feigning surprise.

"That horse is a right fine buy, Pa. That's my old horse, Emma."

"*No*. Is *that* Emma?" Pa says, as though in disbelief. He makes the sound for *tsk, tsk, tsk*. "Well, she sure has *aged*."

"She's got four perfect shoes."

"Only *three*," Pa asserts. "The one on the left hind foot has a nail missin'—second one from the end."

After a tense negotiation, Pa manages to get Clem to knock thirty dollars off his asking price of fifty. Of course, Pa's a little short right now, but he has an idea: "You've tried Ma's jam, haven't you?"

"Yeah."

"Like it?"

"Yeah, but I can't eat twenty dollars' worth."

"No, that's not what I mean. Food prizes at the fair are gonna be bigger than ever this year: a hundred-and-fifty dollars for the jam, a hundred-and-fifty for the bread prize. For twenty dollars, I'll sell you half-interest in Ma."

"*Huh?*"

"Ma would be glad to give up fifty percent for a horse. She'd dearly love a horse to haul her to church on Sunday. And she's a cinch to win the hundred-and-fifty dollars for her jam. And for the twenty dollars you invest, you'll get back seventy-five dollars, and that's better than (*he does some internal ciphering*) six percent!"

"Okay, Pa!" Clem says. "The horse is yours for fifty percent of Ma. And you can take the buckboard along with you. I'll send my boy Marvin over to pick it up Sunday."

Outside again, Pa is mounting the buckboard to take Emma to her new home when Billy Reed arrives on the scene. Offering Pa a piece of hard candy, Billy is asked if he has any that are lime flavored. Billy shakes the glass container holding the candies, making a rattling sound, causing Emma to rear back and whinny.

Watching this at a distance are Clem and Ed. "Maybe I should've warned Pa," chuckles Clem. "Emma was bit by a rattler. Just a little rattlin' noise is enough to set her off."

It is Sunday morning. The bell in the church's steeple is chiming, and the good people of Cape Flattery hurry to be on time for the service. The Kettles are there, of course, being pulled by Emma in Clem Johnson's buckboard. They are all wearing their Sunday best. Watching this with disgust, Birdie Hicks asks her mother, "Did you *ever* see such a disgraceful sight?"

Birdie's mother chides her daughter for her judgmental attitude. "It's a pleasure to see children come to church with smiles on their faces," she says. "It wouldn't hurt for grownups to smile a bit too." Ma issues her standard warning to her restless brood: "First one of you starts cuttin' up in church is goin' to get the hairbrush—and *you know where.*"

Suddenly, a young man approaches Ma. "You must be Mrs. Kettle. I'm Marvin Johnson, Clem's boy."

"Well, haven't you growed!"

"*Ma!*" says the didactic Rosie. "*Not* growed. *Grown.*"

"What have *I* got to groan about?" Ma answers. "Pa! *Pa!* This here's Clem's boy."

"Oh, howdy," Pa says hospitably. "I suppose you come after the buckboard. I took it up to the house."

"Oh, Dad says there's no hurry in returning it."

"Well, thanks, son. Tell yer dad not to worry. I always return things I borrow . . . providin' folks come after 'em."

Ma asks the young man if he would like to sit in church with their family. He demurs—until he gets a look at the blossoming Rosie. The attraction between the two is instantaneous. The boy is sly, too. He gallantly offers Ma his arm as he escorts her into the church. Once everyone has settled in for the service, the pastor addresses the congregation, but his voice is terribly weak. He manages to whisper that, in his many years as pastor, he has always given a sermon. Today, however, he must cede that responsibility to a parishioner willing to accept it. Cut to the Kettles, occupying the first two pews. One of the boys is fiddling with something that looks like a suspender. The boy next to him stretches it out and lets it go, smacking directly into Pa's leg. He reflexively stands up.

"Thank you, Brother Kettle," the preacher says gratefully.

Ma smiles approvingly at her husband as he gingerly approaches the pulpit.

Pa Kettle (standing) unwittingly volunteers to preach a sermon for the ailing pastor.

"I don't know how to preach a sermon," he opens modestly. "I can quote from scriptures. Although I know all the words, I wouldn't know how to put them together. But I can speak from my heart. I can say how thankful I am that I have Ma and my kids. I'm thankful for the food we get, and the clothes we wear. A lot of folks are always askin' God for somethin' instead of being grateful for what they've got. I figure if He wants you to have it, it'll come because you deserve it. He gave us the mountains and the trees, the water, and the fertile land. He gave men the ability to make things and grow things. He put gold and silver, coal and oil, under the ground. All man has to do is dig 'em up. Why, I figure that He kind of wants you to help yourself a little; He don't want to do it all. If I found out right now there was oil under my land, would I be lazy? No, sir. Right away, I'd get Geoduck and Crowbar to start diggin' an oil well. The whole world could be a better place to live in if everybody would do like I do. Each morning, when I wake up, I say, 'I thank You, God, for letting me live to see another day.' And at night, when I go to bed, I say, 'Dear God, please let me live to see another tomorrow so I can prove to You that I can be a better man than I have been today. Amen."

Ma, Pa, and Rosie show up at Town Hall to register for the county fair competitions. Marvin, looking fine in his letter jacket, is coming out of the building just as the three Kettles show up. After exchanging pleasantries, Marvin asks Ma if she will be participating in any of the events. Ma tells him that she is going to take part in the bread-and-jam contest. Marvin tells her that his dad is entering his horse, Peter J.

"Entering a *horse* in a *jam* contest?" she says, aghast.

"*Ma!*" says Rosie, constantly embarrassed by her mother's gaucherie. "Marvin means the *harness meet*."

"*Harness meet?*" Ma says crankily. "My goodness, what're they gonna cook up next?"

At the entrance to the town hall, she comes face to face with Birdie Hicks.

"You gonna make an entry?" Birdie asks.

"I don't know about an *entry*," Ma replies sharply, "but I'm gonna make an *entrance*—*if* ya' get outta the doorway."

"Too bad your horse is too *old* for the harness meet. I'd just *love* to see her race my horse, Dixie."

"If Dixie can run as fast as your tongue can wag, you're sure to win the race."

While these two old bats bicker, the young lovers make a date for the fair.

Pay close attention: we're approaching another plot development.

In a room with a sign on the door reading "Harness Racing," Clem Johnson has just finished officially entering Peter J. in the race, and he hasn't a doubt in his mind that this young horse will take first place. As Clem departs the room, he leaves the door open. The side of the door, now facing front, reads, "Jam Making," and has an arrow pointing to the harness-racing registration desk. Ma approaches the man stationed there.

"Well, good morning," the man says. "Would you like to make an entry?"

"Yes, sir."

"Name?"

"Kettle. Ma Kettle."

"Entry?"

"Crabapple-Plum."

"Nice name. *Age?*"

Ma is taken aback. "Do I *have* to tell?"

"The entry calls for it. *Age?*"

"Fifty-two," she says sullenly.[29]

"Oh, come now, you're joshing. It couldn't be over twenty-one."

"Oh, *now,*" she says, clearly flattered.

"Well, there," the clerk says, completing the registration form. "I guess that takes care of everything."

"If I win," Ma says shyly, not making eye contact and running a finger along the edge of his desk, "I'll bring you some of my entry in a jar."

"Oh, that would be *delightful!*" replies the clerk reflexively.

Ma has left by the time the clerk plays back in his mind what that nice lady had just said. He frowns, confused.

The fair on opening day is a joyous occasion for young and old alike. A barker can be heard yelling above the calliope music. The fairgrounds are simply jammed with people: the women wearing their best hats and bows in their hair; the men wearing old-fashioned boaters. Ma and Pa, caught up in the excitement, even take

---

29 Marjorie shouldn't look so downcast. The writers have taken a full decade off her real age.

a ride on the dark Tunnel of Love. It may have been *too* dark for them, in fact.

"Say, Ma?" Pa asks at the ride's conclusion. "When did you start wearing lip rouge?"

"I ain't *never* used lip rouge," she says, feeling her roughened face. "Since when did *you* start raisin' a mustache?"

"Why, I shaved clean this morning."

They then exchange awkward glances with the couple standing next to them.

Homemade jams in glass jars are lined up on a cloth-covered table, each one bearing an identification number. Some stone-faced male judges in business suits are sampling a spoonful from each jar.

Ma is unusually subdued. "Oh, Pa, I'm so *nervous*. The judges have been smackin' their lips over that jam for an hour. Wouldn't ya' know Birdie Hicks'd be right up there in front?"

The judges have clearly made a taste discovery. "Ladies and gentlemen, your attention, please. The winner of the jam contest is . . . *Ma Kettle!*" Pa hugs Ma and gives her a congratulatory kiss on the cheek. All the onlookers applaud enthusiastically—all, that is, except Birdie Hicks.

Ma is urged forward by the presiding judge, who says, "Let me have your entry blank so that I can attach the prize-winning seal; then you can collect your money." The winner seems humbled. Looking closely at a piece of paper, the judge looks alarmed. He immediately confers with his colleagues. Speaking to the crowd again, he says, "Uh, we regret to announce that Ma Kettle has been disqualified."

"*Disqualified?*" Ma says. "What do ya' mean by 'disqualified'?"

"This form is for the *harness race*, Ma, *not* the jam contest," the judge explains. "You've got a *horse* entered, not *jam*. Sorry." Ma's expression is one of sadness and disbelief.

This time, the judge announces: "The prize goes to Miss Birdie Hicks for her lemon-strawberry."

There is only tepid applause from the spectators. Ma walks toward Pa as though in a daze. "Oh, I'm so mad I could *hit* somebody," she says.

"Never mind," Pa says consolingly. "I'll round up the kids and we'll go home. I'll meet ya' at the entrance."

Marvin and Rosie step up to a concession stand, where Marvin asks for two vanilla ice cream sodas. The Kettle kids pop up out of nowhere.

"Make it *thirteen* more," the good-natured Marvin says.

"Make it *two!*" Ma says. "You kids come home before ya' spoil your dinner. Leave Rosie and Marvin alone."

"Oh, *Ma*," says one little girl. "One ice cream soda won't spoil our dinner."

"Well, all right," acquiesces Ma with a smile. "One ice cream soda . . . *and thirteen straws!*"

Home again. Ma, Pa, and Rosie sit together on the patio, drinking coffee and speaking in serious tones.

"Don't worry about it, Ma," Pa says.

"It's not just losin' the prize money that worries me," she says. "Now that my jam ain't officially the prize jam, Billy Reed won't be sellin' it. Guess he'll be peddlin' Birdie's instead." Nothing Pa or Rosie say or do helps Ma's morale. Standing up with some difficulty, she announces, "Now I gotta go do some bread bakin'." She makes her way to the kitchen.

Out from the cupboard she removes the flour tin to prepare the dough for the loaves of bread. Pouring what little flour remains in the can, she says to herself, "I could have *sworn* I had flour on that list Pa took to Billy Reed's." She opens another cupboard and retrieves a different tin—the one Pa had filled earlier with porcelain cement. Seeing that it is filled with what appears to be flour, she says, "Oh, he put it in the wrong tin."

If this were an episode of *I Love Lucy*, you would hear a member of the studio audience yell out, "Uh-oh!"

As Ma begins the baking process, a delivery arrives at the front door. That nasty Hicks woman has sent along a snide "gag" basket, containing liniment, crutches, and bandages for the aging Emma. This tasteless joke makes Ma so angry that she calls her antagonist and lets her have it. Pa attempts to calm down his irate wife.

"I can't help it," Ma says, "that Birdie Hicks is one woman who really sets this Kettle boilin'!" When Pa doesn't join her in laughing at her own joke, she asks if he still has his sense of humor.

"Not at a time like this," he answers seriously. "Emma's no racer. We couldn't race her against Dixie or any other racehorse."

"Oh, I'm *tired* of hearin' ya' say ya' can't do *this*, and ya' can't do *that*," Ma says, totally fed up. "I bet they told George Washington that he couldn't build that big bridge in New York, but he built it, didn't he?" Using this argument, she pledges to turn Emma into a racehorse.

But no matter how much Ma and Pa cajole, Emma simply will not break into a run; a gentle stroll is all she'll take. Even Geoduck and Crowbar, running four miles as a demonstration, fail to inspire her to go faster. Still, Ma persists. Seated on the buckboard hitched behind Emma, she says that no matter what, Emma is going to be in that race—even if she has to tie wheels on her and *push* her around the track.

Geoduck tries to help by introducing Pa to a medicine man he knows. This horse whisperer is, he says, a "very powerful man," one who can turn Emma into a racehorse. When the medicine man arrives, wearing an immense hat resembling a buffalo head, he is as unprepossessing a fellow as one can imagine.

Greeting Pa, he says, "How."

"Any way you want to, just so you make her run," Pa answers.

After performing what appears to the naked eye to be a pointless ritual, the medicine man shakes some beads in front of the horse, creating a rattling sound. Emma instantly rears back and takes off, with Ma struggling to take control of the reins.[30] Birdie, who just happens to be out for a jaunt in her horse-powered buggy, is shocked to see Ma and Emma traveling at breakneck speed. The

---

30 This sequence, with rousing orchestral music on the soundtrack, has Marjorie Main, in medium shots, with a rather convincing process shot behind her. Doubling for the actress in the long shots is once again former serial queen Helen Gibson.

first step has been accomplished. But if Pa is going to race this horse, Geoduck says, he must get a horse cart or, more accurately, a sulky. And Billy Reed just happens to have one.

"Pa, you aren't *really* going through with this horse race, are you?" Billy Reed asks.

"I sure am, Billy. How much for the sulky?"

"Well, you owed me twenty-five dollars, Ma's grocery list brought it up to thirty, and the sulky's worth twenty. That'll be fifty dollars."

"I'll need some cash for odds and ends," Pa says. "Suppose you give me twenty-five, and that'll make my bill seventy-five."

"Pa," answers the tired-sounding Billy, "I've only got ten dollars in cash."

"Well, give me the ten and you'll owe me fifteen."

Billy wakes up. "*I'll* owe *you* fifteen? You owe *me* fifty dollars!"

"Now, Billy, let's not change the subject."

"All I can give you is five dollars."

"Well, give me the five and you'll owe me twenty."

"Now look, Pa—"

"Fair's fair, Billy. How much did you ask me for?"

"Twenty-five dollars."

"How much ya' gonna give me?"

"Five."

"Well, that makes twenty *you* owe *me*. Take that twenty off the fifty *I* owe *you* and I'll owe you thirty dollars. Just make out a receipt, though."

"*Hmm*," Billy says, thoroughly confused. "Now look, Pa, you're not gonna outsmart me. The sulky's gotta be a cash deal."

"I'll give ya' fifty percent of everything Ma makes at the fair."

"Ma's already lost the jam contest," Billy argues.

"But this afternoon's the bread contest. You've tasted Ma's bread."

"Yeah. Okay, Pa, the sulky's yours for half interest in Ma, but only because I don't want to miss seeing you driving this sulky with Emma trying to pull it." He laughs at the thought of it. "You know, Pa, you ought to put Emma in the driver's seat and *you* do the pulling!"

"Billy, what's that got to do with the five dollars you was gonna give me?"

Still laughing uproariously, Billy says, "Oh, that's right; excuse me, Pa," and reaches into his wallet for the fiver.

"Thanks, Billy," says Pa. "Take it away, boys." And just like that, Geoduck and Crowbar slide the sulky out of the store.

Billy stops laughing and suddenly looks completely flummoxed.[31]

Ma is struggling to remove a loaf of bread from the oven. She places it on the kitchen counter with a *clang.* "I'm jinxed," she tells Pa. "All day I been turnin' out bricks instead of bread." She then orders Pa to get those loaves out of the house; they make her sick just to look at them. "You'd think they was made out of cement instead of flour," she adds.

Ma (right) seems to approve of Marvin Johnson (James Best), the neighbor boy with a yen for Rosie (Lori Nelson, left).

Marvin Johnson is at the door, wearing what looks to be his father's suit. "Hello, Ma," he says cordially. "I came by to see if Rosie could go with me to the fair again."

---

31 This, not surprisingly, is a variation on another Abbott and Costello routine. Given the horse racing subplot, it's almost surprising that Ma and Pa didn't do the "mudder/fodder" bit, used in the A&C films *It Ain't Hay* (1943) and *The Noose Hangs High* (1948). You know the one: "How can a mudder be a fodder?" etc.

"Won't that be nice?" says Ma pleasantly. "Sit down; I'll call her. Um, *Rosie*! Marvin's here to take you to the fair. Come on down."

In the kitchen, Pa has (not surprisingly) corralled Geoduck and Crowbar into hauling the heavy loaves of bread away. In the living room, meanwhile, Rosie is complaining to her new beau. "What am I going to *do*, Marvin? Ma's determined to race Emma just to spite Birdie Hicks. We'll be the laughingstock of the town."

Marvin tells her not to be so sure. "*Birdie Hicks* is liable to be the laughingstock," he says. "Her horse, Dixie, doesn't stand a chance. In fact, Birdie doesn't know it yet, but her horse is gonna lose by a mile."

"You think Emma's that *good*?" asks Ma, who has obviously been eavesdropping.

"Not Emma. *Peter J.*, my dad's new horse. Bought him in Missouri. Won every prize there last year."

Ma is still pleased. "Well, that outta bring Birdie down a peg or two."

Pa, feeling encouraged, wants everyone to join him on the fairgrounds, where he plans to give Emma a good workout. But Ma has no intention of going, not with *her* run of bad luck.

"Not even to try the bread contest, Ma?" he asks. "What can you lose? Don't cost nothin'. They give you the flour and all."

To encourage her to come along, Pa gives her the lucky charm the medicine man had used on Emma. Ma agrees, but she does not hold out much hope.

Marvin asks Ma, rather quietly, to please keep what he said about Peter J. to herself.

"My mouth's a closed book," she says.

In a standard comic juxtaposition, the very next scene has Ma whispering to a neighbor lady about Peter J. being favored to win the harness race. And *that* woman swears her neighbor to secrecy, and so on and so forth. All these gossiping women, including Ma, are using the ovens and baking ingredients provided by the fair. Two of the judges approach Ma and ask how things are progressing. "Should be done," she says with a complete lack of enthusiasm.

She then pulls out the rack, on which rests her loaf of bread. The judges are complimentary of its appearance. "Just try *liftin'* it," she says. One of the judges does so, pronouncing it "light as a feather."

"*Well, I'll be . . .*" she says in disbelief. Ma reaches into her apron pocket and takes out the lucky charm. Maybe this thing is working after all.

Back at the stables, Geoduck tells Pa that Emma is no racehorse without the medicine man's charm. Pa explains that he gave it to Ma for luck in the bread contest. At that moment, he notices that Marvin has some hard candies, not unlike the kind Billy Reed had earlier. Pa asks for one—orange flavored, this time. Naturally, this leads to a shaking of the container, which leads to Emma taking off again. Rosie and Marvin watch in amazement at this impressive display of speed.

At the stables, the always-industrious Geoduck and Crowbar are pitching hay. At one point, Geoduck feels something heavy and solid beneath the hay on his pitchfork. Without stopping to see what it is, he throws it into the growing stack. In a later, completely unfunny scene, horses and crows in the field outside the stables are doing their best to consume Ma's loaves made with the porcelain cement. Loud crunching is the accompanying sound effect. A crow belches twice. When one of the horses whinnies, the crows go to fly off, but they're weighed down by the bread.

Pa is at the stables with Emma when he is approached by Billy Reed. "You've been trying out the sulky, Pa—how do you like it?"

"Surprised myself," replies Pa. "Did all right."

"Good. Next thing, you'll be betting on Emma."

"Mm, maybe."

"I just bet two hundred myself."

"On *Emma?*"

"*Nooo.* Listen, Pa," he says, leaning in confidentially. "I want to give you a tip on a sure thing." He takes Pa to Peter J.'s stall. "Now, don't let this go any further, but Peter J. was a Missouri champ."

"*No!*"

"Lay everything you've got on Peter J.'s nose."

"How 'bout laying a few dollars on his tail? In case he comes in backwards?"

"*Pa!*" It's Ma, holding up some cash. "Pa, *look!* I won the bread prize. A hundred-and-fifty dollars! Ain't that *grand?*"

"It sure is wonderful for the stockholders!" Billy says. "Man, oh, man! Fifty percent!" He takes the money from Ma and peels off seventy-five dollars for himself. "Thanks, Ma," he says, leaving in a hurry.

"Pa, ain't ya' gonna stop him? Did you *see* that? He made off with half my money!"

"That's 'cuz he's got fifty percent of the stock."

"*What* stock?"

"Yours. Ma Kettle's. I had to give Billy *something* for the sulky."

"Ya' mean . . . ? Pa, I'm gonna have to lock ya' up if ya' don't stop doin' foolish things." She stops her rant, looking down. "Seems I'm always scolding ya'."

"I know, Ma," Pa says. "You do all the barkin', but it's *me* that's always in the doghouse."

"Well, I guess it could be worse. We *still* got seventy-five dollars. That's more'n we've seen for a long time."

Along comes Clem Johnson. "Howdy, Ma. Pa."

"Did ya' hear the news?" Ma asks excitedly.

"He ain't interested in things like that, Ma," Pa says, sensing imminent danger.

"Oh, course he is," says Ma. "*I* won the bread contest!"

"That's great, Ma. How much did ya' get?"

"A hundred-and-fifty dollars! But I only got seventy-five left."

Taking it into his own hands, he says, "Seventy-five dollars, all counted out! You must've been expecting me! Guess I'll go see how the boys are doing with Emma."

Alone with a seething Ma, Pa says, "Gue-ess I'll go see how the boys are doing with Emma."

"*Pa!* Come here! *Another* stockholder?"

"I had to give fifty percent for the horse."

"Fifty to Billy for the sulky, fifty to Clem for the horse." A beat, for timing. "Ya' give me all away!"

"Yep," he says, slinking off.

For the first—and only—time in the series, Ma breaks the fourth wall as she says directly into the camera: "*Sold*—for a horse and buggy." She then angrily removes the blue ribbon pinned to her dress and throws it on the ground.

Early the following morning, Clem Johnson shows up at the stables to check on Peter J. When he opens the stall door, he notices immediately that something is ailing this young champion. Meanwhile, Tassie, another horse in the competition, isn't doing so well either; in fact, she can't seem to stand up. Her owner calls out to Clem. Both men are distraught by their obviously ill steeds. Billy Reed, who is passing by the stall at the time, overhears Clem and Tassie's owner commiserating. Without making himself known, he joins a gathering of men outside the stables. "With Peter J. out of the race, Birdie's got the race in her pocket," Billy says. "I'm switching my bet to Dixie." This sets off a consensus.

Pa and Ma in the stable just prior to the all-important harness race.

Ma and Pa are in the stable.

"The horse looks all right," she laughs. "But let's take a look at *you*. Here," she adds, handing Pa some racing gear, "put this on. Nice of that fella to loan ya' this outfit. Wonder why *his* horse ain't runnin'?"

"A horse is like a human," says Pa, suddenly the world's expert on all equestrian matters. "Might've ate somethin' that didn't agree with it."

Once Pa is wearing the shiny racing jacket (and a wonderful smile), Ma tells him to back up a bit; she wants to get a good look at him.

"Well, *I'll declare*," she says, "ya' look as good as ya' did the day we was married, thirty years ago."[32]

Just then, Geoduck and Crowbar show up.

"Where've you two been?" asks Ma. "Pa needs ya' to help hitch up Emma."

"Bet-um two dollar on Emma," says Geoduck.

"Make-um much money," adds Crowbar. "Nobody bet on Pa. Whole town bet-um big on Dixie."

"On *Dixie*?" asks Ma in surprise. "How come? You said *Peter J.* was a champion."

"Now, big champ sick," explains Geoduck.

"Dad's horse, *sick*?" Marvin asks, concerned. He and Rosie leave to offer their support.

"So, Birdie's horse is the favorite," says Ma. "I'd bet against her for spite, if my luck wasn't so bad and I was a bettin' woman … *and* if I had some money."

"Here, Ma," Crowbar says generously. "Seventy-five dollars."

"Where'd *you* get seventy-five dollars?" she asks.

"I find it in, uh—in the stable."

Ma accepts the cash. "This is just borrowin', Crowbar. But if bettin' means sendin' Rosie to college, I guess it wouldn't be *such* a big sin. Thanks. Now, go help Pa hitch up the sulky."

Once Ma has left, Geoduck asks Crowbar: "Where you find seventy-five dollars in stable?"

---

32 An odd continuity error: earlier in the same film Pa had said that he and Ma had been married for *twenty-four years*. The number of years of their union seems to change from film to film, although it is usually in the range of twenty-five to thirty.

"In Clem Johnson's pants pocket."

"Oh. I thought maybe you *steal* it."

Speaking of Clem Johnson, he is saying to Marvin and Rosie: "That's racing luck, son. Emma may still have one good race left in her. I hope so, for your folks' sake, Rosie. Run along now. They'll be on the track soon."

"We'll see you later," Clem says.

"Bye, Mr. Johnson."

"Bye."

Once they leave, Ma shows up. "Hello, Clem."

"Howdy, Ma."

"Sorry about your horse. How is he?"

"Well, the vet's makin' a check now."

"Uh, Clem, if you was bettin' now and needed to win, who would ya' bet on?"

"Why, on *Dixie*. In fact, I figured on betting seventy-five dollars right now, but seventy-five dollars disappeared out of my pocket."

"*Seventy-five dollars?*"

"Yeah."

"That's funny," Ma says, putting two and two together. "Crowbar found seventy-five dollars in the stable. Wanted me to find the owner." She hands him the money.

"Why, thanks," he says. "Aren't *you* gonna bet, Ma?"

"No," Ma says, her shoulders sloped in defeat. "I changed my mind, Clem. If I bet on Pa, I might lose the money. If I bet on Dixie, I'd feel I'd wronged Pa."

"Ah."

"So, I guess I'll just keep hopin' he'll win the purse." She slowly walks away.

"*Clem!*" calls one of his fellow breeders.

"*Huh?*"

"The vet says all our horses have been fed something."

"What?"

"I called the sheriff. He's already figured the whole thing out."

"Yeah," concurs another horse owner. "Somebody didn't want those horses to win."

"*I* could've figured that out," says Clem. "The question is, *who* is that *somebody?*"

The trumpet sounds. It's the call to the post.

Under a beautiful, cloudy sky, the jockeys guide their horses onto the track.

The spectators in the stands talk among themselves. The clear favorite is horse number two, Dixie. Ma takes a seat in the bleachers with her kids.

"*Look, Ma,*" Benjamin says enthusiastically, "*there's Pa!*"

"Looks as good as the rest of 'em," Ma says proudly. She stands up and yells, "GOOD LUCK, PA!"

"Good luck, Pa!" all the kids—including Rosie and Marvin—echo in support.

Pa, looking smart in the sulky, tips his derby to his loyal following. Just then, Emma turns around and begins trotting in the opposite direction on the track.

"Say, you fellas are goin' the wrong way," Pa says to his competitors.

Ma jumps up, shouting, "*PA!* WHERE YA' GOIN'?"

He turns around.

"Why didn't you leave him alone?" asks Birdie Hicks, seated with her mother in the winners' circle. "He'd have stood a better chance coming in first that way. Then we could have called him 'Wrong Way' Kettle."

"Birdie," Ma says calmly. "I thought all the horses had to be on the track."

"They *do,*" she answers.

"Then how come they let a nag like *you* out here?"

"End of the chute, men," says the judge in a wooden tower on the track. "Bring 'em up easy and keep an even line!"

"All set, Ma?" asks Billy Reed, just entering the stands. "The race should begin any minute."

"I hope so! I'm a nervous *wreck.*"

"So am I. I just put a pretty bundle on Dixie's nose. So did *everybody* else."

And ... *they're off!*

Emma is far behind, with Dixie out front. Pa then gets an inspiration: the good luck charm! He rattles it, and Emma comes from behind and straight into the lead!

Realizing that Pa may well come in first after all, Billy tells Ma that such a result would bankrupt the entire community. Ma realizes she has to take action, and fast! Standing behind a garbage can, she lifts her dress and removes a garter. Holding it in her hand like a slingshot, she says sadly, "Hate to do this to ya', Pa." She then pulls back the band and shoots a pebble at Emma, hitting her on the side. Immediately, she loses her stride and breaks into a trot. Dixie wins.

Slowing down, Pa says dejectedly, "Well, Emma ... we tried."

The spectators leave the stands in droves to collect their winnings. Rosie is devastated. So are Geoduck and Crowbar, and, perhaps more so than anyone, is Ma.

Ma and Pa Kettle, two of the most decent citizens of Cape Flattery, are blatantly accused of poisoning the competing horses to gain an unfair advantage. Clem Johnson is the leading accuser, and the sheriff believes that their motivations seem quite clear. When presented with a partial loaf of cement bread, Ma admits that *she* made it, but she certainly did not feed it to any of the horses. Clem adds that one of the stable boys saw Pa's Indian friends dump the bread, mixed with hay, by the horse barn yesterday. Pa accepts responsibility for *that* mishap; after all, it was *he* who gave Geoduck and Crowbar the bread.

Birdie Hicks, predictably enough, joins the chorus of accusers, saying that the Kettles must have figured that with all the other horses sick, an old nag like Emma could win the race. But they had not foreseen that Dixie would refrain from eating the tainted bread. With all this circumstantial evidence, the sheriff says he will have to put both Ma and Pa in custody.

"Well, thanks, Sheriff," says Pa. "For a minute I thought he was gonna put us in jail."

In custody—and in jail—Ma sits glumly on the bunk while Pa stands against the bars. Sam, the inept-but-well-intentioned deputy, tells them, "That Birdie Hicks *sure* can get people riled up. Like the time she blamed Jeb Harris for poisonin' her dog. Why, she got folks so steamed up, they wanted to string Jeb up by the neck. Of course, *your* case is different."

"I hope so," Pa says flatly.

"Yeah, hurtin' a horse is a *bigger* crime than poisonin' a dog." The deputy thinks about what he just said and chuckles slightly. "That *ain't* cheerin' ya' up."

"No," Pa says quietly, "but if you tell us they're gonna hang us, that *would* give us a lift."

"If you could just get out of town until folks cool off, you'd be all right."

"I guess we would," says Ma. "Folks is kinda hotheaded now."

Sam is clearly sympathetic to these good people, neither of whom has it in their constitution to harm an animal or cheat in a competition. He does the bit of leaving the keys in the cell's lock, hoping they take the hint and escape. But the hopelessly honest Ma and Pa repeatedly call him back, reminding him to take the keys. Suddenly from outside comes the sound "*Psst!*" It is the ever-loyal Geoduck and Crowbar.

"*Ma, Pa,*" Geoduck says quietly. "We come to help you make getaway, quick." Through the bars, he slips Pa a baguette before disappearing into the night.

"We got plenty of *bread*," says Ma cluelessly. "We don't need *that*."

Pa goes to toss it back when out from the end slips some tools, including a hacksaw.

"Durned Indians!" Ma says with irritation. "We could've bitten that bread and broke a tooth!"

At the station, the sheriff is handing a long rope over to Clem Johnson. Birdie Hicks and Billy Reed stand in the background. "Here's your tow rope. County don't buy me a new car soon, I'm gonna have to go back to ridin' horses." Everyone chuckles. The door opens, and in walks Ma and Pa, accompanied by Sam.

"Now look here, Sheriff," says Ma brusquely, grabbing the rope from Clem's hands. "If there's gonna be a hangin', hang *me*! *I* baked that bread with the cement in it, but I didn't do it to hurt the horses!"

"Sheriff," Pa begs, taking the rope from Ma and wrapping it around his neck, "hang *me*! Let Ma go! It was *my* cement that got into the bread, and I'm to blame for the Indians putting the bread near the horses!"

It takes the sheriff a few minutes to calm down the noble Kettles long enough to explain that he and a few representative citizens are there *not* to hang them, but to *thank* them. Clem Johnson explains that "Billy Reed told us the wonderful thing you did, Ma. You saved the town from a financial upset."

Ma has a guilty look on her face.

Pa asks, "Did *Ma* do that?"

"She certainly *did*," testifies Billy Reed. "I saw Ma make a slingshot and deliberately shoot a pebble at Emma, making Emma break pace, and letting Dixie win the race."

"Ma," Pa asks his wife quietly, "did *you* help Dixie to win?"

"I had to, Pa," she confesses tearfully. "When Billy told me the whole town would go broke, I just *had* to. You'd have nobody to borrow from."

"That's all right, Ma," Pa says, comforting her.

Birdie walks toward her sworn enemy. "Ma, I'm sorry for all I did. Dixie won, but the victory really belongs to *you*. For losing, you made yourselves dearer to the hearts of all your townspeople. So, I—Well, I, I—"

"I never knew ya' to be at a loss for words before, Birdie," says Ma, again on the verge of tears.

"Oh, I know it, Ma," she says, truly humbled. She then reaches into her purse, saying, "Here's the money that Dixie won. Now *you* take it. That'll get Rosie started in college."

Ma takes hold of her hand. "That's mighty nice of ya', Birdie. Pa and me thank ya'."

Birdie heads toward the door, but Pa stops her. "We'll just borrow it, Birdie, till I go to work."

Birdie merely rolls her eyes and leaves the office.

"And Ma," Billy Reed adds, "I sent a sample of your jam to Mr. Potter of the A&A stores and, if you don't mind, he'll carry a whole line of Ma Kettle's jams and jellies."

The Kettles, the sheriff, Clem, and Billy share a good laugh.

"Ain't it funny, Pa?" Ma says, "I go to enter a jam contest and get in a horse race!"

Pa tops her: "We get into a horse race and we get into a jam!"

Ma tops him: "And now that it's all over, everything jells!"

The Payoff

With *Ma and Pa Kettle at the Fair*, the series reached its apex, at least from a commercial standpoint. The film, which was shot in December 1950 and released in July 1952, was the highest grossing entry, raking in $2.5 million in the United States alone. It also received some of the best reviews of the series, many of which came from everyday people. When the film was previewed at the Warner Theater in Los Angeles on March 6, 1952, an audience made up of seventy-eight males and thirty-nine females, ages eighteen to forty-five, submitted the following comments:

- "We need more of these harmless types of pictures; fun is needed, not guns!"
- "My sides hurt from laughing!"
- "The Indians were a scream!"
- "Very entertaining and a relief from war pictures."

Even the stuffy *New York Times* (July 7, 1952) had this to say:

Loyal followers of those amiable rustics, the Kettles, won't be disappointed in the Palace's screen supplement to the vaudeville show, "Ma and Pa Kettle at the Fair." The latest in Universal-International's family comedy series is basically almost identical with its predecessors, being as wholesome, folksy and unsurprising as a hayride in a clapboard wagon. Yesterday morning's customers, a predominantly family audience, were delighted with the homespun antics of Marjorie Main and Percy Kilbride, whose seasoned gawkiness by now has gone beyond the point of professionalism. This offhanded familiarity also applies to the director, Charles Barton, and two scenarists, Richard Morris and John Grant, whose story, with a few new gags, simply backs the Kettles up and starts them over again . . . Judging by their featherweight tribulations, they may, in fact, outlive us all. Rosie Kettle, played by Lori Nelson, craves a college education. So, with fair time approaching, Ma starts warming up for the jam and bread culinary prizes and Pa rehearses the family nag for a trotting race. The race is lost because Ma learns that the whole town has bet against them and, as insurance toward continued borrowing, nicks Emma (the horse, and a sure enough Kettle) with a garter slingshot. The grateful townspeople compensate this gallantry and Rosie goes on to higher learning. Plunked down bodily from time to time are such time-worn clichés as mixing cement with flour, a nosy neighbor, Pa's milquetoast bargaining astuteness and Ma's ear-splitting butchery of the English language. And in addition to Miss Nelson, James Best, Esther Dale and Emory Parnell all help to keep the humor and general flavor at sod level. The surprising thing about the film, as has happened before, is that Pa and Ma Kettle somehow manage to survive this contrived tomfoolery as characters rather than caricatures. Could be Mr. Kilbride's rock-hewn quietness or the kindliness underlining Miss Main's leathery grimacing. At any rate, one sequence in which Mr. Kilbride delivers an impromptu sermon is both touching and genuinely amusing, two qualities that may yet make the Kettle family synonymous with something more than a ticket stub.

Chapter 7
Ma and Pa Kettle on Vacation
(1953)

Released by Universal-International, April 20, 1953. 75 minutes. Alternate title: *Ma and Pa Kettle Go to Paris*. Directed by Charles Lamont. Written by Jack Henley. Produced by Leonard Goldstein. Musical Direction: Joseph Gershenson and Herman Stein. Director of Photography: George Robinson, A.S.C. Film Editor: Leonard Weiner. Art Direction: Bernard Herzbrun and Robert F. Boyle. Set Decorations: Russell A. Gausman and Joe Kish. Dances: Harold Belfer. Costume Design by Rosemary Odell. Make-Up: Bud Westmore. Hair Stylist: Joan St. Oegger. Sound: Leslie I. Carey and Corson Jowett.

Cast: Marjorie Main (*Ma Kettle*); Percy Kilbride (*Pa Kettle*); Ray Collins (*Jonathan Parker*); Bodil Miller (*Inez Kraft*); Sig Ruman (*Cyrus Kraft*); Barbara Brown (*Elizabeth Parker*); Ivan Triesault (*Henri Dupre*); Oliver Blake (*Geoduck*); Teddy Hart (*Crowbar*); Peter Brocco (*Adolph Wade*); George Arglen (*Willie Kettle*); Alex Ball (*Club Patron*); Eugene Borden (*French Desk Gendarme*); Nick Borgani (*Club Patron*); Margaret Brown (*Ruthie Kettle*); George Calliga (*Club Patron*); Steve Carruthers (*Club Patron*); Jack Chefe (*French Waiter*); Billy Clark (*George Kettle*); Russ Conway (*Cmdr. Fordyce, Naval Attaché*); Gino Corrado (*French Maître d'*); Paul Cristo (*Club Patron*); Andre D'Arcy (*Apache Team*); Jean De Briac (*Chief Chantilly*); Lawrence Dobkin (*U.S. Agent James Farrell*); John Eldredge (*Masterson*); Carli Elinor (*Orchestra Leader*); Franklyn Farnum (*Club Patron*); George Ford (*Plane Passenger*); Jon Gardner (*Benjamin Kettle*); James Gonzalez (*Plane Passenger*); Harold Goodwin (*U.S. Agent Harriman*); Dick Gordon (*Club Patron*); Charles Hagen (*Club Patron*); Chuck Hamilton (*Gendarme*); Sam Harris (*Plane Passenger*); Rosario Imperio (*Apache Team*); Gary Lee Jackson (*Billy Kettle*); Jackie Jackson (*Henry Kettle*); Sherry Jackson (*Susie Kettle*); Alice Kelley (*Stewardess*); Colin Kenny (*Club Patron*); Jack Kruschen (*Jacques Amien*); Eddie Le Baron (*Wine Steward*); Donna Leary (*Sally Kettle*); Jenny Linder (*Sara Kettle*); King Lockwood (*Waiter*); Alphonse Martell (*Restaurant Manager*); Torben Meyer (*Doorman at Hotel Louis*); Beverly Mook (*Eve Kettle*); Rita Moreno (*Soubrette*); Jack Mower (*Dr. R. B. Schriner*); Roger Neury (*Waiter*); Jay Novello (*Andre*); Gloria Pall (*French Girl Walking Poodle*); Manuel París (*Gendarme*); Waclaw Rekwart (*Club Patron*); Suzanne Ridgeway (*Club Patron*); Mark Roberts (*Teddy Kettle*); Ronnie Rondell Jr. (*Dannie Kettle*); John Roy (*Plane Passenger*); Elana Schreiner (*Nancy Kettle*); Ken Terrell (*Cab Driver*); Dave Willock (*Franklin*); Zacharias Yaconelli (*Maître d'*).

Marjorie Main would occasionally treat herself to a meal at a diner on Hollywood Boulevard.

By 1953, Marjorie Main and Percy Kilbride were firmly established in the public's mind as partners; there were even naïve souls in the hinterlands who believed the two were married in real life. In fact, the actors had virtually no contact with each other once the cameras stopped turning. Goodness knows there was no animus between them; they simply led separate lives. On one occasion, however, the two accidentally met. Marjorie, who was always impeccably groomed and dressed when in public, would occasionally take in a matinee on Hollywood Boulevard. Following this, she might venture into a nearby soda fountain. While strolling the boulevard on this afternoon, she noticed a gentleman about a half-block away. "There was something vaguely familiar about the way the fella carried himself," she told a reporter, "something about the tilt of his derby hat that struck a chord of memory." Marjorie stepped up her pace a bit to reach this man. Tapping him on the shoulder, she said, "*Percy?*" Turning around with a blank expression was, of course, Percy Kilbride. The two laughed about the coincidence and proceeded to spend part of the afternoon together. Imagine how thrilled a tourist would be to walk into a shop, only to find Ma and Pa Kettle having ice cream sodas together.

The premise of their newest film—Ma and Pa take a trip to Paris, France—gave screenwriter Jack Henley the opportunity to employ the "fish out of water" situations that had worked so well for the Kettles, comedically at least, particularly in *Go to Town* (1950). Unlike that New York adventure, the current project did not allow for any location work in the storied City of Love. No—the Paris street on Universal's backlot would have to suffice. And instead of grappling with bank robbers, they would now be caught up in an international spy ring. Clearly, this was an attempt to make box-office gold from a retread of a tried-and-true hit. What they ended up with is a funny, if derivative, entry.

The Cast

There are return appearances by Ray Collins and Barbara Brown as the Parkers, and Oliver Blake and Teddy Hart as Geoduck and Crowbar. Other supporting players include:

Sig Ruman as Cyrus Kraft . . .

Sig Ruman.

Sig Ruman (1884–1967) was an actor with a lengthy list of credits in both dramatic and comedic roles. Born in Hamburg, Germany, he had served with the Imperial German Forces in World War I before coming to the United States in 1924. Befriending playwright George S. Kaufman and critic Alexander Woollcott, Ruman was cast in a succession of Broadway plays. With the advent of talkies, he became a favorite of the Marx Brothers, appearing as a foil for the zany team in *A Night at the Opera* (1935), *A Day at the Races* (1937), and *A Night in Casablanca* (1946). With his German accent, he was also a regular in several World War II espionage thrillers, including *Confessions of a Nazi Spy* (1939), *They Came to Blow Up America* (1943), and *The Hitler Gang* (1944); he also gave a superb portrayal of Schulz, the two-faced guard in *Stalag 17* (1953), directed by Billy Wilder.

Bodil Miller as Inez Kraft ...

Exotic actress Bodil Miller (1928–2017) was born in Nørresundby, Denmark, as Bodil Jørgensen. A stunning beauty, she made her acting debut onstage in Copenhagen. Following her training, she ventured to Hollywood in search of stardom. She was signed by U-I and groomed as a starlet, appearing in a few films. Apparently unhappy in Hollywood, she returned to her homeland to continue her career. That career dipped precipitously due to her involvement in an internationally produced science fiction fiasco called *Reptillicus*, (1961). Married only once, to Eugene Solow, Bodil Miller died at eighty-nine on September 16, 2017.

Bodil Miller.

And Gino Corrado as a French Maître d'.

In a career dating back to silent films, Italian-born Gino Corrado (1893–1982) can be seen in four hundred pictures, usually cast as a waiter or a chef. The screen workers strike of 1947 convinced producers to stop using lavish sets and hundreds or thousands of extras, which made it difficult for Corrado to find work. At that point, he made the transition from movies to real life in the restaurant business, in the role of waiter, chef, and even owner. You might say he was one actor who typecast himself.

Gino Corrado.

The Storyline

The film opens on an unfamiliar sight: Pa Kettle is wearing an apron as he works away in the kitchen. He is preparing breakfast for Ma, all the while contentedly singing a children's rhyming ditty called "Lazy Mary."[33]

Ma is obviously getting on, as the expression goes. After a hard day of washing, she remains in bed for the better part of the following morning. Pa is sympathetic to her growing fatigue; so much so that he vows to help with the laundry. "Starting today, I'm gonna make a clean shirt go for a month instead of two weeks," he says nobly.

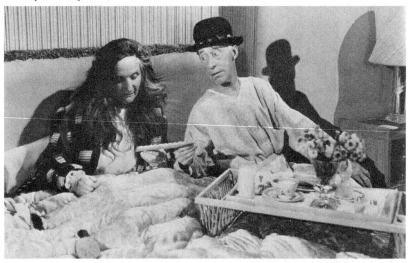

Pa enjoys the breakfast he made for the long-tressed Ma.

On the breakfast tray is an envelope postmarked Boston; it must be from Kim's folks, Jonathan and Elizabeth Parker. Ma tears open the envelope and takes out two airline tickets to New York, and then to Paris. While Pa eats the meal he made for his overworked wife, Ma reads the letter from Jonathan and conveys to Pa that the Parkers would like to treat them to a trip to Paris.

"Paris, *France?*" he asks excitedly.

"Well, it ain't Paris, *Kentucky!* Two of their friends were goin' with 'em, but after buyin' the tickets, their friends can't go. Now they want *us* to go with 'em."

It turns out that Pa had wanted to see Paris since 1917, when America declared war on Germany. When Ma asks, "What

---

33 This children's rhyme was said to have originated in England. It has the same melody as "Here We Go Gathering Nuts in May" and "Here We Go Round the Mulberry Bush."

stopped ya'?" Pa answers, "Don't know. They said I couldn't go till they scraped the bottom of the barrel."

As was the case when they won a trip to New York City, Ma is worried about the kids. Pa, who is elated by the prospect of this new vacation, tells Ma to leave it to him—*he'll* find someone to look after the little darlings. After all, his previous choice, the notorious bank robber "Shotgun" Munger, did not result in any fatalities—although the kids nearly succeeded in killing *him*. Pa gets up from the bed, the breakfast tray now holding a dirty plate and utensils, an empty eggshell, and assorted toast crumbs.

"*Thanks for the breakfast,*" Ma says with heavy sarcasm.

"Oh, don't mention it, Ma," says Pa, gracious (and oblivious) as ever. "I'll fix ya' up a good lunch too."

Pa is on a quest. He must find someone to look after the kids or he can kiss Paris *adieu*. He shares his predicament with Geoduck and Crowbar. Geoduck claims to know someone, "a young squaw who will papoose-sit for four dozen eggs a week."

"Kinda steep, ain't it?" says the parsimonious Pa.

In a hushed tone, Geoduck says, "Pa, don't forget to bring us some postcards from Paris."

"I thought neither of you fellas could read," Pa says innocently. "Who has to *read*'em?" Geoduck replies.

Pa dutifully gets inoculated and has his passport photo taken. Ma asks each of the kids what they want them to bring back from Paris. One daughter says a small bottle of perfume ("if it isn't too expensive"). Ma laughs and hugs the girl affectionately. A young boy asks for Ma to bring home French fries. More laughter, more hugs. She follows this up by saying, "If you'll all be good while Ma's gone and do what Little Red Fawn tells ya', I'll bring every one of ya' a present when I come back."[34] The kids cheer, and the taxi arrives to whisk Ma and Pa off to the airport in Spokane.

---

34 Little Red Fawn, incidentally, is a heavyset, taciturn Native American woman, who just stands there without uttering a word. Her role is so nondescript that she is not even credited on the exhaustive Internet Movie Database (IMDb).

The reunion with their in-laws at Idlewild Airport (later, the John F. Kennedy International Airport) is warm and friendly. Although Pa and Jonathan got along from the first moment they met (during *Back on the Farm*), the tension between Ma and Elizabeth was downright unpleasant, even for a comedy. In addition to their newfound unity, it is also a relief to have these four mature individuals to focus on without having to contend with their whiny adult kids, Tom and Kim. Elizabeth explains their absence by saying Kim and the baby are currently visiting Tom in camp, but that they wish Ma and Pa *Bon Voyage*.

"That was nice of 'em," says Pa. "Did you wish them the same thing for us?"

"Yes, of course!" Jonathan says kindly.

As the ladies make their way together through the airport, Pa and Jonathan stay back for just a moment. "Pa, you old son of a gun," says the jovial Jonathan, "will we have a good time in Paris!"

"Paris, *France!*" says Pa with a knowing wink.

In the stock footage used to establish the interior of the TWA jet, we see the wide, comfortable seats and ample leg room then accorded to travelers—a far cry, sadly, from the cramped misery of flights in the 21st century. A stewardess (this was before they were known as flight attendants) approaches Ma and Pa and asks them to please fasten their belts.

"Don't wear any," says Pa in earnest. "Would it be all right if I take a tuck in my suspenders?"

"She means this belt, *here*," Ma says impatiently.

Pa is enjoying every minute of the flight. As it turns out, he loves airplane food. Ma, on the other hand, can barely digest it. Feeling bilious, she tells Pa that if he plans to light up "that smokestack" (his pipe), she would prefer that he do so in a different section of the plane. (In another nod to an earlier period, it was common for passengers to smoke freely in every part of a commercial airliner.) The always-agreeable Pa immediately sets out to find another seat, this one located toward the back. He finds himself seated next to a pleasant man who introduces himself as Adolph Wade. Mr.

Pa offers sympathy when Ma announces that airline food does not agree with her.

Wade is a slight gentleman, with a carefully trimmed mustache and a pronounced French accent. The two men hit it off almost instantly. When the Frenchman asks Pa where he will be stopping, he answers, "Louie's fourteenth."

"You mean the *Louis Quatorze.*"

"No, this is Louie's fourteenth hotel, I'm sure."

"Mr. Kettle—?"

"Pa's the name."

"Pa. You look like a man who can be trusted."

"Been chargin' tobacco at Billy Reed's store for twenty-five years."

"Good. I want to give you something. That is, if you do not mind doing me a favor?"

"Always believe in bein' neighborly."

Wade asks Pa to bring the letter to him in his room (number 408) the following night at eight. Pa logically asks why he would want the letter brought to him when he is already in possession of it. Wade explains patiently that he is subject to dizzy spells brought

During the flight to Paris, a Frenchman named Adolph Wade (Peter Brocco, left) entrusts Pa (right) with a mysterious envelope.

on by his having been shell-shocked during the First World War. Sometimes, he tells Pa, he barely knows what he's doing.

"Don't feel too bad about it," Pa says kindly. "Ma says I'm that way all the time."

The man laughs politely before adding, "It's amnesia."

"Ma says with me it's dumbness."

We are treated to some ancient stock footage of Paris from the sky as the plane (more stock footage) descends for a landing.

After registering at the Louis Quatorze, Jonathan, who is apparently footing the entire bill for the far-less-solvent Kettles, asks the clerk to convert some American bills to francs. Meanwhile, Pa wanders off. In the far end of the hotel lobby is a large poster advertising the show at La Café d'Eté, provocatively illustrated with silhouettes of shapely can-can girls.

A Frenchman sidles up and says, *"Magnifique! N'est-ce pas?"*

Turning around, he says, "How'd ya' know my name was Pa?"

Pa is clearly in his element while posing with a line of shapely can-can girls in this publicity shot for Ma and Pa Kettle on Vacation.

"*Pardon?*"

"You just called me 'Pa.'"

"No, no, no, monsieur, I said, '*n'est-ce pas.*' I mean, your taste, it is good."

Pa sighs and looks back at the poster. "What I wouldn't give to be fifty-nine again."

The man then tells Pa he has a wonderful bargain to offer: twelve authentic postcards, showing the beauty of Paris. And all for the unheard-of price of one American dollar. And these postcards are—how do you say?—*sen-sa-tion-al!*

As Pa reaches for his change purse, Jonathan intervenes, shooing the man away.

"Hello, Jonathan," says Pa. "I was just going to buy some postals from this young fella here."

"I don't think you want *those* postals, Pa. But there's a much better selection over here at the newsstand." Jonathan is determined that both Pa and Ma have a wonderful time. He also plans to protect them from being fleeced.

In the Parkers' suite, Jonathan pops open a bottle of champagne in preparation for Ma and Pa's arrival. There is a knock at the door. Jonathan answers.

"Hello, folks!" says a cheery Ma.

"We're all set in our best bib and tucker," adds Pa, looking smart in a black tuxedo.

"Ma, you look simply *lovely!*" says the gracious Elizabeth, admiring Ma's tacky feather boa.

"You'd never think she was the mother of fifteen kids, would ya'?" Pa says with pride.

"Come right in, folks," Jonathan says, "and join the festivities!"

"Oh, Ma, I simply can't get over how *wonderful* you look!"

"Thanks, Elizabeth," Ma says. "You look kind of highfalutin yourself."

"Folks," Jonathan announces, "we're going to start the fireworks with a little champagne."

"Well, ain't ya' got any buttermilk?" asks Ma.

Jonathan chuckles.

Pa sits down, and his dickey pops out of his jacket, hitting him square in the face. The Parkers act as though nothing out of the ordinary has occurred.

Offering Pa a glass of champagne, Jonathan says, "Down the hatch!"

Pa drains the saucer in one gulp. A pause for timing, and then he hiccups, sending his dickey into his face again.

Shortly after Adolph Wade checks into his room, he receives some sinister-looking visitors: a bald, goatee-wearing Teutonic man and a sultry-yet-severe young lady. Later that evening, when a slightly tipsy Pa attempts to deliver the envelope to Mr. Wade, we see this foreboding couple moving Wade's murdered corpse behind a couch. Pa knocks on the man's door, and when no one answers, he walks in. He is immediately struck on the head from behind, knocking him cold, as his dickey once more hits him in the face. Ma and Jonathan show up next, and Ma begins to yell for Pa while simultaneously banging her knuckles on the door.

That Pa would forget his own head if it wasn't attached, Ma says; he went over to Mr. Wade's to deliver an envelope, but he absent-mindedly left it behind. Once again met with silence from the other side of the door, Ma lets herself and Jonathan into the room. There they discover Pa, slumped on the couch, unconscious. When he comes to, he explains that the lights went out the moment he entered the room. Jonathan and Ma are quite concerned, naturally. Ma adds that she *knew* that letter was going to get Pa into trouble.

The German knocks on the open door and, accompanied by his female companion, enters the room. He introduces himself as Cyrus Kraft, a close friend of Mr. Wade; the young lady, he says, is his daughter Inez. When Pa explains the story behind the enve-lope, Herr Kraft says that if Pa would give *him* the envelope, *he* would see to it that Mr. Wade gets it. Ma is reluctant to hand it over to him. A quick glance from Jonathan confirms her doubt. Thanking the gentleman for his offer, she sticks the envelope into her décolletage.

Jonathan, worried that Pa might be too shaken to go out, sug-gests he cancel their reservations for the show that evening.

"What show ya' talkin' about?" Pa asks, rubbing his sore scalp.

"Well, *you* know," Jonathan says, trying to be discreet. "The one with the beautiful, uh—the beautiful—the beautiful . . . *pictures* you saw in the lobby."

Pa straightens himself up, immediately feeling better. "Oh, we outta *go*," he says seriously. "I wouldn't *think* of spoiling Ma's fun."

"What show are you going to see, if I may ask?" inquires Kraft.

"The one at La Café d'Eté."

"What a coincidence! *We* are going there too. Allow me to take you as my guests." With arrangements quickly put out of the way and Ma, Pa, and Jonathan having left, Kraft turns to Inez and says with great urgency, "*Get Jacques!*"

La Café d'Eté. The champagne is flowing for everyone (except for Ma, who is still waiting on her buttermilk), and the featured entertainment is about to begin. A soubrette, with a line of can-can girls behind her, literally kicks off the show.[35] Kraft, the evening's genial host, keeps up his somewhat obsequious charm throughout dinner, believing full well that he can easily get that letter from these crude Americans. After a delay, Kraft and Inez are escorted over to their party's table. The two are seated and ask their guests if the show is living up to their expectations.

Pa speaks up: "Never was anything like this at Lem Tellett's Saturday-night keg parties."

Jonathan asks Kraft if he was able to contact Mr. Wade. He answers that he did not, but that he left a message, inviting him to join them for dinner. "By the way," Kraft inquires gingerly, "did you happen to bring the envelope with you?"

"*Sure* did," says Ma, indicating her neckline. "*Right here.* I ain't like Pa."

"I'm glad you're not, Ma," says her by-now tipsy husband.

The floorshow ends, and the orchestra begins to play a rhumba. Kraft rises from his chair and approaches Ma. "Mrs. Kettle, may I have this dance?" he asks with old-world manners.

"Oh, my goodness!" says a delighted Ma. "I haven't done much outside of square dancin' since I was a girl."

"Don't pay her no mind, Mr. Kraft," Pa interjects. "In her day, she was a mighty fancy stepper. Won a cup once for doin' the hoe-down."

This is followed by a truly hilarious sequence. While dancing, Kraft athletically bounces Ma up and down, hoping that the letter will make its way down her neckline and out the bottom of her dress. When an alarmed Ma asks Kraft what he is doing, he tells her that he is simply carried away by her charms. Without achieving his aim, the two return, disheveled and exhausted, to their table. Suddenly, the lights go out, plunging the dining room into blackness. A woman's blood-curdling scream pierces the dark. It is the beginning of *La Danse Apache*, performed by a young man and woman in traditional Parisian garb.[36] Predictably, Ma is angered by

---

35 The soubrette is twenty-year-old Rita Moreno, born on December 11, 1931. She is one of a select group of artists who have won all four major American entertainment awards: the Emmy, the Oscar, the Tony, and the Grammy.

36 A traditional if bizarre form of entertainment, *La Danse Apache* depicts a "violent conversation" between a pimp and a prostitute.

the way the man is throwing the lady around, dragging her by the hair, and striking her.

"That ain't no way to treat a lady!" she says indignantly.

"It's just an *act*, Ma," Jonathan assures her. "It's all rehearsed. They're probably man and wife."

The dance continues, and the pseudo violence escalates.

Ma interrupts La Danse Apache when she believes the male dancer (Andre D'Arcy) is genuinely mistreating his female partner.

"Even if they *are* married, that don't mean he can beat her up!" Ma says, fit to be tied. She jumps up before Jonathan can stop her and rushes to the girl's rescue. Grabbing the shocked male dancer by his shoulders, Ma pushes him down, causing him to slide along the floor and through the kitchen's double doors, from which emanates a crashing sound. Ma then offers a hand to the confused female dancer. The audience goes crazy, thinking this is part of the entertainment. Ma returns to her seat.

"Oh, Ma, you shouldn't have done that," says Jonathan, suppressing a laugh.

"And why *not?*" Ma says defensively.

The manager approaches the table. Kraft stands to buffer the condemnation. But the manager insists that everyone *loved* the display. As far as *he* is concerned, Ma can join the act on a nightly basis.

Pa's leisurely breakfast in bed is interrupted when Jonathan and Elizabeth Parker (right) inform the Kettles that the mysterious Mr. Wade has been murdered.

The following morning finds Ma and Pa in their room, enjoying the good life. Ma is at the vanity table, fixing her hair. Pa, wearing his night shirt (but no derby), is sitting up in bed, leisurely enjoying his breakfast on a tray. Their reverie is interrupted by a knock at the door. It is Jonathan and Elizabeth, still in their bathrobes. Jonathan shows Pa the morning paper, the headline of which announces the untimely death of Adolph Wade. His body was found in the River Seine. Foul play is suspected.

"Too bad," Pa says softly. "He was a nice man." He contemplates this for a moment before saying, "I can't give him the envelope now."

Jonathan strongly suspects that the envelope is the key to Wade's murder. He also believes that Cyrus Kraft and his "so-called daughter" are mixed up in it. After giving the situation considerable thought, Jonathan believes that the envelope should be turned over to a friend of his at the American Embassy. Ma agrees. Jonathan says that, when everyone is dressed, they can rendezvous in the hotel lobby.

In another room, Kraft is seated in a chair, that day's newspaper in his hands. Standing before him are some truly threatening-looking characters: one is Henri, a tall, lean, well-dressed individual with a nasty scar on his cheek; the other is Jacques, a short, stout henchman with a black mustache and a leather cap.

"If the Kettles see this, we are in trouble," says Kraft.

"You shouldn't have killed him," says Henri.

"I had no choice," Kraft insists. "He was armed." Gesturing accusingly at Jacques, he says, "If *you* had done a better job disposing of the body, this wouldn't have happened."

"There was no time," argues Jacques. "It was almost daylight."

Standing up quickly, Kraft announces, "We *must* get that envelope before they turn it over to the police."

"Quiet, *quiet!*" hushes Inez. She is on the telephone. "You say that Mr. and Mrs. Kettle do not answer? ... *Oh*, they *left* the hotel?" Do you know *when* they'll be back? ... I see." She hangs up. "They left ten minutes ago with the Parkers. There's no telling *where* they went."

Looking at Jacques again, Kraft says sternly, "It's *your* business to find out where. Check with the cab drivers. Talk to the hotel doorman. We will wait for your call there."

In an office at Paris's U.S. Embassy, the Kettles and the Parkers stand by while the consul reviews the contents of the mysterious envelope. There are some typed pages and a set of blueprints, although he does not appreciate their significance. As a backup, he has asked the naval attaché, Commander Fordyce, to look it over. Following a brief examination, he says, "Well, it's part of a missing file. The most *important* part." The commander then tells Pa that he has been under considerable danger. Now that he knows the risk, would he be willing to go on for a few days more? Pa, a true patriot, consents immediately. He is instructed to continue carrying the envelope on his person; only now it will be filled with dummy plans. The commander wants Pa to have it when he is next around Kraft and Inez. When they ask for the envelope again, Pa is instructed to hand it over. This will provide the feds with the evidence needed to close in and clean up the spy ring. When Jonathan asks for more assurance, he is informed that two of the government's best agents will be following Pa—day and night.

The two couples are strolling one of Paris's boulevards (the one situated on Universal's backlot), doing a bit of window shopping. Elizabeth, a woman of elegant taste, notices a black gown in a shop window that she believes would look lovely on Ma. She takes Ma into the shop to try it on. Pa and Jonathan, says Pa, are going to smoke out some spies. Of course, that is hardly an activity one can do on an empty stomach. The two gentlemen stop and are seated at an outdoor bistro. Pa sees two French dandies seated at another table, doffing their hats at him. Those must be the agents, he deduces. By the process of elimination, the serious-looking men seated at a table on the opposite side of the bistro must be the spies. Just then, Kraft's henchman pulls by in his car, spotting Pa and Jonathan. He reports this information to his superior. Kraft and Inez are soon at the café, running into them, supposedly by chance. Inez immediately leaves Kraft to dine with the men while she catches up with Ma and Elizabeth at the dress shop.

Kraft gets right to the point, asking if they had read the morning paper. Before Pa can answer in the affirmative, Jonathan claims ignorance. Kraft hands him the paper, commenting on what a great shock he experienced upon learning that Wade's body had been discovered. "One of my *best* friends," he says plaintively. Jonathan asks if a motive for the murder had been discussed. Could it possibly have had anything to do with the letter he had entrusted to Pa? "Ya' mean *this* letter?" Pa says, tantalizingly removing the envelope from his jacket pocket.

"What do you think Mr. Kettle should do with it?" Jonathan asks Kraft.

At first more than willing to take the letter under the pretense that he will deliver it to Wade's widow in the States, Kraft changes his mind abruptly after catching a glimpse of the two federal agents seated nearby.

"How stupid of me!" he says abruptly. "I just remembered I have an important meeting to attend. So, if you'll kindly excuse me—"

Ma and Pa, dressed up and tuckered out.

The Parkers await Ma and Pa in the hotel lobby later that evening. Pa enters, well groomed, and dressed like a gentleman; Ma, with the affected bearing of the Queen of Sheba, is showing off her new gown, the one Elizabeth had noticed in the shop window. Ma also thanks Jonathan for her corsage.

"I love mine too," says Elizabeth.

Jonathan says grandly, "They are the, um—the *pièce de résistance.*"

"Well, that's funny," Ma says, perplexed. "The man who brought 'em said they was orchids."

When Ma, Jonathan, and Elizabeth leave the lobby, Pa stays back for a moment to purchase those French postcards from the shady fellow he had spoken to on their first day in Paris. He hands Pa a sealed envelope (oh, please, not *another* envelope! Those are almost as bad as black bags!) and tells Pa he must not open it until he returns to the States.

Pa rejoins the group and, almost immediately, they run smack dab into Kraft and Inez. Pa again offers the envelope to Kraft, who again is on the verge of accepting it when Inez (noticing the ubiquitous federal agents) suggests that it would be safer if Mr. Kettle were to hold onto it for a while longer. Kraft concurs. This time, he asks Pa to personally deliver the envelope to Mr. Wade's widow and extend their condolences. And, once again, they beat a hasty retreat.

The two couples enter a limo and are whisked away to La Café Robespierre. They are immediately followed by the two agents, traveling by taxi.

Seated at a table in another elegant restaurant, with lovely music emanating from the string section, Pa becomes wistful. Leaning in close to his beautifully dressed wife, he tells her it reminds him of the song he played on the gramophone the night he proposed to her. After a momentary silence, he says, "Ma, if anything should happen to me while I'm bein' a G-man, I just want you to know that I think you're the most wonderful girl in the world."

"Oh, nothin' ain't gonna happen to ya', Pa."

"Can't tell. I'm on a pretty dangerous mission, ya' know."

Ma begins to cry softly. "Oh, now, go on with ya'," she says, knowing she would be lost without her husband.

"Oh, here comes our Crêpes Suzette!" says Jonathan, hoping to lighten the mood. "Watch the way the maître d' makes them, Ma and Pa." As happens in any number of slapstick comedies when the brandy is lit, Pa jumps up, takes off his jacket, and begins to douse the flame. He is roundly castigated by Ma, who says angrily, "A *fine show* you gave us, Pa!" She has apparently forgotten about her intervention in the domestic dispute between the Apache dancers.

Ma meets Elizabeth and Miss Kraft in the lobby. "I'm all set," she announces.

Inez is nearly in a panic when she realizes that Monsieur Kettle will not be joining them. Ma explains that she has just dropped Pa in the bathtub. Besides, he don't like to shop—he only likes to borrow. With no other alternative, Inez allows Jacques to drive them to the perfume shop. Once inside, they are greeted by Henri.

"Mademoiselle Kraft," he says, "what a delightful surprise!"

"I brought my friends because of the liberal discount you gave me last year," the fashionable Inez says ingratiatingly. "Will you make the same arrangement now?"

"*Certainement, mademoiselle.*" He beckons the ladies into another room, where he claims to have a much better selection. A mirrored panel opens automatically. After everyone has entered the room, the door shuts, giving way to a much less friendly air. Kraft is there, asking, "Why didn't you bring Mr. Kettle along?"

"Mrs. Kettle is going to phone him to join us," offers Inez.

"Will somebody tell me what these shenanigans are all about around here?" Ma says, cutting through the charade.

"The idea is this, Mrs. Kettle," Kraft says, dropping the charm act. "We are going to hold both of you as hostages until we get that letter Mr. Wade gave to your husband."

"Well, *Pa's* got it! *I* ain't."

"So I gathered. I'll get him on the phone for you. *You* are going to tell him to bring that letter *here*." Into the receiver, he says, "Hotel Louis Quatorze, please."

"You *will* make it *urgent*, won't you, Mrs. Kettle?" Inez threatens.

"*Hmm*," mutters Ma, "I should have known better than to trust a woman with black hair and blonde roots!"

"Mr. Kettle, please?" Kraft says into the receiver, after which he hands it over to Ma. "Mrs. Kettle?"

Ma, at first, walks over to Kraft. On second thought, she steps back toward Elizabeth and, taking her protectively by the hand, returns to the phone. "HELLO, PA!" she yells.

Pa, on the other end of the line, blanches. "Yeah?" he answers quietly. "This is Pa. Where ya' at, Ma? . . . I see. Four hundred and fifteen Rue de Rivoli. Mm-hmm . . . *Huh*? The *letter*? Well, for heaven's sake, Ma, what do you want the *letter* for? You know there's nothin' in it."

"NOW, PA, DON'T ARGUE!" Ma says, continuing to yell. "YOU GOTTA BRING THAT LETTER *HERE!*"

Kraft whispers: "And tell him to come *alone*."

Jacques opens his switchblade, pointing it at Ma. Elizabeth gasps.

"And Pa," Ma says a bit shakily, "you come *alone*." There is a momentary silence, followed by more yelling: "I DON'T CARE *IF* YOU'VE GOT A DATE WITH JONATHAN! *BUST IT*! . . . WHAT'S *THAT*? LISTEN! THE EIFFEL TOWER'LL *STILL* BE THERE!" And with that, she slams down the receiver.

Pa walks over to Jonathan, who is seated in the lobby. "Jonathan, that—that was Ma, but she don't make sense."

"What do you mean, Pa?"

"Well, she told me to bring the letter to Four-fifteen Rue de Rivoli. Said I was to bust a date I had with you to see the Eiffel Tower."

"We—we had no date," Jonathan says, taking a moment to think. "*I get it*! It was Ma's way of making sure you'd tip me off! She couldn't talk—she was being intimidated! Pa, it means that Ma and Elizabeth are in trouble!"

"*Trouble?*" Pa says. "Well, what are we standin' *here* for?"

On their way out, Pa passes the two French dandies. "Come on, fellas," he says confidentially. "Follow us."

The men, wearing suits, homburgs, and carrying walking sticks, look at each other, shrug, and do as they are told. Jumping into a cab parked in front of the hotel, Jonathan tells the driver their desired destination. The serious-looking men hail the next cab; the dandies hail the one after that. Pa, saying that the spies are closing in, encourages the driver to lose them. He does.

Stymied by the language barrier, Pa does his best to convince the prefect of police that his wife is in grave danger.

Passing by a police station, Jonathan yells for the driver to stop. He tells Pa to go into the station and get as many policemen as possible and then meet him at the shop at 415 Rue de Rivoli. Pa jumps out of the car and runs into the station, where five gendarmes are lounging. Panting, he goes directly to the desk sergeant and says, "Ma's in trouble, boys! I mean, *my wife*! Follow me!"—and he begins to run out. Realizing that no one is following him, he returns, this time speaking with a pseudo-French accent to make himself better understood. "*Spies! Spies!*" he says urgently. "*Come on*, will you! It's life or death!" To further make his point, he attempts to pantomime the danger afoot, generating little more than blank stares. This man is *fou* (loony), they surmise. Pa gets an inspiration. Picking up a heavy object, he hurls it through the glass window leading into the station. *That* gets their attention. They pick up their truncheons and give chase to this little American vandal. Pa, never so active in any series entry before or after, runs along the boulevard with no assistance from a double. Spotting two gendarmes, he stomps on one's foot, and then the other. Enraged, they join the chase.

Pa, desperate to rescue Ma from the clutches of international spies, uses every trick in the book to cause the gendarmes of Paris to chase him.

In the hidden, soundproof chamber of the perfume shop, the situation has grown dire. Elizabeth is dissolved in tears at one point, forcing the far stronger Ma to tell her to quit "puddlin' up." Jacques asks what will happen if Pa does not show—or worse—if he goes to the prefect of police. Kraft calmly explains that if they see *any* indication of trouble through the one-way mirror, their guests, after Jacques has done his work, will simply vanish. Just then, Pa can be seen through the glass panel, running into the shop. Realizing that no police are with him, he runs back outside, while Kraft orders, "*Stop him!*" Ma begins to yell to Pa that they are in the back room, but Kraft informs her that he can neither see nor hear her. Pa has found the police, whistled for them, and they once more give chase. Pa just precedes them into the shop, where Henri is standing. Asking where his wife is, Pa tackles the much taller man, knocking him to the ground.

"ATTABOY, PA!" Ma yells.

As Pa is apprehended by several of the gendarmes, he frantically explains that his wife is being held in this shop and she needs help! Realizing the jig is up, Kraft orders Jacques to exterminate

Ma and Pa are happily reunited just as the film winds to an end.

the hostages. Elizabeth screams as Ma starts swinging a table pedestal, knocking Jacques cold and breaking Kraft's arm. Jonathan arrives at the shop, as do the agents. He tells the gendarmes to "arrest these men—they're spies." The agents present their credentials, convincing Pa that they are, in fact, the G-men. Pa begins to call out for Ma. She answers by using that trusty pedestal to break the two-way mirror. She and Elizabeth are free.

The agents congratulate Pa on a job well done. "Just doin' what any red-blooded American would do," he says. He then reaches into his jacket pocket to remove the envelope. At first taking out the one containing the French postcards, he looks guilty and quickly switches it for the correct one.

Very few things in this movie turn out to be what everyone thought. We know that the "spies" who were constantly trailing Pa were the federal agents. What we did *not* know is that the "federal agents" were a couple of con men, hoping to rope a gullible American tourist into a promotional scheme involving salad dressing. And perhaps the biggest disappointment of all? The French postcards were of the Eiffel Tower and the Arc de Triomphe!

The Payoff

Ma and Pa Kettle on Vacation struck box-office gold, with U.S. and Canadian rentals adding up to $2.2 million. The film, despite its plot contrivances, continues to make viewers smile. Our favorite online critic of classic films, Samuel Stoddard, awards *On Vacation* three stars and describes it thusly: "Ma and Pa Kettle take a trip to Paris this time, with culture-clash gags aplenty. There are mix-ups with international spies, too; this installment seems to be trying to recapture what made *Ma and Pa Kettle Go To Town* work so well. Some of the humor works and some does not, but the film is as charming as its ever-likable characters. Watch for the scene on the dance floor, one of the series' funniest."

Chapter 8
Ma and Pa Kettle at Home (1954)

R eleased by Universal-International, March 10, 1954. 81 minutes. Directed by Charles Lamont. Produced by Richard Wilson. Story and Screenplay by Kay Lenard. Music by William Lava.
Director of Photography: Carl E. Guthrie, A.S.C. Film Editor:
Leonard Weiner. Art Direction: Bernard Herzbrun and Robert
Boyle. Set Decorations: Russell A. Gausman and Ruby R. Levitt.
Director of Make-Up: Bud Westmore. Hair Stylist: Joan St. Oegger. Assistant Director: William Holland. Sound: Leslie I. Carey
and Robert Pritchard.

Cast: Marjorie Main (*Ma Kettle*); Percy Kilbride (*Pa Kettle*);
Alan Mowbray (*Alphonsus Mannering*); Alice Kelley (*Sally Mad-
docks*); Brett Halsey (*Elwin Kettle*); Ross Elliott (*Pete Crosby*);
Mary Wickes (*Miss Wetter*); Oliver Blake (*Geoduck*); Stan Ross
(*Crowbar*); Emory Parnell (*Billy Reed*); Irving Bacon (*John Mad-
docks*); Virginia Brissac (*Martha Maddocks*); Richard Eyer (*Billy
Kettle*); Marjorie Bennett (*Corset Saleslady*); Edmund Cobb (*Jef-
ferson*); Edgar Dearing (*Perkins*); Tony Epper (*Donny Kettle*);
James Flavin (*Motorcycle Cop*); Helen Gibson (*Ranch Wife*); Coral
Hammond (*Eve Kettle*); Whitey Haupt (*Henry Kettle*); Donald
MacDonald (*Benjamin Kettle*); Betty McDonough (*Ranch Wife*);
Patrick Miller (*Teddy Kettle*); Donna Cregan Moots (*Ruthie Ket-
tle*); Patricia Morrow (*Susie Kettle*); Robert Nelson (*Motorcycle
Cop*); Carol Nugent (*Nancy Kettle*); Judy Nugent (*Betty Kettle*);
Gary Pagett (*George Kettle*); Ken Terrell (*Indian*); Rick Vallin
(*Indian*); Guy Wilkerson (*Jones*); Hank Worden (*Indian*); Nancy
Zane (*Sara Kettle*).

On April 8, 1953, the following headline appeared in newspapers across the United States:

'PA KETTLE' TO QUIT FAMILY FILM SERIES
By Bob Thomas
Hollywood UPI——Ma and Pa Kettle and their mas-
sive brood are hitting the movie trail for the last time.
    Most movie series play more final engagements than
Sarah Bernhardt. But this is really the last one for the

Percy Kilbride as Pa Kettle.

sloppy Kettles and their 15 kids. So says Pa, otherwise known as Percy Kilbride.

The Kettles have had an amazing success. The characters were pulled out of "The Egg and I" and put into a low-budget comedy. It was an instant success, and one picture led to another. Dollar for dollar, they have been the best movie investment in recent years. Made on a quicky budget, they have outgrossed the majority of the high-priced epics.

It seems that everyone likes the Kettle series except Marjorie Main and Percy Kilbride, who play the leading roles. Last year, when they made their [most recent] one, an unreleased film about Waikiki, they swore it would be their last. But here they are making another, "Ma and Pa Kettle Hit the Road Home."

I asked Percy, how come?

"Wal," he said in his famous twang, "the studio offered some inducements that were too appealing to pass up. For one thing, they now have a limousine to transport me to and from the studio. I don't drive, you see; I always had to take a taxi before. I am allowed to quit work at 4:30.

"Also, I only have to work five days a week; I get a day off besides Sunday. And the studio offered a nice little nugget as added inducement. So, I agreed—on the stipulation that this would absolutely be the last one."

What is his objection to continuing with the Kettles?

"I had my training on the stage, where I did a variety of roles. That's the fun of being an actor: to meet the challenges of creating new characters.

"But old Pa Kettle is always the same. He can do anything; there is no need to establish any motivation. There's no kick in doing him over and over again.

"I have had dozens of offers to do television series, but I have turned them all down. I might do one-shot appearances, but I won't let myself get tied down to one character."

Percy has reason to dislike being typed. Although he played a variety of roles on the stage, he has generally played a taxi driver or a farmer in movies. He cannot drive and he has never lived on a farm.

Furthermore, he has been cast as the parent of 15 progeny in the Kettle series. He is actually childless.

Percy said that Miss Main blows hot and cold over continuing with the Kettles. But he is firm in his resolve, and no added moola will sway him.

Was it merely fatigue with the role of Pa Kettle that led the veteran actor to make this decision? It's doubtful. Percy Kilbride suffered from heart disease, which limited how much he could work. From 1949 on, he waited patiently to make just one Kettle film per year and was rarely offered any other film projects, so typecast had he become.

It became screenwriter Kay Lenard's duty to provide the departing star with a script that was truly "one to go out on." Judging by the results, she succeeded mightily. Kay Lenard (1911–1997) was the only woman to provide a script for not one, but two, Kettle films. She began her writing career with the *San Francisco Chronicle*. Relocating to Los Angeles, she turned out a few screenplays, including this one, *The Kettles in the Ozarks*, and the Marjorie Main–Chill Wills vehicle *Ricochet Romance*. Throughout the 1960s she wrote for such episodic television series as *The Donna Reed Show* and *Combat!* In 1976, she received a Daytime Emmy for her work on *The Young and the Restless*. In all, she has an impressive six hundred credits to her name. For this film, Lenard gets back to basics with the Kettle clan. The settings are not in the least exotic (no scratchy stock footage of Paris or Honolulu in this one), it has a more-or-less plausible premise (no bank robbers, international spies, or kidnappers), and even shows the rural family and their many friends and neighbors celebrating Christmas. In fact, the story takes place entirely in the month of December, although it was shot in April 1953.

The Supporting Cast
Brett Halsey as Elwin Kettle . . .

Brett Halsey and Alice Kelley are the film's likeable romantic leads.

Brett Halsey was born Charles Oliver Hand in Santa Ana, California, on June 20, 1933. A handsome kid, he was working as a page for CBS Television when he had the good fortune to meet comedian Jack Benny and the president of Universal Studios. The next thing he knew, he was put under contract, along with other future stars Clint Eastwood and David Janssen. Universal decided to change Charles Hand's name to Brett Halsey as a nod to his uncle, the famed World War II admiral William "Bull" Halsey. He was soon apprenticing in a string of Universal pictures, including one as a victim in the sci-fi horror *Revenge of the Creature* (1954, co-starring fellow Kettle kid Lori Nelson). His first featured role was as Elwin Kettle in *Ma and Pa Kettle at Home*. "I had seen a couple of the Kettle films and liked them very much," Halsey told the authors in June of 2020. "They might have been B-pictures, but they starred great actors, such as Marjorie Main, Percy Kilbride, and, in this instance, Alan Mowbray. What a learning experience that was for me! Here I was, just a green kid at the time; I hadn't even turned twenty-one yet."

What does he recall about working with Marjorie Main? "She didn't seem too well during the shoot," he said, frankly. "I believe she had a kidney ailment, and she was always running to the bathroom. In fact, she insisted that a Honeywagon be within sight of the set at all times."[37] He also recalls that she was rather distant with the rest of the cast, remaining in her trailer between takes. He has fonder memories of Percy Kilbride, whom he says was a warm, talkative, friendly man. One day, Brett arrived late to

Seasoned pro Percy Kilbride (right) lectures newcomers Brett Halsey and Alice Kelley on the importance of being on time for a shoot.

the set, prompting an anecdote from Percy. "Never was late to the theater, not even once," he said proudly. "I remember one incident, oh, I must have been just about seventeen at the time, and I was still living in San Francisco. Took quite a bit to get to the theater, not just on time but at all. Nevertheless, I made it, with minutes to spare before curtain. Only trouble was, the roof of the theater had caved in; as a matter of fact, the whole structure was destroyed. The date was April 18, 1906, the day of the great earthquake."

---

37 Honeywagon® is a brand name for a line of portable toilets.

Working with Alan Mowbray, too, was a pleasure, Halsey says: "He was just a wonderful guy—friendly, open, and helpful. He was always there, giving advice that I really needed. God, was I green when I was on that film! And I was really flattered when he gave me a nice little art piece he had done. Unfortunately, someone stole it out of my locker at Universal."

Alan Mowbray as Alphonsus Mannering . . .

Alan Mowbray.

Alan Mowbray (1896–1969) had this to say regarding his own background: "I must confess that around the turn of the century, in London, England, I was born of mixed heritage—a mother and a father." This wonderfully droll character actor, best known for playing pompous Brits, was born Ernest Allen to a non-theatrical family. After acting in London's West End, Alan Mowbray (his stage name) came to the United States, where he toured the country with the Theater Guild from 1923 to 1929. He also appeared in several Broadway plays, including the comedy *Dinner is Served*, which he wrote. It was not a success, closing after just four performances. His excellent diction, however, made him a natural for sound movies. A member of the "stiff-upper lip" school of British acting, he could be counted on to turn in finely etched performances in such movies as *My Man Godfrey* (1936), or as "the surprise killer" in B-movie murder mysteries. One of his favorite roles was that of a con man in the television series *Colonel Humphrey Flack*, which ran on the Dumont network in 1953. A member of the Royal Geographic Society and active in several theatrical fraternities, Mowbray also was one of the founding members of the Screen Actors Guild.

Alice Kelley as Sally Maddocks . . .

Alice Kelley (1932–2012) had been a professional model for print advertising since the tender age of twelve. She was also a titled beauty queen, being named "Miss Junior Miss 1948." At twenty-one, she married Ken Norris, a lieutenant in the U.S. Air Force Reserves. He later inherited Norris Industries from his father and became a leading philanthropist in the Los Angeles area, contributing an estimated $70 million to various charitable causes. She and Norris had two sons together and were later divorced. He subsequently died in a boating accident.

Irving Bacon as John Maddocks . . .

Irving Bacon.

Irving Bacon (1893–1965) was a longtime secondary player who could be counted on to convey a friendly, comic air as timid mailmen, milkmen, clerks, chauffeurs, cab drivers, bartenders, soda jerks, carnival operators, and handymen. His role in *At Home* is something of a departure for him, playing as he does an ogre of a man, John Maddocks, whose Scrooge-like attitudes are challenged, and ultimately reformed, by Ma Kettle.

Virginia Brissac as Martha Maddocks . . .

Virginia Brissac.

Virginia Brissac (1883–1979) was a popular American stage actress who later had a long second career as a character actress in films and on television. A versatile artist, she was cast as farm women and rancher's wives, aristocrats and society women, and various nurses, seamstresses, and landladies. She is probably best remembered for her role as the grandmother of Jim Stark, the troubled teenager played by James Dean, in *Rebel Without a Cause* (1955).

Marjorie Bennett as the Corset Saleslady . . .

Marjorie Bennett plays the landlady in this scene from Limelight *(1952), with the film's director and star, Charlie Chaplin.*

Marjorie Bennett (1896 –1982) was an Australian actress (born in York), although she worked primarily in the United Kingdom and the United States. Marjorie's sisters, Enid and Catherine, were also actresses (Enid Bennett, in fact, would marry silent film director Fred Niblo). Although Marjorie had appeared in some films as early as 1916, she did not fully invest herself in an acting career until 1946, when she was hired by Universal to play a shop assistant in *Dressed to Kill*, the fourteenth, and final, entry in the Sherlock Holmes series starring Basil Rathbone and Nigel Bruce. Bennett began appearing regularly in minor roles in some major films, including two features by Charlie Chaplin, *Monsieur Verdoux* (1947) and *Limelight* (1952), and in Robert Aldrich's camp thriller *What Ever Happened to Baby Jane?* (1962).

Mary Wickes as Miss Wetter . . .

Mary Wickes.

A lanky, unlovely lady, Mary Wickes (1910–1995) played cooks, housekeepers, and other subservient occupations in the least servile way possible. No one, regardless of their rank, was spared her blunt assessments and wisecracks. She is seen by many traditionalists each year as the nosy desk clerk in the perennial favorite *White Christmas* (1954). One of her most noteworthy final roles was as an octogenarian singing nun in *Sister Act* (1992), a megahit Disney comedy.

And Richard Eyer as Billy Kettle.

The adorable Billy Kettle (Richard Eyer) seems to have done something to displease Ma. The photo is inscribed to the authors: "To Lon and Debra from one of Ma's kids Richard Eyer."

Richard Ross Eyer, a clean-cut, all-American type with a face full of freckles, was born in Santa Monica, California, on May 6, 1945. His first acting role came in 1952 when he was cast as Bobby Sharon on *The Roy Rogers Show*. Sci-fi fans will recall him as having the title role in *The Invisible Boy* (1957), producer Nicholas Nayfack's independently made sequel to MGM's *Forbidden Planet* (1956). In *The Desperate Hours* (1955), with its taut direction by William Wyler, Richard plays Ralph, the youngest member of a suburban family being held hostage in their own home by a trio of escaped convicts, headed by the psychotic Glenn Griffin (Humphrey Bogart). In *Ma and Pa Kettle at Home*, Richard's character, Billy, unlike the other children in the cast, had ample dialogue and bits of comic business. In an interview with the authors in 2020, the seventy-five-year-old Eyer was able to recall only a handful of details about his experiences on the set of *At Home*, but the memories he *does* have are pleasant ones. Alan Mowbray, as the fussy Mr. Mannering, and Billy share some charming scenes together, mostly involving the mischievous boy putting his pet frog Oscar in Mannering's water pitcher and, later, in his bath. Richard remembers Mowbray, as well as all the adult actors in the film, as being friendly to him, although he corroborates Brett Halsey's observation that Marjorie Main kept her distance from the other cast members, hiding out in her trailer between takes. He also recalls that Oscar the frog was only real in the close-ups; otherwise, a rubber substitute was used. Richard's favorite memory

Ma, Pa, and the kids.

of the two Kettle pictures, however, was having so many other children on the set to play with. That group of children (there is not one familiar Kettle kid in the cast) include Coral Hammond, Whitey Haupt, Donald MacDonald, Patrick Miller, Donna Cregan Moots, Patricia Morrow, Gary Pagett, Nancy Zane, and real-life sisters Carol and Judy Nugent.

The film's premise, involving someone writing a fanciful account of their life and then having to back it up, had been used effectively in the wartime holiday movie *Christmas in Connecticut* (1945), starring Barbara Stanwyck and Dennis Morgan. Unlike today, studios had no qualms about releasing holiday-themed films in months other than December. *Christmas in Connecticut*, for instance, was released by Warner Bros. on August 11, 1945. This Kettle film which, as stated earlier, takes place during the yuletide season, was released on March 10, 1954. The working title, according to the quoted news item, was "Ma and Pa Kettle Hit the Road Home." It was ultimately shortened to *Ma and Pa Kettle at Home*.

The Storyline

"Is that bull wearing a derby?" Pa is asked. "Sure is," he answers. "Looks good in it, don't he?"

Pa, Geoduck, and Crowbar are at the old place to get some eggs for Ma's latest baking project. Pa greets Nick, their bull, who wears a derby not unlike the one resting on his owner's head. The three men enter the hen house, which looks like it would fall over if someone blew on it. Pleasant orchestral music can be heard.

"Where music come from?" asks Geoduck.

Pa points to a shelf on which sits an old speaker he had rigged up. The music, he explains, makes the hens happy and helps them lay more eggs. Geoduck, checking some nests, says, "Not many eggs."

"Must be too many commercials," reasons Pa.

As only happens in movies of that time, an announcer states: "We interrupt this musical program with the following flash news. Today, in New York, the *National Magazine* announced that two Cape Flattery high school seniors, Miss Sally Maddocks and Mr. Elwin Kettle, have been awarded one hundred dollars each for writing the prize-winning essays on 'My Life on a Typical American Farm.'"

"Land o' Goshen!" says Pa.

The announcer continues: "The regional grand prize is a four-year college scholarship. The contest judges were greatly impressed by Elwin Kettle's vivid description of his family's farm 'with the chicken house made of glass brick and filled with a flock of prize fat hens. The well-kept grounds, which feature everything an efficient, modern farm can boast—the redwood silo almost bursting with grain . . .'" We see a poorly constructed silo, its boards full of dry rot, leaning at a 45-degree angle. "The spanking-clean white barn . . ." We see a barn whose roof has almost fallen in, due in part to the debris (including discarded tires) on its surface. "The sleek milk cows, contented hogs, prize goats, a satiny black champion bull . . ." Nick, derby in place, stands on the junk-covered grounds, mooing.

With his trademark straight-faced understatement, Pa says, "Seems maybe Elwin exaggerated a mite here and there." This is something he needs to tell Ma about right away. It is at this inopportune moment that Nick chooses to jump a fence and head toward the neighbor's property. "He's after the Maddocks's Bessie," Pa states with resignation. "Can't keep Nick away from that cow." And then, to Geoduck: "Careful with them eggs."

Pa enters the house by way of the front door, calling out, "Ma, oh, *Ma*! Heard somethin' mighty surprisin' on the radio a while back."

Ma and their teenaged son Elwin are seated on the couch together. Both are obviously down in the dumps. Pa asks why. Ma holds up an envelope, saying that there is a hundred-dollar check inside, but there is also the news that two contest judges are coming from the magazine in New York to Cape Flattery to spend a week on each farm. "The way our farm looks is gonna count in the judgin' too," she explains to Pa. "The old place ain't exactly as Elwin says it was in his essay." If Ma and Pa are concerned, Elwin is downright humiliated. In fact, he had no desire to enter the contest in the first place, but his teacher made all the seniors do it. The only thing he wants to do now is withdraw. Without his saying so, Ma knows his prime reason is that he does not want to compete against Sally Maddocks, the neighbor girl he is sweet on. Pa

Elwin Kettle (Brett Halsey) and Sally Maddocks (Alice Kelley) have a friendly relationship, despite having to compete for a college scholarship.

points out logically that Sally's father, John Maddocks, is the richest man in the county. The tightest, too, Ma says. Elwin, a sensitive, intelligent young man, decides to go and discuss the situation directly with Sally. He walks to the rigorously maintained Maddocks farm, with its clean, white outbuildings and picket fence. Sally runs out to greet him, although she cannot stay long, she tells him; she has to clean out the chicken house. Elwin tells her that he has been thinking about withdrawing from the contest.

"No, you mustn't!" she says. "I told Dad *I* wanted to withdraw, but he won't let me."

The sound of a rifle shot spoils the peacefulness of the moment. John Maddocks is chasing Nick, who has just bounded through his fence. Maddocks, an old grouch if there ever was one, immediately confronts Elwin: "Why in the devil can't you Kettles keep that bull locked up? Next time he comes around here, botherin' Bessie, I'll use buckshot instead of rock salt!"

"Sorry, Mr. Maddocks," Elwin offers.

"*You* get outta here too," he says. And to his daughter: "*You* get back to your chores."

Because there is so much that needs to be done to make the old place presentable for the judges, Elwin gives Pa his prize money to purchase supplies from Billy Reed. Instead, Pa spends the entire amount on four goats he buys from Maddocks. Ma, naturally, rails against her husband for squandering their son's money. But Pa has found a way to restore his credit with Billy Reed. The salesman is renting the model home while the Kettles prepare to move, temporarily anyway, back to the farm. Pa arrives at the old place to meet Geoduck and Crowbar and begin the renovations.

Meanwhile, in New York City at the offices of *National Magazine* ("The Journal of the Home"), Garden Editor Alphonsus Mannering is extolling his own virtues for the benefit of the magazine's photojournalist, Pete Crosby: "For a city-bred man, I have a remarkable instinct for growing things. That's one of the reasons our publishers selected *me* as one of the contest judges." For the benefit of the viewer, the pompous Mannering tells Pete that the reasons *he* was chosen as co-judge had to do with his photojournalism credentials, naturally, and because of his farm background and activities in the 4-H Club, an organization that gets a huge plug in this film.[38]

Pa instructs Ma to clean up the interior of the house while he (or, more accurately, Geoduck and Crowbar) sees to the grounds.

38 According to their website, the 4-H Clubs of America, founded by A. B. Graham in 1902, is a U.S.-based network of organizations whose mission is "engaging youth to reach their fullest potential while advancing the field of youth development." Its name is a reference to the occurrence of the initial letter "H" four times in the organization's original motto "head, heart, hands, and health."

Mannering is prepared—one might say *over*prepared—for his fortnight in the rugged Pacific Northwest. He has even purchased a pistol. It is, after all, the Wild West, and they might just encounter bears—or even, God forbid—Indians. In the same vein, he's increased his life insurance, he's scheduled an anti-mosquito shot, and he's planning to take along his electric blanket—it gets very cold at night in the state of Washington, he has heard. Once he has dismissed his secretary and Pete, Mannering muses on what a paradise the Kettle farm must be. He even reads aloud from Elwin's essay: "From my bedroom windows I can see across our lush, green meadowland, on which contented cows are pastured." Ma takes up the reading in Cape Flattery: "Our herd of prize goats graze by the stream that flows through the south meadow, where at day's end I sometimes go fishing, catching fighting trout for the family's supper."

"Heavens to Betsy!" Pa says, impressed. "I never knew there was *fish* in that creek."

But Ma isn't fooled by such hyperbole. "This job'd be a lot easier if Elwin's imagination hadn't been so good."

Pa, however, is filled with confidence. He tells Ma to take care of the house while he, Geoduck, and Crowbar see to the grounds. Unlike earlier Kettle films, the children are oddly obedient, as they willingly clear away the junk on the property. To clean the wood floors in the house, the children have wire brushes strapped to the bottoms of their shoes, skating around on the soapy surface.[39]

When Ma goes outside to inspect the work that Geoduck and Crowbar have done, she is amazed by the addition of such new structures as a white smokehouse. Not heeding Pa's warning, she touches the wall, which rattles. "Why, this ain't nothin' but *cardboard!*" she says in disbelief.

"Well, it's for lookin'," Pa says irritably, "not *pushin'!*"

Other outbuildings, which Pa assures Ma are *not* made of cardboard, are only façades, not unlike the exterior sets used in studio films. Such is the case with the machine shop, used (Pa begins to quote from the essay) "to house the tractor and other mechanized

---

39   A similar gag had been performed by Marion Davies in *The Red Mill* (1927), a Cosmopolitan picture produced by King Vidor and directed by William Goodrich, the alias used by Roscoe "Fatty" Arbuckle.

Ma (right), Pa (center), and the gregarious corset saleslady (Marjorie Bennett, left) enjoy a moment of spontaneous fun just prior to the magazine judges' visit.

equipment." But *where's* the equipment? Ma wants to know. That, apparently, had not occurred to Pa. Acting on instinct, he makes a tour of his neighbors' farms, asking if he can borrow items as small as milk cans ("They're nice and shiny") and as large as a tractor. He even borrows livestock, including pigs, and the corn to feed them. The house, too, is in ship shape, with Ma acting like a drill sergeant, albeit a benevolent one. The kids seem to take well to this more regimented approach. As they are finishing their latest inspection, in which Ma checks to see if they have washed properly behind their ears, she orders them to play outside for a while, but to stay clean. She is determined to impress those New York judges.

Just then, there is an unannounced visit from the corset lady. A pushy little distaff version of Billy Reed, she opens a large case containing her latest wares, some real "beauts," as she describes them. While talking a mile a minute, she tightly laces up a corset over Ma's dress. Wanting to get something for their daughter Rosie, Pa is willing to model a pair of women's undergarments, also worn over his clothes. And just as they have gotten into these snugly secured unmentionables—wouldn't you know it?—the judges show up.

Looking at this elderly farm couple, both in women's underwear, and their horde of young kids, Mannering turns to Pete and says, "Do you think this could be a *mirage?*"

Ma sees to her guests' comfort by setting them up in a spare bedroom. Looking around, Mannering asks his colleague if this farm looks like the paradise described in the boy's essay.

"Well, you might say that Elwin writes more like an advertising man than a factual reporter," Pete says tactfully.

"Perhaps after we've made a complete inspection of the farm,

The Kettles, a traditional Christian family, say grace before dinner. It seems that, after making the checkered tablecloth, Ma had enough material left over for a shirt for Elwin (right, standing).

I'll feel differently."

Ma has prepared a sumptuous lunch and called in the kids, with the usual chaotic results.

Overhearing from the guest bedroom, Mannering says, "It sounds like the Charge of the Light Brigade."

"Working on a farm gives you an appetite," says the more down-to-earth Pete. "C'mon, lunch is ready."

Once seated at the nicely laid table (with a checkered table-cloth and everything), the family waits for the paterfamilias to offer grace.

"Dear Lord, we thank you for the vittles we are about to eat," Pa says respectfully, his derby lifted in supplication. "And Elwin would be much obliged if he gets to go to college. Amen."

"Dig in, Mr. Mannering," Ma says hospitably. "Help yourself."

"Mr. Kettle, don't you *ever* remove your hat?" he asks.

"Oh, I'm sorry," says Pa. He tips his hat at his guest. "Howdy. Just call me 'Pa.'"

"You're a marvelous cook, Ma Kettle," Pete says. "I haven't had a meal like this since I left my father's farm."

Ma is humbled by such praise.

The only one at the table not eating is the fussbudget Mannering. He announces that, being on a strict eating program, he cannot digest such heavy fare. He asks instead for some plain crackers or Melba Toast. Ma, at a loss, says she doesn't *have* any plain crackers or Melba Toast.

(Left to right) Elwin, Mannering (Alan Mowbray), Pa, and Pete Crosby (Ross Elliott) tour the Kettle barn.

"Ma," Pa says, "there's that sample box of biscuits Billy Reed left the other day. You know, the Bright Hart's Delight?"

"They're *dog* biscuits, Pa!"

"But, *Ma*," Pa says decorously, "we could spare a few for a *guest*."

Later that afternoon, Pa and Elwin take Mannering and Pete on a guided tour. As a way of controlling what the judges see, Pa is carrying a large black umbrella. He explains that it will keep the sun out of their eyes.

Inside the barn, Mannering says, "Now let me see if I remember the words exactly: 'A modern, sun-flooded, machine-equipped dairy barn housing a herd of blue-ribbon cows.' Well, I don't see any machinery, and does *one* cow make up a herd?"

"The essay described the farm as I hope it *will be* someday," offers Elwin.

Pete says empathetically, "The 4-H Club taught me to fix up the place the way I wanted it."

Elwin says that he wishes there were a 4-H Club nearby. He could use the advice when it comes to doing some experimental grafting on apple trees.

Mannering makes the mistake of bending over to inspect some grain when he is charged by a goat, knocking him down. Pete and Elwin rush to his aid. As he is having hay brushed off his suit, Mannering says irritably, "I've had more than enough for today; I'm going to my room. We shall continue our inspection at nine forty-five tomorrow." And with that highly specific proclamation, he flounces off.

Walking back out onto the grounds, Pete takes notice of Nick. "Is that bull wearing a derby?" he asks, perplexed.

"Sure is," says Pa. "Looks good in it, don't he?"

Nick hops the fence, as usual, and heads for the Maddocks place.

"Ah, he's gonna meet Bessie again," Pa says. "C'mon. We'd best go after him or Maddocks will be mad."

Sally greets Elwin, Pa, and Pete: "I heard Dad yelling at Nick and I figured you'd be along after him."

"Sally," says the always-proper Elwin, "this is Pete Crosby, one of the contest judges."

"How do you do, Sally? I'm glad to see the two contestants are friendly rivals."

A rifle shot. Fortunately, Maddocks's aim is off.

"You and your *bull*!" he says angrily to Pa.

"If you'd stop tryin' to keep Nick and Bessie apart, you'd save yourself a heap of trouble," Pa says.

"I'm not lettin' my prize cattle get mixed up with that mangy bull of yours," Maddocks counters.

"Let love have its way, I always say," offers Pa.[40]

"Dad," Sally interrupts, "this is Mr. Crosby, one of the contest judges."

The surly man's demeanor changes perceptibly when he hears this. "Nice to meet you, Mr. Crosby. You'll be glad when your week with the Kettles is up. I'll show you what life on a *real* farm is like."

"I'm enjoying my stay with the Kettles very much," says the diplomatic Pete before leaving with Pa and Elwin.

Ma retrieves her pet hen, Jenny, from the bed of her fussy houseguest.

---

40 This subplot is something of a bovine version of *Romeo and Juliet*, with the Kettles as the Montagues, the Maddockses as the Capulets, Nick as Romeo, and Bessie as Juliet. Who says the Kettle films aren't Shakespearean?

As Mannering goes about his nightly ablutions, taking his pulse and his final medications for the day, he settles into bed, the springs creaking noisily with his every movement. Sliding his feet beneath the counterpane, he suddenly lets out a scream. Something is in the bed with him! Ma runs in to investigate. It turns out her pet Sussex hen, Jenny—her best layer, too—is up to her old tricks again. A female of no little confidence, Jenny simply refuses to nest with the other chickens. Ma gently encourages her pet to leave their guest alone so that he might have a peaceful night with pleasant dreams. What she doesn't realize is that Jenny has managed to stay in the room when she closes the door behind her. Mumbling to himself, Mannering has no sooner adjusted his battery-operated electric blanket and affixed his sleep mask when he lies back and *splat!*—a newly laid egg falls from the rafter, directly onto his forehead.

This simply has not been his day.

The following morning—at precisely 9:45, no doubt—Ma, Pa, and Elwin continue the farm tour that had been cut short the day before. When Mannering appears to be heading off course, Ma asks where he is going. "I'd like to see the other side of the silo," he says. Just like that, Pa opens the black umbrella, blocking his view.

"Will you get that umbrella out of my way?"

"Might rain," Pa says. "You wouldn't wanna get wet, would you?"

Refusing to be distracted, Mannering turns to leave.

"Where ya' goin', Mr. Mannering?" asks Ma, holding onto his arm.

"I'm going to look at the machine shed."

"Oh, the buildings can wait," she says roughly. "It's the pigs' feeding time." And, in her best "affected" tone, she recites, 'And outside of a sunset, there's nothing quite so pretty as a bunch of hungry hogs a-sloppin'.'" And then, in her own coarse tone: "Feed the pigs, Elwin."

"Okay, Ma."

"They're a healthy bunch, Mr. Mannering, just like Elwin said in his essay. C'mon!"

In the pen, a line of piglets suckle on their mama. Picking up a squealing young'un, Ma hands it to Mannering, saying, "They're pretty, ain't they?"

Taken aback, he (*not* his double) falls backward, directly into a large mud puddle. Pete and Elwin help the sopping-wet Mannering back on his feet.

"I'm afraid you'll have to take a bath before ya' do any more inspectin'," Ma says, a mischievous grin on her face.

No easy process, Ma prepares Mannering's bath. Starting from the kitchen, she forms an assembly line comprised of the kids, passing a bucket of hot water from one to the next to fill the tub in the bathroom. Finally, Billy makes the announcement: "It's *full*, Ma!" Ma summons Mr. Mannering, who appears at his bedroom door, wearing a striped robe and carrying his bathing supplies. There follows the previously discussed sequence involving Billy—that little rapscallion—putting his pet frog Oscar into the tub with the skittish Mannering. This results in prodigious splashing and high-pitched male screaming.

When all is said and done, Pete assures Ma that Mannering "will get over it." As she pulls some freshly made biscuits out of the oven, Pete snaps her picture. Ma is curious to know why. Pictures will be used to illustrate the forthcoming article about the contest, he explains. Ma asks if he took any shots of the outbuildings. Pete says that he did, but he only photographed them from their "good side."

"We hate foolin' anybody, Pete," says Ma seriously. "But Elwin's only chance to go to college is to win the scholarship."

"I understand," he replies.

"Besides," she adds, a touch defensively. "Ya' can still raise kids without a fancy place for 'em to live in."

"I see what you mean."

"But Mr. Mannering, he's—"

She stops talking when the man himself, a blanket draped about his head, walks into the room. "I'm catching cold," he announces forlornly. "After I've medicated myself, I'll continue the inspec-

Mannering (far left) alerts Ma, Pa, and Pete (far right) to the fact that wild Indians (actually, Geoduck and Crowbar) are in the vicinity.

tion." Once outside, Mannering comes close to more minutely examining one of the outbuildings. But Nick the bull, clearly in Elwin's corner, chases him off. During another attempt, Mannering is startled by the sudden appearance of Geoduck and Crowbar.

"*Indians!*" he cries.

The two Native Americans obligingly do a war whoop.

Mannering runs to the front of the house, where Ma, Pa, and Pete are lounging on the porch. Barely able to speak, the tenderfoot exclaims that Indians are on the warpath! He then runs into the house to retrieve his pistol.

Dropping by for a visit is Miss Wetter, a maiden librarian "who knows all about books, but nothing about cooking." Ma steps into the house to get some loaves of bread she has made for this gangly lady. For her part, Miss Wetter has a book on how to grow fruit trees, which Elwin had requested. Ma takes her latest guest to meet the contest judges.

"Oh, Mr. Mannering," Miss Wetter gushes, "I'm simply *thrilled* to meet a literary figure of your stature!"

"Thank you," he says.

"I'm a *devoted* fan of yours," she elaborates. "I read your *beautiful* column every month. Through you, culture has come to Cape Flattery, and I for one am *speechless* with delight."

"Here's your bread, honey," Ma says. "And don't forget you're coming to the Christmas Eve party." Addressing both Miss Wetter and Mannering, she adds, "Since you're both interested in literature, it might be right nice for ya' to be partners at the party."

"It'd be a pleasure," Mannering says, his head clearly turned.

"It *would?*" Miss Wetter asks meekly. "Well, I'll be *dreaming* of Christmas Eve. 'Bye."

Back to business, as usual. "I'd like for you to show me the machine shed now," Mannering demands.

Ma hedges by saying that Pa found a skunk in there this morning. Stepping outside, Mannering suggests, "Suppose you show me the smokehouse?"

Above his head, a black umbrella opens. "Looks like rain!" Pa warns.

"Then we shall see it *before* it does," Mannering says, quickly losing patience.

"But those Indians might still be around," Pete says, trying to be helpful.

"I'm ready for them this time," Mannering says, patting his pistol inside his jacket pocket.

A cloud burst occurs at that very second, forestalling the inevitable once again. Ma, Mannering, and Pete seek shelter in the house. Pa stays back a bit, looking up to the skies and saying, "Thank ye!"

Cut to the roof, where two of the Kettle boys are spraying hoses.

When Mannering turns down another "nice, hot bath," Ma suggests a strong cup of coffee. To this he has no objection. Pa, meanwhile, sees that the water is still coming down in buckets. He walks out front, umbrella in hand, and shouts, "*That's enough*, kids!" When he hears a mighty thunderclap, he realizes that Someone Else has been helping as well. "Thank Ye," he calls out reverently.

Ma has taken out some of her prize-winning quilts. With evident pride, Pa tells Pete and Mannering that Ma is the "best needle woman in the county," and relates how she had taken first prize at the annual fair. Ma, even more proudly, shows off a lovely lace tablecloth her daughter Rosie had made for her. "Sure value it a lot," she says.

Mannering says that he believes his sister is an enthusiast for such handmade items. He offers to pay Ma well for them.

Ma, Pa, and Elwin look concerned. "Well," Ma says with much uncertainty, "all ri—"

"Oh, *no*," Elwin says firmly. "These things mean too much to Ma."

"We couldn't allow her to part with *those*," Pa agrees.

"Well," the self-centered man says, "it's a small matter. I'm going to bed now and take care of my cold."

"Elwin," Ma says, "it's about your bedtime, dear."

"Okay, Ma. Good night, Pete." Ma and Pa turn in as well.

Pete smiles. He is touched by this display of family unity.

When the rooster crows, signaling the beginning of a new day, Mannering awakens and looks out the bedroom window. What he sees astonishes him. The rain had done its worst to the makeshift, cardboard edifices meant to fool the judges. Everywhere he looks, in fact, is another rain-soaked, wet-cardboard disaster. He wakes up Pete and has him look out as well. No Indians or umbrellas can help the Kettles this time; the farm has been exposed for exactly what it is: a run-down shanty. While Pete says there must be some explanation, Mannering, not surprisingly, feels they have been hoodwinked. He storms into the kitchen, where Ma, Pa, and Elwin are gathered.

"Well, what have you got to say?" he demands.

"Kinda damp, ain't it?" Pa says, rocking in his chair and smoking a pipe.

"Your fraudulent actions are exposed completely. I'm moving to the Maddocks farm *this morning*."

No one says a word.

As Mannering is carrying out his suitcases, neighbors are arriving to reclaim their equipment. The rain had apparently done enough damage to one man's property to necessitate the return of his tractor. Another neighbor needs his wheelbarrow back; his kitchen is half-full of mud. And the man who had loaned Pa the pigs is there as well.

"Well," Pa says sadly, "it looks like the storm cooked our goose."

"You tried your best, Pa. That's the most that any man can do."

"Thanks, Ma."

Mrs. Maddocks is clearing the table following dinner. John walks out, saying to Mannering and Pete, "See you at the barn. Come out when you're ready."

While Mannering professes to like the skimpy meal that had just been served to them, Pete clearly misses Ma's ample breakfasts, with those fresh-baked biscuits dipped in gravy. Also, Maddocks is a grouch, running the farm like a dictator. While Mannering feels this recent change of locale is a step-up in quality, Pete wishes *he* were back with the hospitable Kettles.

Seated in the wagon are the doubles for Percy Kilbride, Alan Mowbray, and Ross Elliott. Each stuntman has his head lowered to avoid detection in this action still from Ma and Pa Kettle at Home.

To impress Mannering, Pa comes up with an idiotic plan. And he needs Geoduck and Crowbar to help him carry it out.

The next morning, Pa invites Pete and Mannering to go with him into the woods to chop down a Christmas tree. He is driving his ancient, horse-drawn cart. *This* should be a good spot, Pa announces. They dismount. Pa asks Pete if he would give him a hand with the tools; Pete agrees. Just then, coming from the opposite direction is a large group of Indians—straight out of Central Casting—on horseback. And these Injuns are clearly on the warpath.

An alarmed Mannering says, "Oh, *why* didn't I bring my pistol along?"

A candid shot of Percy Kilbride (left), Alan Mowbray (center), and Ross Elliott (right) reveals the affection Kilbride's co-stars obviously felt toward him.

Pa, in the manner of a 19th century melodrama actor, says heroically, "Don't worry! *I'll* save you! *Giddup!*"

The chase is on, and Mannering is falling for it, hook, line, and sinker. Pete, on the other hand, senses that someone is playing a joke on them. At one point, Geoduck orders his men to halt:

"We're crowding Pa too much." Some of the ersatz Indians are complaining, objecting to, as one member of the tribe calls it, "this kid stuff." Another says, "I wish *I* had the money to send Elwin to college myself. It'd sure be easier than *this!*"

A couple of arrows stick to Pa's wagon. Removing the projectiles, Pete discovers that the arrowheads are topped with corks.

"Don't *touch* it!" says the terrified Mannering. "It might be *poisoned!*"

Pa accidentally steers the horses onto the main road.

"He went that-a-way!" yells one of the Indians.

"He should have gone *that-a-way!*" says another, indicating the woods. "He shouldn't've gotten on the main highway!"

"We gotta keep chasing him," announces the loyal Geoduck. "Pa gotta prove himself a hero. *C'mon!*"

In a remarkably staged sequence, cars whiz by Pa's wagon and the Indians. Drivers and passengers stare at this display, which has seemingly been taken out of a John Ford western. Two highway patrolmen on motorcycles join the chase. Eventually catching up to these miscreants, the tribe is told to stop on the side of the road.

"We in heap big trouble," Geoduck admits.

An officer approaches Pa, who has an arrow sticking through his derby. Before he can get a word in, Mannering is babbling on about being chased by these "terrible Indians!" The officers turn their attention to the Wild Bunch.

"It was all in fun," Geoduck says.

The cops hardly view it that way; they plan to run *everybody* in. Pa, to his credit, readily admits to having orchestrated this demonstration so that he could appear heroic in his guest's eyes. Mannering, naturally, is furious, but Pete convinces him to drop the matter; if the newspapers pick up on the story, they would come off as prize fools, which would reflect badly on the magazine. Walking back to the officer, Pete says, "Mr. Mannering and I are going to write this story for the *National Magazine.* We'd like to include you officers. Would you pose for us?"

"Well," says the cop with a shrug, "if you guys don't sign a complaint, I got nothing I can hold Pa and the Indians on."

"Good," says Pete. He begins snapping pictures.

It is now Christmas preparation time at the Kettles. The kids are divided between the kitchen table, making homemade ornaments, as another group hangs them on the family's large, fresh-cut tree. Ma is removing another batch of cookies from the oven as the guests start to arrive. Sally Maddocks and Pete show up first and are welcomed warmly. Elwin is especially happy to see the lovely Sally, their relationship none the worse for all the trouble with the contest and Sally's vindictive father. She is just as pleased to be there as Elwin is to have her. She simply loves trimming Christmas trees, but there isn't one at her parents' home: "Dad thinks they're silly." She also tells Elwin that she wants *him* to win the prize scholarship. Elwin says that is just not possible given Pa's actions earlier that day. And speaking of Pa, *where* is he?

"He's in bed," Ma explains. "He says he don't feel so good."

"Mannering's not feeling too well himself," Pete says. "He says he's not coming to the party tomorrow night."

"Oh, that's *awful*," Ma says, disappointed. "We'll all be disgraced if one of the guests of honor don't show up. I've got to do *somethin'* to get him to change his mind."

The following morning, Christmas Eve, Ma is at the Maddocks farm, talking to Mannering. She plays to his massive ego by saying that a smart man like him could *never* have fallen for a stunt like the Indian attack. She then tells him that, if he doesn't attend her party, she will be ashamed before everybody. Properly softened up, he agrees to be there. Just then, Maddocks walks by.

"Mr. Maddocks," Ma says, approaching him, "since you folks ain't havin' a tree, you can put your wife's and Sally's presents under ours."

"Ain't got no presents," he says tersely. "Too busy to waste my time shopping. They get the necessities all year." He walks away without another word.

Ma, deeply saddened by what she has just heard, returns to Mannering. "Takes all kinds," she says. "Don't it?" Watching her leave, Mannering smiles at this good woman.

"Sally's asked me to put these under the Kettles' tree," says Pete conspiratorially. "Surprise presents she and her mother bought for Maddocks." At that moment, John and his wife walk into the house. "Can't we take a ham to the Kettles?" she asks.

"What for?"

"It's *Christmas*, John!"

"They don't need anything from us."

When John looks up and sees Pete and Mannering's disapproving expressions, he turns to his wife and says abruptly, "Get the ham." And then, out of camera range: "You'd better hurry, Sally. Everybody's nearly ready."

The Kettle home on Christmas Eve seems an idyllic place to be. The older kids are helping to serve the guests while the younger ones sneak a peek at their stockings, hanging from the fireplace mantle. The house smells wonderfully of Ma's cooking, and everyone, a whole houseful of neighbors and friends, is made to feel like one big family.

Miss Wetter excitably runs up to Mannering and says, "I've been waiting for you! *You* are going to be my partner at supper."

"I've not forgotten," he says kindly. "I, too, was looking forward to it." She leaves to get him some refreshments.

"Folks," Ma says, "everybody's here now but Pa. He'll be along soon. I'm really glad to have you here tonight and all us Kettles hope you have a good time."

Everyone applauds.

"Me and the kids have written a poem," she announces. "Of course, none of us is a Shakespeare, but I'll be *darned* if we didn't make everythin' rhyme." She begins: "Tis the night before Christmas, but it won't be so quiet, not with us Kettles—we make such a riot." Each subsequent stanza is custom-tailored to an honored guest. Acknowledging neighbor John Maddocks, Ma reads that she's "hoping at last, he'll say 'Okay' now, when Nick wants to go courtin' with Bessie, his cow." Miraculously, this line even gets a smile out of the brooding Maddocks. Billy Reed is thanked for letting Pa run up endless credit at his store. Geoduck and Crowbar are given much-deserved love and appreciation. Pete is acknowl-

The Kettles' farm on Christmas Eve. Pictured from left to right are Mr. Mannering, Elwin Kettle, Mrs. Maddocks, Ma, Geoduck, Pa/Santa, Miss Wetter, and the latest batch of Kettle kids.

edged as a great guy who loves Ma's cooking. Miss Wetter, the spinster, receives the wish that she lands a husband. And "poor Mr. Mannering, whose stomach's not strong," is gifted with an egg from Ma's hen Jenny, in hopes that "it cures whatever is wrong."

Just then, the sound of sleigh bells emanates from outside. Ma encourages everyone to go out to the front porch to welcome a special visitor. They are greeted by the sight of an old wagon pulled by a horse, a bull (with a derby), and four goats. Seated at the reigns is old St. Nick—Pa, of course, wearing his dyed-red long underwear and a lengthy, white beard.

"*Santa Claus!*" the littlest children scream.

Pa robustly calls out, "Merry Christmas, everybody!"

Hurrying into the house with a big sack over his shoulder, he places presents under the tree. The Kettle kids, meanwhile, form two rows and begin singing "Silent Night." Pa soon joins them, conducting, while Ma stands next to him, singing along (horribly) at one point. When the kids segue into "Jingle Bells," even old man Maddocks gets caught up in the holiday spirit, much to his wife's delight. Miss Wetter, noticing the mistletoe hanging just above Mannering, gives him a peck on the cheek. Although in shock, he joins in the chorus as well.

Following this homespun musical interlude, Pa asks everyone to gather round while he hands out the presents. He turns and leans over to retrieve the packages when—you guessed it—one of the goats escapes from the harness and runs into the house. Although we don't actually see Pa being charged, a close-up of Mannering laughing heartily tells us exactly what just happened. Pa laughs it off as well, saying that it's just the goat's way of wishing him "Merry Christmas."

The grateful recipients then receive their presents. Martha Maddocks is overjoyed to unwrap her gift, saying, "Oh, *John*! You bought Ma's prize-winning quilt!" The gift John supposedly got his daughter is just as precious. Holding up the handmade lace tablecloth Rosie Kettle had made for Ma's birthday, Sally asks, "Dad! How did you *ever* get Ma to part with *this*?" John, of course, is at a loss. Ma and Pete exchange knowing smiles.

"Go on, open up your package, Mr. Mannering," Ma says encouragingly.

He does so; it is a feathered headdress from Geoduck and Crowbar.

"Put it on," she urges.

As Mannering clearly has no idea how to affix such an adornment, Geoduck walks over and assists him with it.

"This make you honorary chief of our tribe," he says.

"Ma," John Maddocks says. "You've made us all very happy and taught me something I've needed to learn."

"I'm glad, John," Ma says, warmly taking her neighbor's hand.

"Ma," he continues. "I'm taking Sally out of the competition and sending her to college myself."

Sally turns to her boyfriend and says joyfully, "You *win*! We can *both* go!"

Mannering, still wearing the headdress, confers briefly with Pete before announcing: "Ladies and gentlemen, my colleague and I are very happy at Mr. Maddocks's announcement. However, we can't agree. It wouldn't be fair to Sally. After all, it is a very high honor to enter college on a scholarship. We therefore declare the contest . . . a *tie*—each one to receive a two-year scholarship."

Ma and Pa hug. "Isn't it wonderful, son?" she says, hugging him as well.

"You know," Pete says, "if there were a 4-H Club around, those two kids could earn enough for the last two years."

"You're *right*!" chimes in Miss Wetter. "The 4-H Club has all sorts of money-raising projects. Where the members can learn by doing."

"By golly, *I'll* start one," says John, his transformation complete. "I'll teach farming if Ma will teach how to make a happy home."

Ma laughs and says, "You can sure count on me, John!"

Inspired by all this yuletide goodwill, Pa resolves to make some changes, too. "I'm gonna fix up this old place real good . . . soon as Geoduck and Crowbar get the time."

Everybody laughs, with the obvious exception of Geoduck and Crowbar.

Billy seeks forgiveness from Mr. Mannering for having put Oscar into the tub with him. The Brit accepts the boy's apology with grace. Billy then wordlessly hands their honored guest a small package, tied up with wrapping paper and string. Opening the box, he comes face to face with Billy's pet frog, which croaks a greeting.

Mannering smiles. "And a happy New Year to you, too, Oscar."

The Payoff

Samuel Stoddard writes: "This is one of the best in the Ma and Pa Kettle series and certainly the warmest. *Too* warm for some, possibly, but cynical viewers won't have made it this far in the series anyway." Leonard Maltin, in his longtime best-selling *Movies on TV* ratings books, awards the film three stars and calls it "the best entry in the series ... One slapstick gag follows another, leading to a wild climactic chase; there's some homespun sentiment, too, as we spend Christmas with the Kettles." The box-office numbers were down from the previous entry (*At the Fair*), but the $1.75 million take was still substantial. U-I officials, not surprisingly, wished the main stars would commit to an endless number of additional entries. To show just how resolute he was about retirement, however, Percy Kilbride turned down a million-dollar bonus—an absolutely unheard-of amount at the time (closer to $10 million by 2021's calculations)—as an incentive to continue in the role. The studio was convinced that it would easily make back that money, and then some, were Percy to reprise his role again. At the time, Ma and Pa Kettle were considered the thirteenth-biggest box-office-draw in America. Fortunately for the studio, it had one more Main-Kilbride film sitting on the shelf, awaiting release.

Chapter 9
Ma and Pa Kettle at Waikiki
(1955)

Released by Universal-International, April 1955. 79 minutes. Directed by Lee Sholem. Produced by Leonard Goldstein. Assistant Director: Tom Shaw. Story by Connie Lee Bennett. Screenplay by Jack Henley, Harry Clork, and Elwood Ullman. Musical Direction: Joseph Gershenson. Director of Photography: Clifford Stine. Film Editor: Virgil W. Vogel, A.S.C. Art Direction: Bernard Herzbrun and Eric Orbom. Set Decorations: Russell A. Gausman and Ruby R. Levitt. Make-Up: Bud Westmore. Hair Stylist: Joan St. Oegger. Sound: Leslie I. Carey and Corson Jowett. Gowns: Rosemary Odell.

Cast: Marjorie Main (*Ma Kettle*); Percy Kilbride (*Pa Kettle*); Lori Nelson (*Rosie Kettle*); Byron Palmer (*Bob Baxter*); Russell Johnson (*Eddie Nelson*); Hilo Hattie (*Mama Lotus*); Loring Smith (*Rodney Kettle*); Lowell Gilmore (*Robert Coates*); Mabel Albertson (*Teresa Andrews*); Fay Roope (*Fulton Andrews*); Oliver Blake (*Geoduck*); Teddy Hart (*Crowbar*); Esther Dale (*Birdie Hicks*); Claudette Thornton (*Rodney Kettle's Secretary*); George Arglen (*Willie Kettle*); William Bailey (*Board Member*); Faire Binney (*Party Guest*); Margaret Brown (*Ruthie Kettle*); Dee Carroll (*Secretary*); Ben Chapman (*Passenger*); Billy Clark (*George Kettle*); Helen Dickson (*Passenger*); Bob Donnelly (*Clerk*); Bonnie Kay Eddy (*Susie Kettle*); Norman Field (*Dr. Fabian*); Jon Gardner (*Benjamin Kettle*); Cindy Garner (*Secretary*); Kenneth Gibson (*Board Member*); Arthur D. Gilmour (*Bradley, Butler*); Pat Goldin (*Painter*); James Gonzalez (*Ship Passenger*); Harold Goodwin (*Dr. Barnes*); Herschel Graham (*Barbershop Customer*); Alan Harris (*Barber*); Timmy Hawkins (*Teddy Kettle*); Grace Hayle (*Party Guest*); Myron Healey (*Marty, Kidnapper*); George Hoagland (*Ship Passenger*); Jackie Jackson (*Henry Kettle*); Byron Kane (*Prof. Gilfallen*); Kenner G. Kemp (*Ship Passenger*); Donna Leary (*Sally Kettle*); Rudy Lee (*Billy Kettle*); Jenny Linder (*Sara Kettle*); Leon Lontoc (*Rickshaw Driver*); Charles Lung (*Papa Lotus*); Luukiuluana (*Doreen, Masseuse*); Frank Marlowe (*Chauffeur*); Charles Mauu (*Doorman*); Timothy A. Miguel (*April Lotus*), Beverly Mook (*Eve Kettle*); George Nardelli (*Barber*); Dorothy Neumann (*Miss Pennyfeather*); Ralph Peters (*Barber*); George Piltz (*Outrigger Driver*);

Ezelle Poule (*Party Guest*); Richard Reeves (*Lefty Conway, Kid-napper*); Ric Roman (*Chuck Collins, Kidnapper*); Ronnie Rondell Jr. (*Donnie Kettle*); Cosmo Sardo (*Barber*); Elana Schreiner (*Nancy Kettle*); Sandra Spence (*Pa's Secretary*); Ben Welden (*Shorty Bates, Kidnapper*); Judy Wiard (*Secretary*); Lois Wilde (*Boat Passenger*); Lawrence A. Williams (*Board Member*); Sally Yarnell (*Clerk*).

The year is 1955. Moviegoers are just settling into their seats when the familiar strains of the Ma and Pa Kettle theme song can be heard. A black-and-white title card appears on the screen. It reads:

**The Schine Theaters
Present
two of your old friends,
Ma and Pa Kettle**

(*The setting is the interior of a shed. Marjorie Main, in the guise of Ma Kettle, enters the frame, wearing a house dress and a pleasant smile.*)

Ma: Hello, there! (*She turns to her right*) Pa, say hello to the folks.

(*Percy Kilbride, outfitted as Pa Kettle, has a corn cob pipe in his mouth and is wearing his usual derby. He doffs it for the audience.*)

Pa: Howdy.

Ma: For a long time, Pa and I and the twelve—uh, *fif-teen*—kids have wanted to thank you for the way you've received the Kettle pictures. It's gratifying to know that we've been able to make you laugh and forget your cares for a while. You know, once a year, along about spring-time, we're liable to bust in on ya'! Just like a spring tonic! I'm molasses, and Pa's sulpur! (*She laughs raucously at her own joke.*) That's a good one, ain't it, Pa?

(*The exact same footage of Kilbride as Pa is used again.*)

Pa: Howdy.

Ma: Pa's in a conversational rut today. But we're both excit-ed over the fact that the Schine Theater circuit is going to have a world premiere of *Ma and Pa Kettle at Waikiki* in fifty theaters, in fifty states. And we hope you'll all come see what the Kettles do when they're on vacation (*laughs*). Good-bye, and good luck. Say good-bye to the folks, Pa.

Pa: Howdy.

This trailer—as different from contemporary coming attractions as one can imagine—was made to advertise a film made three years earlier, with footage of Percy Kilbride from a movie made two years before that. This was U-I's ragged attempt to put together a campaign in the hopes of enticing the public with one last entry, *Ma and Pa Kettle at Waikiki*. The series' producer, Leonard Goldstein, had died suddenly from a cerebral hemorrhage on July 23, 1954, at the age of fifty-one. This was a major blow to the franchise that he had overseen since its beginning. The very concept of the Ma and Pa Kettle movie series, in fact, had been his.

Lee Sholem.

Someone else missing in action was Charles Lamont. His director's chair would be temporarily filled by Lee Tabor Sholem (1913–2000). Sholem, a patient, generous director, did his level best to make a film set an enjoyable place to be. During his forty-year career, "Roll 'Em" Sholem directed upwards of thirteen hundred projects, both features and TV episodes, without ever once going over schedule. He had begun his career in the cutting room in the thirties. A lengthy association with producer Sol Lesser brought him into contact with the celebrated production designer William Cameron Menzies (*Gone with the Wind*), from whom Sholem learned the key to expedient production, and later led to his first directorial assignment, *Tarzan's Magic Fountain* (1949).

It was at this time that Marjorie Main began to slow down professionally. As she is quoted in a U-I report of September 21, 1952: "I've been doing five pictures a year for fifteen years. As far as I'm concerned, those days are behind me. One or two pictures a year for me is all I'm looking for." Her heart simply was not in acting anymore. This is demonstrated by an on-set anecdote involving an exchange between Ma and her longtime adversary Birdie Hicks. Marjorie's line was straight-forward enough: "That's what *you* say, Birdie Hicks!" But it took several takes to get it right. On the first take, she said, "That's what *you* say, Bennie Hicks!"

"*Cut!*" said Lee Sholem. "The name is *Birdie* Hicks, Marjorie."

Take two: "That's what *you* say, Betty Hicks!"

"*Cut!* Try it again. At least we're using a woman's name now."

Take three: "That's what *you* say, Sarah Bernhardt!"

Marjorie laughed to cover her embarrassment. "And to think I started in the theater playing Shakespeare!"

Like Marjorie, Percy Kilbride was not at the top of his game. In their most recently completed film, *On Vacation*, he was a positive whirling dervish of activity, running from an ever-growing group of policemen. But a heart condition would slow the sixty-five-year-old Kilbride considerably. For various scenes in the film, Sholem accommodated Percy by having him in a prone position, whether in his hammock at home, or on a deck chair during an ocean voyage. There were also a few instances in *Waikiki* when he had to be doubled to complete scenes involving physical comedy, such as taking a fall, fully clothed, into a swimming pool. Like all Kettle films, slapstick gags occur at incongruous times, calling for Ma (or, more specifically, her double, Helen Gibson) to take a violent fall, or in an early scene in the kitchen, having flour blown around by the air conditioning unit, which Pa had inadvertently hooked up backward.

Ma's demeanor in general is more raucous than in previous entries. This may be attributed, at least in part, to the script contributions of Memphis-born Elwood Ullman (1903–1985). Through the assistance of screenwriter Jack Natteford, Ullman began writing for two-reel comedies, and was eventually hired by the Columbia Pictures short-subjects department in 1936. In that capacity, he provided scripts for the Three Stooges, Andy Clyde, and Charley Chase. He left Columbia in 1951 to concentrate on writing features, including several for the Bowery Boys at Monogram, before retiring from the business in 1966.

The Supporting Cast[41]

Loring Smith as Rodney Kettle . . .

Loring Smith.

A favorite of George S. Kaufman and Ruth Gordon, Loring Smith (1890–1981) was a regular on Broadway between the years 1940 and 1964. He appeared in five hit original productions, including *John Loves Mary* and *The Solid Gold Cadillac*. He also had supporting roles in such A-pictures as *Shadow of the Thin Man* (1941) and *Pat and Mike* (1952).

Mabel Albertson as Teresa Andrews . . .

Mabel Albertson.

Mabel Albertson (1901–1982) is the elitist Teresa Andrews, who is simply appalled by the Kettles. Mabel, who was actor Jack Albertson's sister, had a long and varied career in show business, beginning with vaudeville in the twenties, radio in the thirties, and the legitimate theater—as both an actress and a director—in the forties. It was not until she turned fifty, however, that she truly found her niche, playing, according to the IMDb, "the ultimate haughty, judgmental (often wealthy) mother-in-law (or mother, or stepmother, or auntie)" in

41 *At Waikiki* marked the final appearance of Esther Dale in her signature role as Birdie Hicks. She died on July 23, 1961, at the age of seventy-five.

an impressive array of films, TV movies, and sitcoms. She is best remembered as the overbearing mother of Howard Sprague (Jack Dodson) on four episodes of *The Andy Griffith Show* (1960–1968) during its sixth, seventh, and eighth seasons.

Russell Johnson as Eddie Nelson . . .

Classic sitcom fans will also recognize Russell Johnson (1924–2014) in one of the many roles he essayed before becoming inextricably linked to the character of the Professor on *Gilligan's Island* (1964–1967). He had key supporting roles in such sci-fi classics as *It Came from Outer Space* (1953) and *This Island Earth* (1955).

Russell Johnson.

Byron Palmer as Bob Baxter . . .

Byron Palmer and Lori Nelson supply the requisite romantic interest in Ma and Pa Kettle at Waikiki.

Providing the film's requisite romantic interest are Lori Nelson and Byron Palmer. During World War II, Palmer (1920–2009) joined the Army Air Forces and ran a radio station on an island in the Pacific. In addition to reading news items, he also sang tenor on the air with a quartet called the Music Mates. The fan mail he received from soldiers encouraged him to take voice lessons after the war. After acting as master of ceremonies for a touring "Hollywood on Ice" show, he got his first big break in 1948, co-starring in the Broadway show *Where's Charley?* with Ray Bolger. Although *Ma and Pa Kettle at Waikiki* was his official film debut, he was first seen by audiences in *Tonight We*

Sing, released by 20th Century-Fox in 1953. Other films in which he appeared include *Man in the Attic* (1953), starring Jack Palance as the suspected Jack the Ripper, and *The Best Things in Life Are Free* (1956), starring Gordon MacRae. On television, he had guest roles on several series, including dramas, but may be best known for his duets with Joan Weldon on KTTV's *This is Your Music*, in 1955.

Hilo Hattie as Mama Lotus . . .

Lending some authenticity to the supposed Hawaiian setting is Hilo Hattie (1901–1979), the legendary entertainer of Hawaiian descent. Hattie (real name: Carol Nelson) demonstrates her musical abilities in this, one of only a handful of films in which she appeared during her long career.

Hilo Hattie.

And the Last of the Original Kettle Kids.

At Waikiki served as a final reunion, of sorts, for nine of the original Kettle kids: George Arglen, Margaret Brown, Billy Clark, Jackie Jackson, Donna Leary, Jenny Linder, Beverly Mook, Ronnie Rondell Jr., and Elana Schreiner.

Beverly Jean Mook, who was reprising her role as Eve Kettle, was born in Los Angeles on August 3, 1940. In addition to the five Kettle pictures, she appeared as an extra in two star-studded films, *The Greatest Show on Earth* (1952) and *Around the World in Eighty Days* (1956); she also had the featured (yet uncredited) role of Judy Coffman in the film adaptation of William Inge's play *Come Back, Little Sheba* (1952), starring Shirley Booth and Burt Lancaster. Her final credit was as a nameless harem girl in *The Three Stooges Meet Hercules* (1962). Margaret Brown, a professional dancer, appeared on three episodes of *The Ed Sullivan Show* (then known as *Toast of the Town*) between 1950 and 1953. Most of her credits, however, were as Ruthie Kettle, in five Kettle pictures.

Jackie Jackson, better known as Henry Kettle, had what must have been fun acting assignments for a typical all-American boy in the late forties. After all, he was able to play baseball (*Take Me Out to the Ballgame* and *Kill the Umpire!*), eat ice cream (*The Good Humor Man*), ride a horse (*The Red Pony*), be on-set with comedian Bob Hope (*The Great Lover*), and be one of those crazy Kettle kids in four pictures. Donna Leary, a.k.a. Sally Kettle, was born in Los Angeles on June 14, 1936. In addition to the five Kettle pictures, Donna appeared as a Bobby soxer, swooning over Frank Sinatra in *Meet Danny Wilson* (1952). She was also in Roger Corman's lurid quickie *Sorority Girl* (1957), which was remade in 1993 (with a different set of sorority girls, interestingly enough).

The Storyline

We open on a sweltering summer day in Cape Flattery.[42] The tulips in a flower box on the Kettles' windowsill droop in exhaustion. Pa's suits of long underwear, hanging in a row from the clothesline, roll up like wallpaper. The thermostat inside the house is no better; it reaches its peak of 130 degrees, causing the mercury to spurt out the top in surrender. "*Hmm.* Couldn't take it, eh?" says a ragged-looking Ma, who has resorted to doing laundry in their "home of the future" on an old-fashioned washboard. Nothing in the house, it seems, is working, and as usual, that includes Pa. Lying outside on a mechanized hammock, he is dictating a letter to Geoduck. Crowbar is above Pa, lying on a board suspended between two step ladders, shooing away flies from his boss with a horsetail on a stick. The letter, to Pa's cousin Rodney, is full of tall tales concerning his financial acumen. As we join in, he is recounting his latest coup—purchasing the First National Bank.

"You bought First National Bank in last letter," Geoduck points out.

"Well, then, make it the second. Gotta keep on expanding."

"Why every time you write your cousin, you tell same big lies?"

"Oh, I ain't lyin'," Pa insists, "just exaggeratin'. 'Course, Ma don't know I'm doin' it, but Rodney is rich and successful. Owns a fac-

---

42 A kitchen wall calendar reads August 1952, a clue for sharp-eyed viewers as to when the film was made.

tory and a mess of pineapples in Honolulu. Me and Rodney both courted Ma when we were young sprouts. I got Ma, and Rodney took the pineapples. Done so good with 'em, he never come back here. No harm lettin' him know I did just as good. Can't have him thinkin' Ma made a mistake marryin' me 'stead of him!" Over some scratchy stock footage of pineapple fields in Hawaii, Pa's expository narration continues: "Yes, sir. May be hard to believe, but over in Honolulu, a member of the Kettle family is wallowin' in money, takin' life easy, with never a care in the world."

The next shot has Rodney Kettle, a balding, overweight, late-middle-aged executive, throwing a heavy object through the glass door of his office. Standing behind his wide desk with a secretary on either side, he is ranting at two men, Robert Coates and Eddie Nelson, who are planning a hostile takeover of Kettle Enterprises. The pineapple business, it seems, is in the red. The bank considers it a bad risk. And Rodney is in danger of having a heart attack. What he needs is a long rest . . . and someone sharp enough to run the business while he recovers. Only one man comes to mind, a man of boundless energy, drive, uncanny foresight—P.A. Kettle, the industrialist in Washington State. He's a mighty busy man, but maybe, *just maybe*, he'll be willing to come to Honolulu for a few weeks to get the company out of its current financial hole and back on its metaphorical feet. To appeal to his mega-successful cousin, Rodney begins to dictate a letter to him. No, too impersonal. *A cable?* That's not right, either. *A phone call?* No, it would be too easy for P.A. to turn him down. There is only *one* way of ensnaring him, and that is to send his assistant general manager, Bob Baxter, to Cape Flattery to visit him in person.

Bob Baxter is on foot in the Kettles' posh neighborhood. Passing by two pedestrians, Birdie Hicks and the equally spinsterish Miss Pennyfeather, he says politely: "I seem to be lost. Can you tell me where P.A. Kettle lives?"

"*P.A.* Kettle?" repeats Birdie, confused by the initials.

"The only Kettles *we* know live down this street," says Miss Pennyfeather, obviously smitten with this well-dressed stranger.

In this sequence, we see an outdoor façade of the Kettle model home for the first, and only, time in the series. The other shots, in earlier films, were done on a soundstage, with the aid of a matte.

"Is *he* the industrialist?" Baxter asks.

"If you consider having children an industry," answers the sharp-tongued Birdie.

Ma and Rosie are discussing the family's finances and baking cookies. Once the batch is removed from the oven, in runs the horde of Kettle kids, their olfactory senses as keen as ever. They want to escape the heat and go to summer camp, but Ma explains that there are twenty reasons they can't go. The first is, they haven't got the money—the other nineteen don't count. The kids settle for playing in the sprinklers. This leads to some unexpected guests— Birdie, Miss Pennyfeather, and Bob Baxter—getting soaked when the water pressure is turned on.

Pa is, not surprisingly, scared to death of having his bluff called, but Rodney instructed Bob not to take "no" for an answer. To cover expenses, he has issued a check to P.A. for two thousand dollars (which would be worth more than ten times that by contempo-rary standards) as well as the promise of a generous stock bonus once he puts the company back on its feet. Ma would love nothing more than to get away from her washboard and take a trip to "Hiwaii," as she mispronounces it. She even forces Pa to agree to go as well. ("Up to now, Pa Kettle," she says, "you've been nothin' but lazy, shiftless, careless—" Taking offense, Pa says, "*Careless?*") Ma says she still believes in him, but if he doesn't go, she's packin' up the kids and leavin' him. That ultimatum works: Pa *will* go. While the fourteen younger kids are enjoying themselves in summer camp, Ma and Pa will be traveling with their eldest daughter, Rosie, so the film can have a romantic subplot.

This unflattering shot of Ma in her tennis outfit was one of the photos Marjorie Main routinely sent to fans who requested an autograph.

The scenes on shipboard are played for yocks, as they say, with Ma stuffed into a tennis outfit, carrying a racket and ball, and yelling (and we do mean *yelling*), "POINT–GAME!– SERVICE!" This is followed by an overhead swing, smacking Pa, asleep on a deck chair, square on the noggin. Ma, in fact, has become an exercise fiend, stretching, and working out at a furious pace. Pa suspects, and not without reason, that Ma is trying to get into shape so she can be presentable when seeing her old beau once again. After all, Rodney and Phoebe (Ma's first name, revealed for the first, and only, time in the series) were quite an item in their day. As Ma runs literal circles around the sedentary Pa, he warns her to take it easy: "You don't want to bust something. You ain't no gazelle, you know."

As Ma does the squats, holding the ship rail for support (with bone-cracking sound effects), she expounds, "Sea air *sure* does somethin' for ya'! No doubt about it, Pa. Travel really broadens a person. Meetin' people and seein' things makes you spread out. Maybe this trip'll make *you* change your whole life." Suddenly noticing that her husband has dozed off, she shakes him by the shoulder and yells, "PA! *WAKE UP!*"

"What's *wrong?* We ain't *sinkin'*, are we?"

"Ya' haven't heard a thing I've been sayin'."

"Heard every word."

Folding her arms, she says, "What'd I say?"

"Well, you said, travel makes you kinda broad. Eatin' makes you spread out. And maybe this trip will make me . . . change my wife."

Beginning to run in place, Ma says, "You gotta do better than that when we get to Hi-waii."

The "fish-out-of-water" concept is called into service for the scenes involving fellow passengers Fulton Andrews, president of the Honolulu Bank (and the one on whom Rodney is counting to approve a loan on the strength of Pa's performance), and his unbearably stuffy wife, Teresa. Ma first encounters this unhappy woman on the deck when she takes the seat next to her.

"D' ya' mind if I sit down here?" Ma asks. "Gee *whiz*. New shoes *sure* make my feet sore." She begins to untie them. "I'd as soon have a *toothache* as a foot ache!" Looking at her dour companion, she says, "The name's Kettle, Ma Kettle. What's yours?"

"Mrs. Fulton Andrews," she responds, blue-bloodedly. "You're the wife of that *peculiar* little man that sleeps on deck, aren't you?"

"That's Pa," Ma says with obvious pride and affection. "He's goin' over to Honolulu to take over a big factory."

"How interesting," she says, showing no interest at all. "Does he sleep *all* the time?"

Ma chuckles and answers, "Oh, just about . . .'cept around mealtime. But put a fork in his hand with a pork chop on it, and he'll come to, all right . . . Oh, that's my daughter up there! HELLO, ROSIE!" she shouts, causing passengers to bolt upright in their deck chairs.

Rosie is on the upper deck, mooning over Bob Baxter. "Oh, hi, Ma," she says.

Baxter recognizes Ma's reluctant companion: "Say, that's Teresa Andrews, wife of the president of the Honolulu Bank! I didn't know *she* was on board."

"Trust Ma to make friends with *everybody*," Rosie says.

As Mrs. Andrews attempts to make a getaway from this coarse person, she is run into by Pa (or at least their doubles run into each other), sending them both into the pool, fully dressed.

Having arrived on the island, Ma and Pa are unwinding after dinner in their Honolulu hotel suite (with its table lamps resembling large pineapples). Pa, wearing a bathrobe, is tinkering with his radio, which he brought along. Attempting to start it, he sits in a chair nearby. Lifting the chair beneath him, he lets it land with a *thud*. Nothing happens. *Hmm*, that's *strange*, he says; always works at home. Ma is in her robe as well, soaking her feet in a tub of hot water.[43] There is a knock at the door. Ma is too tired to get up to answer it; as for Pa, he says, "Can't do two things at once, Ma."

"COME IN!" Ma yells.

It's Bob Baxter, dressed in a white dinner jacket; Rosie is a vision in her white evening gown (by U-I costumer Rosemary O'Dell). They make a hasty exit, leaving the stage in time for a funny sequence.

Rodney shows up and is surprised to find P.A. and Phoebe so informally dressed.[44] He wants them to put their best foot forward, so to speak, given that Mr. and Mrs. Fulton Andrews will soon be dropping by to pay their respects. Cut to a shot of the hallway outside the suite, with the high-toned couple approaching. Teresa, who has already had enough of those "impossible people," receives not the slightest bit of sympathy from her pragmatic husband. He knows that P.A. is rich, and he wants the Kettle money in his bank. So, to his wife, he says, "Don't be yourself. *Be nice.*"

Rodney, desiring to impress Andrews to get that all-important bank loan, is trying to make his casual cousin and former girlfriend seem a bit more refined. (Good luck with that, Rodney.) He covers Ma's feet ("What, ain't she never had sore feet before?")

---

43 This scene presented a challenge for Marjorie Main, who was concerned that keeping her feet wet for an extended period would lead to her catching cold.

44 Something is clearly missing here. Apparently, the scene in which the two former sweethearts meet after a twenty-five-year separation is still somewhere on the cutting-room floor.

and encourages Pa to put on a clean shirt. The guests arrive and introductions are made.

"Phoebe, dear," Rodney says gallantly, "this is Mr. Fulton Andrews and his charming wife."

"Mrs. Kettle and I have met," says Teresa frostily.

"We sure have!" Ma says. "Hi' ya', Tessie!"

Standing by Phoebe, Rodney says to Mr. Andrews that he "was once madly in love with this enchanting creature." Ma giggles shyly.

Ma (seated, far left) and Pa (center) are formally introduced by Rodney Kettle (Loring Smith, left) to bank president Fulton Andrews (Fay Roope, right) and his haughty wife, Teresa (Mabel Albertson, far right).

"Well, I can understand that perfectly," Andrews responds with an almost imperceptible eye roll. "Where is your husband?"

Ma yells, "PA! COME ON IN. COMPANY'S HERE!"

Pa walks in the room half-dressed, wearing his long underwear, over which his pants are about ready to fall down. (Fortunately, for modesty's sake, he also has on his derby.) Pa has a tea kettle in hand, telling Ma the treatment is no good unless the water stays hot. The water he then pours into the tub is apparently scalding, judging by the sheer volume of Ma's screams.

"Pa, take it easy!" Ma objects. "I just wanna *soak* my feet, not *boil*'em!"

Rodney introduces Pa to Andrews.

"It's a great privilege, P.A."

"Pa's the name."

"You and Teresa met on board, I understand."

"Believe we did," says Pa, tipping his hat to the lady. "In the *pool*, wasn't it?"

Mrs. Andrews is not amused.

"Teresa just dropped in to invite Mrs. Kettle to a cocktail party at our home," explains Fulton.

"That's real neighborly of her," says Ma with a genuine smile. "Give me a chance to wear my new dress with the high collar in the back."

"I'm afraid that's impossible, Fulton, I—"

"*Nonsense!* One more won't matter." And then, graciously to Ma: "If you could be there at four o'clock, Mrs. Kettle?"

"I believe we'd better be leaving," says Teresa, putting a hand to her forehead. "I have one of my headaches."

"Stay right here," Ma says, drying off her feet. "I can fix that in a jiffy."

"Oh, no, really, I'd rather—"

"I learned how from a medicine show man who come to our town when I was a girl."

"Please, don't trouble," says Teresa in an urgent tone. "It'll go away."

"Oh, no it won't," says Dr. Ma. "It's no trouble at all." She stands up and, taking Mrs. Andrews by the arm, guides her over to a stiff-backed chair. "Pa can tell ya'. I'm pretty good at curin' up headaches, earaches, chilblains." Teresa looks over her shoulder pleadingly at her husband.

"I'll be all right the minute I get out in the fresh air."

"*Sit down!*" Ma commands. Standing behind her captive patient, she begins to massage her neck roughly. "Just take a deep breath and let go!" Ma puts the afflicted woman in a headlock

Ma (standing, right) uses her chiropractic skills on an ungrateful (and unwilling) patient. Pa (left, standing) is more interested in what song is playing on the radio.

and cracks her neck like a walnut. Mrs. Andrews lets out an ear-piercing scream as the chair rocks sideways, landing with a *thump*. This time, the radio works, blaring out (as always) "Tiger Rag."

"I *knew* she'd work!" Pa says delightedly.

"TURN THAT THING DOWN!" Ma says, shouting over the din.

"Can't," says Pa. "Knob's busted."

As music continues to blare forth from the speaker, Ma remembers that she had forgotten to go into reverse. Putting the woman in another headlock, she cracks her violently in the opposite direction. Another scream, another *thump*. The music stops.

"*There!*" Ma says. "That outta make ya' feel *good!*"

"Never fails," Pa attests. "Cures me every time."

Teresa runs to her husband. "Fulton, take me out of this madhouse!"

"She was only helping you, dear," he says consolingly.

Teresa leaves without another word.

"She'll see you tomorrow, Mrs. Kettle. Good-night, P.A."

"Pa's—"

"Coming, Rodney?"

"In a minute, Fulton."

He takes a few seconds to tell P.A. that the following morning his presence is requested at a special board meeting. It begins at nine o'clock. And he tells him *not* to wear sport clothes; he wants him to wear what he usually wears to work.

Before attending one of the pineapple company's board meetings, Pa (standing, left) was instructed to wear his usual work clothes. Introducing the honored guest is his cousin Rodney Kettle (standing, right).

Pa, in his traditional moth-eaten sweater, baggy black pants held up by a loosely tied rope, and, of course, the ever-present derby, makes his way to Kettle Enterprises in the heart of downtown Honolulu. He is invited to sit at the head of a long, polished table, lined with serious-looking board members. Rodney has taken the liberty of purchasing a smaller, more compact radio for his cousin; he noticed that the one in his suite was not playing too well the night before. Pa is genuinely delighted.

Everyone seems perplexed as to why this hallowed industrialist is wearing a hat indoors. Pa says, "Had it for twenty-two years. Couldn't do a lick of work without it sittin' right here on my head."

Well, what's good enough for P.A. Kettle is good enough for us, Rodney decides. Each board member, Rodney included, gets up, retrieves his hat, and puts it on. With everyone now behatted, Rodney bangs the gavel to begin the meeting.

"Once more, Rodney," says Pa. When the chairman goes to bang the gavel again, Pa is prepared: he has a walnut beneath it that needs to be cracked open.

Fascinated by his new radio, Pa takes a tour of the factory. Rodney Kettle's right-hand man, Bob Baxter, is (ironically enough) at the far left.

Pa is simply enthralled by his new portable radio. He carries it with him everywhere, holding it up to his ear and playing it as loud as he pleases, even while being taken on a tour of the fruit-processing plant. As Rodney explains how the pineapple is cored and packaged, Fulton Andrews interrupts to ask if anything could be done to step up the assembly line; the workers, he believes, are moving at too slow a pace. Rodney is annoyed by this, telling

Andrews frankly that he is overstepping; this is *his* company, after all, and if there was a way of stepping up volume, he would have implemented it sometime during the past twenty-five years. At this very instance, Pa accidentally bangs his radio against a crate of pineapple, cranking up the volume to eardrum-shattering levels. In this case, his inability to turn down the radio has unwittingly doubled, even tripled, production. Keeping time with the swing music, the smiling girls on the assembly line are working more efficiently than ever.

"It's amazing!" marvels Andrews. "A simple thing like music, and we never even thought of it!"

"It's tremendous, Mr. Kettle!" Rodney's secretary tells him.

"Make a note," Rodney says to his secretary. "Loudspeakers in *every* department! It's *wonderful! Stupendous! Colossal!* Congratulations, P.A.! How did you *ever* hit on it?"[45]

Pa, now fully ensconced in his interim position as chairman of the board of Kettle Enterprises, dictates an important letter to two secretaries: "Dear Kids, Me, Ma, and Rosie are feelin' fine. Hoping you're behavin' yourself and you haven't wrecked the camp yet, I remain very truly yours, your father, Pa."

A bespectacled man with a goatee timidly enters the office. Removing his hat, he introduces himself as Professor Gilfallen of the Honolulu College of Agriculture, M.D., Ph.D., D.A., and P.F.

"With all them letters you outta know quite a lot," says Pa, impressed.

"May I speak to you in confidence?"

The secretaries leave the office without being asked.

"Mr. Kettle?"

"Pa's the name."

"Mr. Pa. How would you like to increase the quality of your product one-hundred-and-sixty-five percent?"

"We-e-l-l . . ."

---

45 The satisfying payoff to the sequence prefigures a pattern used regularly on the sitcom *Bewitched* (1964–1972), the one in which boss Larry Tate euphorically tells his hapless employee Darrin, "Stevens, you're a *genius!* How did you ever come up with that idea?"

"*Of course* you would! After three thousand seven hundred and fifty-six grueling experiments, I have struck upon a formula." The professor reaches into his jacket pocket and removes a vial. "Poured into the pressure pump, it brings out and locks in the juice a lost element which I have named XP-two-five-two."

"Ya' don't say," says Pa, lighting his pipe.

"You, being a man of vision and action, I have brought it to you."

"Well, that's right neighborly of ya'."

"I guarantee a quality and flavor of juice no firm on Earth can duplicate."

"Mm-mm. Looks like potato bug poison."

"Experiment today. If it does not fulfill every promise, I demand nothing. When it doubles your sales, a small percentage. My attorney will call on you this afternoon to talk terms. Good morning." And with that, he puts on his hat and leaves the office.

The secretaries return. One asks, "Would you like to continue with your dictation, Mr. Kettle?"

"Not now," Pa says with a sense of urgency, "I got business to attend to. Memo: Have the heads of all the departments meet me in the vat-pressing room in an hour. Get Ma on the phone."

"Yes, sir."

"Never mind, I'll get her myself." He picks up the receiver of one of the three phones on his desk and dials Ma at the hotel.

In the factory, Pa is climbing a ladder in front of a huge vat of finely crushed pineapple. From this bird's eye view, we can see a group of ten (including Ma and Rodney), looking up. Pa pours half of the vial's contents into the mixture.

"Pa sure must have somethin' good this time," says Ma, beaming with pride.

"I hope we'll have the success with this that we did with his music," Rodney says excitedly. To Pa, he says, "P.A., we're sure anxious to see if this experiment works."

"No use rushin', Rodney," Pa says laconically. "Spoils your digestion. Once I set my mind to a thing, I always get results." He then goes to the vat across the way, climbing up that ladder as well. Reaching the top rung, he pours the remainder of the vial into the mixture.

"If this does what you say it does, you'll save this factory from Coates and his crowd," says an even-more-sped-up-than-usual Rodney.

"Get down off that thing, Pa, 'fore ya' fall in!" cautions Ma.

"Now don't go to frettin', Ma," he says, climbing back down the ladder. "Everything's gonna be all right." He walks to the lever and says, "Here she goes!"

Immediately after Pa empties the vial containing formula XP-252 in the vats and flips a switch, a tremendous explosion rocks the factory and douses the onlookers, including Rodney (center, in a state of collapse) and Ma, with a storm of wet pineapple bits. Authors' collection.

An explosion rocks the plant. The onlookers scream in terror. Pineapple bits, millions of them, shoot from every vat. It is a wet, sticky, Hawaiian nightmare.

Ma and Pa, looking like two war refugees, walk slowly down a Honolulu street. Ma is a particular sight, with her hat askew and bits of pineapple stuck to it. To match her ragged appearance, she is in a foul mood.

"Just when I thought you was about to make somethin' of yourself, ya' go and do a fool thing like that."

They sit down together on a public bench.

"Just what do ya' think Rodney'll say when he comes to?" Pa asks.

"Fire ya'. What do ya' *think* he's gonna do? Give ya' a prize for blowin' up his factory?"

At that moment, a sedan occupied by three men, pulls up, stopping in front of Ma and Pa. "How do we get him away from her?" one of the men asks. "They could sit there for hours." The car drives off.

"Ya' know, Ma—" He stops himself when he notices something amiss. "Ya' got a piece of pineapple on your hat."

"Got it down my back, too. If I had some mayonnaise, ya' could serve me up as a fruit salad."

"Can't understand it explodin' like that," says Pa. "Man said it was foolproof."

"Maybe *it* was, but *you're* not. Why do ya' have to do what other people tell ya'? Why can't ya' be more like Rodney?"

"I wish I could. You'd have more use for me then."

"I like his get-up-and-go. He always *did* have gumption. That's something *you* never had."

"Maybe you should have married Rodney instead of me."

"*Mm.* Maybe I should've. Then I wouldn't be sittin' here in a foreign island wonderin' if I'm ever gonna see my kids again."

"Wish you hadn't said that, Ma."

"It's just that ya' make me so doggone mad." She stands up. "C'mon, let's go. Might as well go back to the hotel and pack."

"You go on ahead, Ma. I'm gonna sit here and think."

"About *what?*"

"I hadn't thought that up yet."

"In that case, you'll be here all night!" She begins to walk away, then stops and says, "Just don't sit there till you get cold."

Pa gets right down to thinking. We know his thoughts due to the employment of a voiceover: "Best thing to do is to fix it that Ma marries Rodney . . . But, if I did somethin' to make her proud of me, she wouldn't want to. That's the thing to do, I guess."

Just as Ma leaves, Eddie Nelson, one of the men involved in the attempted hostile takeover, walks up to Pa and asks if he has a match. Pa, deep in thought, fails to notice the man at first. Bringing himself back to the present, he says, "I must've been thinkin'."

"Well, that's a good thing to do," Nelson says affably. "Clears the cobwebs out of your hair."

"That's not cobwebs. That's pineapple."

The man sits down next to him. Pa, looking for someone in whom to confide, tells this total stranger that he has severely disappointed his wife and is thinking of a way to impress her. I've got just the thing right here, the man says. Acting as though he is about to share the world's greatest secret, he takes a map out of his jacket pocket. This, he tells the gullible Pa, is a treasure map for the Island of Kalula. Although *he* would be noticed going to the location himself, he explains, *Pa* would not. All he would have to do is dig up the treasure and they would split the proceeds, fifty-fifty. Pa ponders: Finding a buried treasure—*that* might just make Ma proud of him. Okay, he'll do it. At that moment, Nelson notices that Bob Baxter is approaching, with Rosie. He makes a hasty exit.

"Who was that you were talking to, Pa?" she asks.

"A good friend," he answers cryptically. "Gotta go." And he's off to find a shovel, a pick, and to hire a boat to take him to Kalula and the buried treasure. When renting a boat for ten dollars (five dollars each way), he finds himself joined by the other henchmen, none of whom are talkative enough for the garrulous Pa. Noticing their semi-concealed holsters, Pa asks if they plan to do any shooting on the island.

Reflexively, one of thugs begins to answer before stopping himself short, "Not unless it's absolutely necessar—"

Ma is in a panic: Pa *still* has not come home. And when he misses mealtime, it must be something *truly* serious. Rosie is with her mother in the suite, which resembles a laundromat due to the sheer number of freshly washed clothes hanging from makeshift clotheslines.

"I thought you were mad at Pa, Ma."

Rosie (left) and Ma (right) learn to their horror that Pa has been kidnapped.

"I *am*. But I can be mad at him and fret about him at the same time."

The phone rings. It is Bob. The shot of him at his end of the line has him holding a pay phone receiver in one hand, and his other arm wrapped around Eddie Nelson's neck. Nelson is putting up quite the struggle. Bob manages to tell Rosie that her pa has been kidnapped and taken to the island of Kalula. That is all he has time to say: Eddie has wrested himself loose and taken a powder.

"*Kidnapped?*" Ma says. "*I'll* find him!" Walking out in front of their luxury hotel, she says to the uniformed doorman, "Hey, General! How do I get to Kalamazoo?"

"*Kalamazoo*, madam?"

"Maybe I ain't pronouncin' it right. It's an island."

"Oh, *Kalula?*"

"*That's* it! How can I get a taxi?"

The doorman explains that the last taxi has just left. The only mode of transportation available is a rickshaw. The Japanese boy who pulls it is asleep. Ma wakes him up and, with the doorman

To reach her husband, Ma takes the only mode of transportation available to her: a rickshaw.

interpreting for her, manages to communicate where she needs to go. Ma gets in the contraption and the boy takes off at a dead run. "Faster! *Faster!*" Ma yells frantically.

Meanwhile, an oblivious Pa (right) is taken to a remote island by kidnappers, Ben Welden (left) and Myron Healey (center); Richard Reeves is at the wheel.

Taking a closer look at his new companions, Pa begins to see an opportunity to avoid some manual labor. He strongly implies that he might be on a quest for buried treasure. Maybe these three strong thugs would be willing to dig it up for him. There would be something in it for them—say, *ten percent* of the findings? The men balk at this futile activity, but the boat's driver (their superior) turns back from the wheel just long enough to say that if the man wants you to dig, you'll *dig*. The orders were to treat Pa as gently as possible. This is a hostile takeover, after all, not a murder plot.

The rickshaw puller is exhausted. Slowing down to a trot, he soldiers on. Ma, in the passenger seat, looks like she wants to say something, but dares not. The poor guy is doing his best.

Pa and the men are now on the island of Kalula. Having marked off where the treasure should be, he orders the men to start digging.

"And just what are *you* going to do?" one of them asks.

"Somebody's gotta be the boss, you know," says Pa, obviously having grown accustomed to being a C.E.O.

When the rickshaw driver (Leon Lontoc) runs out of gas, Ma takes over.

A great sight gag. The Japanese boy is in the rickshaw—and *Ma* is doing the pulling. And she is *really* making tracks. They finally reach the shore, where Ma joins two other paddlers on a long tail boat. Together, they power their way to the island. And Pa.

Pa (center) has no idea that his nice traveling companions are, in fact, ruthless individuals, intent on taking over his cousin's company.

After hours of digging, the three men are standing in a wide, deep hole. Pa, having enjoyed a snooze and a couple of bananas, wanders off through the dense vegetation. He comes upon a man, about his age, only of Hawaiian descent, stretched out on the ground, drinking fermented coconut milk through a long straw. They introduce themselves.

"I'm Pa Kettle."

"Hello, Pa. I'm Papa Lotus."

"Nice to make your acquaintance, Pa-Pa."

Papa shares his deliciously intoxicating brew with Pa, who is immediately affected by its high potency. "This is made from sugar cane, ain't it?" he asks. At that moment, a coconut falls from above, hitting him—*conk!*—on the head. "I always thought Lem Tellett's hard cider was powerful, but it never hit me like this," he says, his speech slightly slurred.

Papa Lotus, it seems, has much in common with his new friend. He, too, has a batch of kids, twelve in fact, each one bearing the name of a month: January, February, March, etc. He also has a dynamic wife, Mama Lotus. Mama, like Ma, is a wonderful cook, and she is pleased to have Pa as their honored guest to lunch. After an enjoyable feast, Mama sings a spirited song as her daughters form a line and dance the hula.

While Pa is seated on the ground, watching the floor show, the three kidnappers sneak up from behind and one of the men knocks him cold. They then drag him, unconscious, back to their camp.

A sound can be heard throughout the jungle, a sound so fierce, so shrill, that it could only be made by the banshees of Kalula. The Lotus kids seek protection from Mama, who looks terrified as well. The sound is coming closer. One can almost make out what is being said . . .

"PAAAAAAAAAAAA! PAAAAAAAAAA KETTLE!"

It's Ma, naturally, and she wants to know where her husband went off to. "He was here just a minute ago!" says a baffled Mama. When Ma explains that Pa is in trouble, the resourceful Mama summons her brood to "prepare for battle." They cheer and run for their weapons. In addition to stockpiling enough fruit to pummel the enemy into submission, there are pineapple-shaped hand grenades, which they learned how to make from the soldiers stationed there during the war.

Pa, meanwhile, is still out cold, and being held by the kidnappers. With the stealth of trained guerillas, Ma, Mama, and the Lotus kids make their way through the jungle, weapons in hand. (Papa Lotus, incidentally, decides to stay back; *someone* has to hold down the fort, he reasons.) Holding their position, but unable to see their adversaries, the kidnappers quickly run out of bullets. The resulting showdown sees much thrown fruit, and ends with a stunning explosion, not unlike the one in the pineapple factory.

Mama Lotus (Hilo Hattie, far left) and her resourceful offspring join forces with Ma (far right) to rescue Pa.

"They're runnin' like gophers in a salt sack!" announces a triumphant Ma.

Pa shows up, safe again. Bob, Rosie, and Rodney arrive just in time for Ma's reunion with him.

"Oh, *Pa!*" Rosie says. "I'm so *glad* nothing happened to you!"

"I wouldn't say *nothin'* happened to me," Pa says, wanting credit for his ordeal. To Ma, he says, "I thought you wanted to marry *Rodney.*"

"If I wanted Rodney, I'd be with *him,*" she answers sharply, "not fightin' the Battle of Bull Run for *you.*"

"Congratulations, P.A. You did it again!" Rodney says admiringly.

"What'd he do *now?*" asks an exasperated Ma.

"Fooled us all," he answers.

"Look, Rodney," says Pa. "If you're talkin' about those letters I wrote ya', I've been tryin' to explain—"

"I'm talking about the explosion," he clarifies. "It was a stroke of genius." Rodney goes on to say, "Our chemist analyzed the liquid you used, which homogenized the varied and combined juices into a sensational nectar!"

"Ya' don't say," comments Pa. (Yes, but what about the little man who convinced Pa to use the liquid in the first place? Did they cut him in for a "small percentage" of their sales? And how on earth could causing the factory to explode be considered a stroke of— oh, *who cares?* The movie's almost over.)

"Yes, the bank is showering us with credit. And with no worries, my doctors have given me a clean bill of health. And I'd like *you* to stay with us, P.A., as my partner."

"Well, that's mighty nice of ya', Rodney, but there's pressing business calling me to the mainland."

"That's right, Rodney," concurs Ma. "It sure is pretty here, but it's no place for Pa and me. He's got fifteen important things to take care of in Cape Flattery."

"Well, I'm sorry," Rodney says. "But as our farewell, we'll have a luau tonight that you'll remember forever!"

Ma and Pa say aloha to Waikiki with a luau held in their honor.

Ma and Pa, seated, lotus style, on the ground, are preparing to enjoy the tropical delicacies placed before them, including a batch of fresh poi.

"I always *knew* you'd make good, Pa," says the ever-supportive Ma.

"Have some poi, Ma," says Pa.

"Keep yer fingers outta the food!"

"That's Hawaiian tradition," he says. "*Try* some."

She does.

"Tasty, ain't it?"

"Best wallpaper paste I ever ate," she opines.[46]

A lovely young island girl walks up behind Pa. She gently places a lei of fresh flowers around his neck, and then, ever so gently, kisses him on the cheek.

Ma, looking like a worn and cranky Dorothy Lamour, says sarcastically, "*Another* Hawaiian custom?"

"Well, it sure is," Pa says. And with that, he removes the lei from around his neck and puts it lovingly around hers. He follows this with a sweet kiss, as the picture fades to black.

The Payoff

Ma and Pa Kettle at Waikiki marked the last entry of the Kettle series to star Percy Kilbride as Pa Kettle, and the final film of his career. Samuel Stoddard has this to say concerning one of the story's recurring themes: "Ma finally gets fed up with Pa's laziness and possibly regrets marrying him. It's utter nonsense, and not only because it's only paid lip service, but it is not used in any meaningful way. The whole charm of the series relies on how these two characters, crazy and quirky as they are, have a relationship as perfect as any could ever be. It's the whole reason the comedy works in the first place." Audiences of the time managed to overlook this defect, however; they just laughed and enjoyed the gags, particularly those involving exploding pineapples. And with the film's tie-in to the Schine movie theater chain, it helped to put an additional $1.5 million into the U-I coffers. According to *Variety Weekly* (January 25, 1956), it was one of the top box-office hits of 1955.

---

46 Real poi made the actors sick when they first tried it. The prop department soon replaced it with custard, which photographs in black-and-white the same as poi.

Chapter 10
The Kettles in the Ozarks (1956)

Released by Universal-International on March 14, 1956. 81 minutes. Directed by Charles Lamont. Produced by Richard Wilson. Story and Screenplay by Kay Lenard. Director of Photography: George Robinson, A.S.C. Film Editor: Edward Curtiss. Art Direction: Alexander Golitzen and Alfred Sweeney. Set Decorations: Russell A. Gausman and Ruby R. Levitt. Music Supervision: Joseph Gershenson. Second Unit Direction: Joseph E. Kenney. Make-Up: Bud Westmore. Hair Stylist: Joan St. Oegger. Sound: Leslie I. Carey and Robert Pritchard. Costume Design: Jay A. Morley Jr.

Cast: Marjorie Main (*Ma Kettle*); Arthur Hunnicutt (*Sedgewick Kettle*); Una Merkel (*Miss Bedelia Baines*); Ted de Corsia (*Professor*); Olive Sturgess (*Nancy Kettle*); Dave O'Brien (*Conductor*); Richard Eyer (*Billy Kettle*); Cheryl Callaway (*Susie Kettle*); Joe Sawyer (*Bancroft Baines*); Sid Tomack (*Benny*); Louis Da Pron (*Mountaineer*); Harry Hines (*Joe*); Jim Hayward (*Jack Dexter*); Elvia Allman (*Meek Man's Wife*); George Arglen (*Freddie*); Roscoe Ates (*Townsman*); Bobby Barber (*Barn Dance Guest*); John Breen (*Passenger*); Helen Brown (*Bit Role*); Bob Burns (*Barn Dance Guest*); Janet Comerford (*Miz Hawkins*); Richard Deacon (*Big Trout*); Robert Easton (*Lafe*); William Fawcett (*Old Man*); Bonnie Franklin (Betty); Slim Gaut (*Barn Dance Guest*); Helen Gereghty (*Barn Dance Guest*); Joe Gilbert (*Passenger*); Pat Goldin (*Small Fry*); Chuck Hamilton (*Barn Dance Guest*); Helene Heigh (*Woman with Cat*); Edna Holland (*Bit Role*); Stuart Holmes (*Bald Man*); Ann Kunde (*Barn Dance Guest*); Walter Lawrence (*Barn Dance Guest*); Peggy Leon (*Passenger*); Lu Leonard (*Heavy Woman*); Betty McDonough (*Bit Role*); Mira McKinney (*Bit Role*); William Meader (*Barn Dance Guest*); Patricia Morrow (*Sally*); Jack Mower (*Passenger*); Lillian O'Malley (*Barn Dance Guest*); Sarah Padden (*Miz Tinware*); Eddie Pagett (*Sammy*); George Pitman (*Passenger*); Mike Portanova (*Passenger*); Felice Richmond (*Passenger*); Walter Ridge (*Passenger*); Kathryn Sheldon (*Old Woman*); George Sowards (*Barn Dance Guest*); Ray Spiker (*Barn Dance Guest*); Leslie Turner (*Outraged Woman*); Harry Tyler (*Meek Man*); Joe Walls (*Barn Dance Guest*); Paul Wexler (*Reverend Martin*).

Marjorie Main stars in The Kettles in the Ozarks *(1956), following Percy Kilbride's departure from the series.*

In 1954, Marjorie Main's second seven-year contract with MGM expired. There would be no additional renewal. For the first time in fourteen years, she was a free agent. Universal presented her with an exclusive contract, a one-picture deal, for *The Kettles in the Ozarks*. Apparently, the studio felt there was still some life left in the series, and Marjorie Main was available. *Ozarks* would be the first, and only, attempt at a Ma and Pa Kettle film without a Pa Kettle. Percy Kilbride, a man true to his word, had retired and stayed that way. Marjorie, meanwhile, was not getting any younger. At sixty-five, she was beginning to show her age, but all she had ever known was work, so she continued to accept acting assign-

Marjorie Main simply did not have the same screen chemistry with Arthur Hunnicutt that she had achieved so effortlessly with Percy Kilbride.

ments. One look at this tired woman and the last thing you would imagine her having is a six-and-a-half-year-old child, but that is just one of the many blessings bestowed upon her by screenwriter Kay Lenard in this late entry. She also gains a brother-in-law, a man she has never met in her decades-long marriage.

The Supporting Cast
Arthur Hunnicutt as Sedgwick Kettle . . .

Arkansas-born Arthur Hunnicutt (1910–1979) was a tall, lean, bearded individual who made a career out of enacting humorously wise rustic types. His initial plan was to become a teacher, not an actor. Enrolled at the Arkansas State Teachers College, he was forced to drop out due to a lack of funds. It was then that he

Arthur Hunnicutt.

turned to acting, joining a theater company in Massachusetts. His next stop was New York, where he landed some roles on the Great White Way, including the lead in the original company of *Tobacco Road*, one of the longest-running shows (3,118 performances) in Broadway history. Another stage role of distinction was as Kit Carson in the 1940 production of *The Time of Your Life*, which was written and co-directed by William Saroyan. Hunnicutt's film career took off in the late forties, at which time he gained a reputation as a dependable supporting player. He was perfectly cast in the Howard Hawks western *The Big Sky* (1952), for which he was deservedly nominated for an Academy Award.

Una Merkel as Miss Bedelia Barnes ...

Una Merkel.

Una Merkel (1903–1986), born in Covington, Kentucky, bore a close resemblance to Lillian Gish, so much so that she began her movie career as a stand-in for that gifted silent screen actress in the MGM film *The Wind* (1928). After that, Una performed on Broadway before she returned to movies, working (somewhat ironically) for D.W. Griffith (Gish's beloved mentor) as Ann Rutledge in the visionary director's first all-sound film, *Abraham Lincoln* (1930). Perceptive casting directors saw a comic potential in the aspiring actress that was decidedly lacking in Miss Gish. Usually relegated to supporting roles, Una, with her broad Southern accent and her peroxide-blond hair, gave one of her best performances as a wisecracking but not-too-bright chorus girl in *42nd Street* (1933). A showy part in *Destry Rides Again* (1939), in which she and the fiery Marlene Dietrich engage in a tempestuous hair-pulling catfight, assured Una's screen immortality. For comedy fans, however, an even more memorable performance can be found in *The Bank Dick* (1940), in which she hilariously essays Myrtle Sousé, the melodramatic fiancée to the doltish Og Oggilby

(Grady Sutton), and the daughter of the town's leading tippler, Egbert Sousé (W. C. Fields). After a long hiatus, she made a successful comeback, now cast primarily as middle-aged wives and spinsters. In 1956—the same year she was seen onscreen in *The Kettles in the Ozarks*—Una Merkel won Broadway's Tony Award for her performance in Gail Gilchriest's play *The Ponder Heart*.

Olive Sturgess as Nancy Kettle ...

Olive Sturgess is a petite (five-two) Canadian beauty, born on October 8, 1933, in Ocean Falls, British Columbia. Sturgess is certainly decorative in the *Ozarks* picture, but the script does not give her character much to do. She found more satisfying work on television, appearing in guest roles on numerous episodes of such westerns as *Laramie* (1959–1963) and *Have Gun—Will Travel* (1957–1963). She also appeared regularly on *NBC Matinee Theater* (1955–1958), the most heavily promoted regularly scheduled

Olive Sturgess.

U.S. daytime program of its time; it drew close to seven million daily viewers. The guest stars (a veritable Who's Who of Hollywood) performed time-honored plays, the majority of which were broadcast in color. Sturgess's best-remembered theatrical film is Roger Corman's 1963 horror-comedy *The Raven*, starring Vincent Price, Boris Karloff, and Peter Lorre. After marrying studio musician Dale Anderson, she seemed to lose interest in acting. In fact, she refused a part on the television show *Flipper* (1964–1967) because she did not wish to leave her baby daughter in someone else's care. During the authors' telephone interview with this charming lady in 2020, she said that her most vivid memory of Marjorie Main is of the aging actress riding around Hollywood on a bicycle. She also recalls that when she first met her, Main refused to shake her hand, citing contagions. Once Main had put on gloves, however, Sturgess was granted the privilege of a handshake.

Robert Easton as Lafe ...

Robert Easton.

Robert Easton (1930–2011) first gained the public's attention as one of the scarily bright youngsters on the popular radio show *Quiz Kids* in the early forties. While a student at the University of Texas in the spring of 1949, he was initiated into Phi Eta Sigma, a national honorary scholastic fraternity for men. Throughout the forties, he appeared as various rustics on network radio series. He would go on to play his "hick" character in the Abbott and Costello vehicle *Comin' Round the Mountain* (1951) and on television sitcoms, including *The George Burns and Gracie Allen Show* and *The Beverly Hillbillies*. Much more significant than his early acting career was his later, vaunted reputation as the "Henry Higgins of Hollywood," a master of dialects who frequently coached other actors.

And Pat Goldin and Richard Deacon as Small Fry and Big Trout.

Sedge (Arthur Hunnicutt, center) and his Native American friends, Big Trout (Richard Deacon, left) and Little Fry (Pat Goldin, right), have evidently caught a skunk.

To continue using the characters of Geoduck and Crowbar, without being Geoduck and Crowbar, Sedge Kettle has the same dynamic as Pa with a pair of Indians, in this case Big Trout and Small Fry. Neither of the actors chosen to play these tertiary roles had even a trace of Native American in their lineage. In fact, Pat Goldin (1902–1971), who portrays Small Fry, was Russian born. If he is known to movie buffs at all, it is for his comical presence in a few of the Monogram-produced Jiggs and Maggie pictures in the late forties. Being a diminutive individual, he was also given the role of the alien invader in the 1951 sci-fi opus *The Man from Planet X.*

Richard Deacon.

Richard Deacon (1921–1984), the actor playing Big Trout, grew up in Binghamton, New York. He is well remembered by fans of classic television as the put-upon producer Mel Cooley on *The Dick Van Dyke Show* (1961–1966); he was also Fred Rutherford on *Leave It to Beaver* (1957–1963), and Roger Buell on the second season of *The Mothers-In-Law* (1967–1969). Deacon worked for a time as a contract player at U-I, having to accept pretty much any part he was assigned. Although he did not manage to convey any believability as a Native American, he was no more convincing as an Egyptian in *Abbott and Costello Meet the Mummy* (1955).

The Storyline

Pa's brother Sedge, a resident of the Ozark mountains of Missouri, is in a heap of trouble. His farm is about to be taken over by the bank. Hoping to receive financial aid from his "rich brother," he sends an S.O.S. to Cape Flattery, Washington. Learning that a Kettle is in need, Ma decides to personally travel to the troubled farm, taking along thirteen of her kids, the family dog, and a chicken in a covered bird cage. In a clever sight gag, Ma has a rope tied around her waist, a rope that extends to every one of her kids, to keep them in place. There is pure chaos at the depot, with the dog chasing a cat, all the while dragging Ma's double in circles. There is also bedlam on the train, with a messy bit involving the conductor being hit in the face with a raw egg.

It comes as a relief when Ma, her kids, and their various animals arrive in Mournful Hollow. They are met at the depot by one

The train conductor (Dave O'Brien, standing right) literally has egg on his face, a souvenir of his encounter with the Kettles' caged chicken. Ma (center), daughter Nancy (Olive Sturgess), and Danger, the family dog, offer little-to-no assistance.

Ma and the kids are greeted in Mournful Hollow by the kind-hearted Bedelia (Una Merkel, at the reins) and her lazy intended, Sedge (Arthur Hunnicutt).

of the strangest-looking vehicles ever to appear in a Kettle film: a motor-less old car being hauled by a speckled horse. Sedge is seated in the back, an umbrella shielding him from the noonday sun. Holding the reins in front is Bedelia, a sweet, middle-aged woman, who has been Sedge's "intended" for twenty long years.

Upon inspecting her brother-in-law's cluttered domicile, Ma (right) realizes she has her work cut out for her. Poor Bedelia (left) looks absolutely mortified.

Ma, it soon becomes clear, has her work cut out for her. The house's interior looks like a candidate for the A&E TV series *Hoarders*, and the outbuildings are no better. Ma is there to help Sedge make his property a paying farm again, and—after meeting the taken-for-granted Bedelia—to get him to once and for all make an honest woman out of her. And finally, she is determined to help repair Sedge's damaged reputation. It seems that twenty-five years earlier he had been employed as a wood cutter by a revenue officer, something for which the neighbors have never forgiven him.

Pa Kettle may not be in the film, but he is referred to often enough. The kids point out some obvious comparisons between Sedge and their father, including the way each of them says grace before a meal. Sedge, whose coonskin cap is as much a part of his head as Pa's derby is to his, always removes it respectfully when

Sedge Kettle (standing) bears a strong resemblance to one of his ancestors, a fact pointed out by his nieces and nephews.

giving thanks. Sedge is full of sayings, including one that will be familiar to anyone who has seen the earlier Kettle films. When something reveals itself to be broken (in this case, an exposed

Ma (second from left) attends a Saturday night social in Mournful Hollow. Nancy Kettle (far right) has evidently caught the eye of Lafe (Robert Easton), a local bumpkin.

spring on the parlor sofa), he says laconically, "Gotta fix that one of these days," one of Pa's trademark musings.

A more direct reference to Pa occurs at a Saturday night social. A longtime citizen tells Ma that she well remembers Egbert when he was just a boy. *Egbert?* That would have been an appropriate-sounding name for Pa, but he had already been christened Franklin, or simply Frank. This is but one example of the screenwriters not doing their homework. Pa is also represented by letters he has sent to Ma, which she reads to the kids. In one of these missives (allegedly dictated to Crowbar), he tells his wife of thirty years: "You might not be the prettiest woman in the world, but you make up for it by being a hard worker." This strikes the authors as something the *real* Pa would *never* write or say.

(Left to right) Bedelia, Ma, Benny (Sid Tomack), Joe (Harry Hines), Sedge, Professor (Ted de Corsia), and Jack Dexter (Jim Hayward).

Just prior to the arrival of Ma and the kids, Sedge signed a contract with a shady-looking gent named Jack Dexter, who wanted to purchase his crop of corn (regardless of whether it proves productive) and to rent his barn for six dollars a month. When Dexter says he will pay *seven* dollars, Sedge says drily, "Ya' must have money to burn." As to *why* this outsider wants to rent the ramshackle structure, it soon becomes clear that he and his sleazy colleagues are manufacturing bootleg corn whiskey. Ma finds out about this and confronts the bootleggers—at the point of a rifle, no less. But these fellows—who go by the names "Professor," Joe, and Benny—let her know that the reputation of the landowner and all who reside there is at stake if it gets around that stills are being operated at the Kettle farm. That would be looked on with much disfavor, both from those moralists who oppose making corn whiskey, and the unfair competition it would represent to those who *do* make it. And Sedge's reputation can hardly afford more black marks.

Corn whiskey is made from a mash of at least 80 percent corn and distilled to the maximum strength of 160 proof (80 percent alcohol by volume). Apparently, the process can be a messy one. The challenge of mashing corn is getting a complete gelatinization of the starches so they can be broken down into sugars. As this starts to occur, the entire mixture thickens to a porridge consistency, making it difficult to stir, yet stirring is necessary to keep it from burning the bottom of the mash pot. Disposing of the mash, particularly in areas forbidding the manufacture of moonshine, is an important step in avoiding detection. In the film, the bootleggers simply dump it on the ground, where the livestock consumes it. Indicative of puerile comedy tropes, the rooster, the goats, the pigs, the chickens—even the goose that walks around in men's galoshes—all become roaring drunk. In a later sequence, when the bootleggers attempt to do a better job burying the mash, the man using a pickaxe swings it backward, making direct contact with a hive full of angry hornets. All four bootleggers run screaming through the woods. By the time they return to the farm they are covered in unsightly bumps caused by bee stings.

Ma is determined to get rid of these unsavory individuals by any means necessary. An opportunity presents itself when one of the men takes a nostalgic interest in Ma's cooking saltwater taffy on the kitchen stove. More than anything, he wants to engage in an "old-fashioned" taffy pull with his cohorts. The men seem taken with this odd idea as well. A quick-thinking Ma pours an excessive amount of corn syrup into the pot, making the batch dangerously sticky. Sedge witnesses her adding too much of the syrup

Ma (center) has a late-night conference with Sedge (left) and Bedelia (right) to decide how best to deal with the bootleggers.

Ma ingeniously restrains bootleggers (left to right) Professor, Benny, and Joe by engaging them in an old-fashioned taffy pull.

and attempts to warn her. To keep him quiet, Ma has him sample the taffy from a wooden spoon. The result is quite effective: Sedge cannot open his mouth. When Professor, Benny, and Joe engage in the fine art of taffy pulling, they find themselves hopelessly stuck together. Thus encumbered, they are locked in a shed until Ma can think of what to do with them next.

In the meantime, she has informed Sedge (falsely) that Bedelia is officially fed up with being an unpaid farmhand. An ultimatum is issued: either Sedge agrees to get hitched or Bedelia "ain't comin' round no more."

"Well, if that's the way ya' feel about it, would ya' *like* to get married?" he asks her.

"Oh, *Sedge!*" she says dreamily and without the slightest trace of irony. "This is all so *sudden!*"

After a two-decade-long engagement, Sedge and Bedelia finally tie the knot, with Ma acting as surrogate for Reverend Martin (Paul Wexler). The Kettle kids (left) and Big Trout and Little Fry (far right) serve as witnesses.

The preacher is summoned. Sedge, now with a bad case of cold feet, has an idea of how to postpone the proceedings. He offers him a piece of saltwater taffy. Chewing it, the minister soon realizes his teeth are sealed together. How is he going to conduct the wedding ceremony if he cannot talk? Quick-thinking Ma comes through again when she suggests that the preacher hold the Bible while she lays her hand on his shoulder, thereby serving as his proxy. With Sedge unable to say, "I do," or anything else for that matter, Ma acts as *his* proxy as well. Bedelia and Sedge are pronounced man and wife.

When Ma reads the line asking Bedelia if she takes this man in holy matrimony, she answers sweetly, "I'm *glad* to."

"I now pronounce you man and wife. You may kiss the bride."

Sedge does so, shyly.

"He's *all* mine!" exclaims Bedelia.

Sedge, who has finally managed to pry his teeth apart, says, "Shucks, taint nothin'."

Ma has a great line, which she delivers perfectly: "Let her find that out for *herself*."

While these festivities take place, the three taffy-bound prisoners come undone, remove some loose-fitting boards from a window, and climb out, hopefully to freedom. Instead, by the time the third man sets foot on the ground, the rotted boards beneath them collapse, sending them to the bottom of a deep well with a mighty *splash*. They struggle to climb out, and finally resort to standing on one another's shoulders, creating a human ladder. When the first of the bootleggers rises from the well, he grabs hold of a rope dangling within reaching distance. This rope, when tugged, releases a torrent from the water tower to which it is attached.

Ma, standing at the window the bootleggers had climbed through, turns to the newlyweds and says, "Well, Bedelia, you've had the wedding and now ya' got Niagara Falls!"

The Payoff

The finished film was previewed at the Panorama Theater in Los Angeles on August 3, 1955. The comment cards collected from the audience revolve around one basic question: *Where is Percy Kilbride?*

- "The many references to Pa Kettle are ridiculous. I waited throughout for him to come into the picture. Why build up a character without using him?"
- "One of the best Kettle pictures, but too bad Pa couldn't be in it."
- "I liked the first Ma and Pa Kettle pictures, but this one I had to walk out on before it was over."

In a newspaper interview she gave just a month prior to the wide release of *Ozarks* in 1956, Marjorie was still sounding optimistic about the Kettles. "There is something immensely satisfying about working in a series like this," she said. "That's especially true when you play a character like Ma Kettle, who's both likable and amusing. After all, the main function of an actress is to give pleasure to the people. I've been an actress a long time and I've played many a fine part, but even *I* was surprised by the warmth and evident affection with which I was greeted wherever I went after I started playing Ma Kettle. Aside from this warm regard from the public, another reason I've enjoyed so much working in this series is the comfortable feeling I get from working with pretty much the same people all the time. I suppose that sort of thing depends on what type of person you are. Some actresses may enjoy working with new people all the time. As for me, I have a kind of family feeling about these Kettle pictures and I'd love to have them around for as long as I continue to work."

Marjorie was receptive to the idea of making more films with Arthur Hunnicutt if the new combination caught on. It did not. The disappointing box-office returns saw to that. The film grossed $1.3 million, less than half the take of Kettle films at their 1952 peak (*At the Fair* grossed $2.5 million in U.S. and Canadian rentals alone).

Chapter 11
The Kettles on Old MacDonald's Farm (1957)

Released by Universal-International, May 10, 1957. 80 minutes. Directed by Virgil W. Vogel. Produced by Howard Christie. Screenplay by William Raynor and Herbert H. Margolis. Director of Photography: Arthur E. Arling. Film Editor: Edward Curtiss. Art Direction: Philip Barber and Alexander Golitzen. Second Unit Director: Marshall Green. Music Director: Joseph Gershenson. Set Decorations: Russell A. Gausman and Ruby R. Levitt. Make-Up: Bud Westmore. Sound: Leslie I. Carey and Perry Devore. Special Photography: Clifford Stine. Costume Design: Marilyn Sotto.

Cast: Marjorie Main (*Ma Kettle*); Parker Fennelly (*Pa Kettle*); Gloria Talbott (*Sally Flemming*); John Smith (*Brad Johnson*); George Dunn (*George*); Claude Akins (*Pete Logan*); Roy Barcroft (*J. P. Fleming*); Patricia Morrow (*Bertha*); George Arglen (*Henry Kettle*); Fred Aldrich (*Logger*); Emile Avery (*Logger*); Donald Baker (*Abner*); George Barrows (*Hunter*); Margaret Bert (*Bit Role*); Wag Blesing (*Shaver*); Polly Burson (*Agnes Logan*); Noble "Kid" Chissell; Don Clark (*Shivaree Man*); Roger Creed (*Townsman*); George DeNormand (*Hunter*); Harvey B. Dunn (*Judge*); Clem Fuller (*Townsman*); Helen Gereghty (*Townswoman*); Frank Hagney (*Townsman*); Ethyl May Halls (*Bit Role*); Chuck Hamilton (*Race Starter*); Jean Harvey (*Bit Role*); George Hickman (*Pie Judge*); Hallene Hill (*Granny*); Rickey Kelman (*Elmer*); Tom Kennedy (*Contest Spectator*); Verna Kornman (*Shivaree Woman*); Paul Kruger (*Contest Spectator*); Ann Kunde (*Townswoman*); Russell Meeker (*Contest Spectator*); Frank Mills (*Contest Spectator*); Boyd "Red" Morgan (*Shivaree Man*); Eva Novak (*Woman*); William H. O'Brien (*Hunter*); Carl Saxe (*Hunter*); Edna Smith (*Shivaree Woman*); Cap Somers (*Logger*); George Sowards (*Shaver*); Sara Taft (*Clarabelle*); Glenn Thompson (*Shivaree Man*); Sailor Vincent (*Contest Spectator*); Glen Walters (*Townswoman*); Henry Wills (*Townsman*); Isabel Withers (*Bit Role*).

Virgil William Vogel (1919–1996) began his career at Universal in 1940 as an assistant editor. He worked in that capacity until the mid-fifties, by which time he had tired of the job and pressed U-I executive Edward Muhl for a shot at directing. Vogel was handed the script for *The Mole People* (1956) and told to shoot it. About his directorial debut, Vogel told interviewer Tom Weaver: "I thought the script was pretty good. You've got to remember that I was a young man then, and I didn't know too much what I was doing!" Inexperienced or not, his capable handling of that film led to other assignments at the studio, including the very last of the Ma and Pa Kettle pictures. *The Kettles on Old MacDonald's Farm* is no classic, but it *is* a slight improvement on the previous entry. It was also Marjorie Main's last film (her eighty-fifth), and it seems fitting that she should close out her illustrious career with her most unforgettable character.

The Supporting Cast

Parker Fennelly as Pa Kettle . . .

Parker Fennelly introduces himself to millions of Kettle fans in this publicity shot for The Kettles on Old MacDonald's Farm *(1957).*

To many fans of the series, there can only be one Pa Kettle—Percy Kilbride. But Parker Fennelly (1891–1988), a comic actor with his own unique style, did his best to fill Pa's scuffed-up shoes. Although not a household name, he certainly had a household voice. If your television was on anytime between 1956 and 1977, chances are good that you heard his distinctive New England accent as he uttered the familiar slogan: "Pepperidge Farm remembers." Claiming to have been "born old," Fennelly was playing elderly men even as a young actor. He received classical training in Boston and was tutored by the performing arts educator Leland T. Cowers. An apt pupil, Parker was soon on tour with the Boston Toy Theatre company and the Maud Scheerer Shakespeare Players. In 1919, he and his wife, Catherine, formed the Parker Fennelly Duo, presenting short plays, readings, and impersonations. Beginning in the 1920s, he made his mark on Broadway in *Florida Girl* (1925). This was followed by *Babbling Brookes* (1927), *Black Velvet* (1927), *The Country Chairman* (1936), *Yours, A. Lincoln* (1942), *Our Town* (1944), *Happily Ever After* (1945), *Live Life Again* (1945), *Loco* (1946), and *The Southwest Corner* (1955). He occasionally branched out, writing and directing his own stage vehicles.

Parker Fennelly achieved national fame by playing the fictional Titus Moody, a crusty New Englander, one of the mainstay

(Left to right) Fred Allen, Kenny Delmar, Minerva Pious, Peter Donald, and Parker Fennelly, the cast members of NBC radio's The Fred Allen Show.

characters created by satirist Fred Allen for his weekly radio show feature, "Allen's Alley." Fred would go from door to door in this imaginary neighborhood, visiting such comically ethnic characters as the Yiddish Mrs. Nussbaum (Minerva Pious), Senator

Beauregard "It's a Joke, Son" Claghorn (Kenny Delmar), and Irishman Ajax Cassidy (Peter Donald). When Allen called on Moody, the old codger would greet his inquisitive visitor with a taciturn demeanor and a two-word salutation, "Howdy, bub." Movie roles came along less frequently, but when they did, they tended to be noticed. Alfred Hitchcock capitalized on Fennelly's droll delivery by casting him as a millionaire in the comedy-mystery *The Trouble with*

Parker Fennelly in character as Pa Kettle.

Harry (1955), starring Shirley MacLaine in her film debut. When it was announced that Fennelly was replacing Percy Kilbride as Pa Kettle, the casting seemed ideal. Never attempting to imitate Kilbride, Fennelly brought his own twist to the character. But a weak script (by William Raynor and Herbert Margolis), and a lack of chemistry between Parker Fennelly and Marjorie Main, sank *Old MacDonald's Farm* before moviegoers had the chance to say E-I-E-I-O.

George Dunn as George...

George Dunn.

Hailing from Brownwood, Texas, George Dunn (1914–1981) appeared in vaudeville doing what is now referred to as a "tribute" act. In his case, he was emulating the great American humorist Will Rogers. He even went so far as to spin a rope while uttering homespun philosophies and satirical remarks. As an actor, Dunn, with his pronounced Texas twang, appeared primarily in westerns, including *The Adventures of Jim Bowie* (1956) and *Cimarron City* (1958). Throughout *Old MacDonald's Farm*, the character of George fills the secondary position formerly occupied by Geoduck and Crowbar. George is a garbage man, one very much dedicated to his chosen profession ("Show me a man without garbage and I'll show you a man that hasn't eaten," he says as though expressing a profundity). Dunn was, in fact, reprising the role, having played a variation of it in 1956's *Away All Boats*.

John Smith as Brad Johnson...

The story of John Smith (1931–1995) is an unusual one, even if his name is not. Once upon a time in Hollywood—the 1950s,

John Smith.

to be exact—there was an agent named Henry Willson, who discovered three good-looking, well-built, young men named Arthur Kelm, Robert Ozell Moseley, and Roy Scherer, and changed their names to Tab Hunter, Guy Madison, and Rock Hudson, respectively. As a joke of sorts, he changed his latest find's moniker from Robert Van Orden to John Smith, easily the western world's most common male name. With a name like that, he said, the actor would be "the only one in the business." It turns out he was right. Of Dutch, German, and Irish ancestry, Orden (now Smith) was born in Los Angeles on March 6, 1931. As a youth, he developed a deep, smooth voice as a member of the Robert Mitchell Boy Choir, a singing group that appeared in two Bing Crosby films, *Going My Way* (1944) and *The Bells of St. Mary's* (1945). After graduating from high school, he got a job in the mailroom at MGM, where he was soon promoted to supervisor. Mentored by popular cowboy star George Montgomery, Smith landed a role in *The High and the Mighty* (1954), starring John Wayne, who signed the young actor to his company, Batjac Productions. The following year, Smith was cast in the comedy *We're No Angels* (1955) as Arnaud, a doctor stationed aboard a ship. Aldo Ray, observing the tall, blond-haired Smith in full dress whites, says in his characteristically raspy voice, "He looks like a glass of milk."

Gloria Talbott as Sally Flemming...

Like her sister, model and actress Lori Talbott, Gloria Talbott (1931–2000) was born in the Los Angeles suburb of Glendale, a city co-founded by their grandfather. Gloria would die there as well when she was in her mid-eighties. But in 1957 the world was still full of promise and the former Miss Glendale of 1947 was at the

Gloria Talbott.

peak of her minor career. Growing up near the major studios, she landed small parts in such films as *Maytime* (1937), *Sweet and Lowdown* (1943), and *A Tree Grows in Brooklyn* (1945). After a three-year hiatus (during which she married, gave birth, and divorced; she ultimately married four times), Talbott resumed her career, working extensively in both TV and films. Her best-remembered B-thrillers, *Daughter of Doctor Jekyll* (1958), with John Agar, and *I Married a Monster from Outer Space* (1958), co-starring future novelist Thomas Tryon, have gained cult status in recent years.

Claude Akins as Jim Flemming...

Claude Akins.

Claude Akins (1926–1994) never seemed short of work, appearing in nearly 100 films and 180+ TV episodes in a career spanning more than forty years. A solidly built actor with wavy black hair and a booming voice, Akins finally became a household name, due to his portrayal of the titular role in the redneck television series *The Misadventures of Sheriff Lobo* (1979–1981).

And Three Toes as Himself.

Producer Howard Christie believed correctly that the script needed another element to infuse the proceedings with some zest. This was partially accomplished with the addition of a grizzly bear with an unusual name, one that dates to the early 20th century, when an oversized grizzly known as Ol' Ephraim roamed the

Cache National Forest in Idaho. Due to a deformity on one foot, Ol' Ephraim was also known as "Three Toes." Three Toes is the catalyst to the film's climactic chase sequence and provides the comic wrap-up.

Three Toes.

The Storyline

We join the Kettles on moving day. Apparently, they had sold their ultra-modern house (the sets for which had been struck several years earlier) and purchased a presentable two-story farmhouse. This house, according to a sign on the kitchen wall, was once "MacDonald Manor," Betty and Bob's home for the first year of their roller-coaster marriage. Ma replaces this sign with a new one, reading "The Kettles." She seems pleased with her new home. Her reverie is rudely interrupted, however, by the sound of the family's horse-drawn wagon hitting the front porch overhang. Pa, it seems, wanted to get the wagon, containing all the kids and the family's worldly goods, as close to the house as possible.

Ma prepares dinner for her family. There is no need to push chickens off the table; this place is as well cared for as their most recent home. In fact, when she gives out with her customary "COME AND GET IT!" the kids come walking, not running, in. *What is this?* Ma wants to know. Henry reminds his mother that she had lectured them on behaving in this house; they are only trying to follow

Ma (center) does a double take when she sees her usually ravenous brood amble unenthusiastically toward the dinner table. Pa (Parker Fennelly, seated at the head of the table) and George (George Dunn, far right) seem equally baffled.

Brad (John Smith) and Sally (Gloria Talbott) are rudely interrupted on their way to the bedroom.

orders. Ma, however, takes this lack of enthusiasm as a slight. "If that's all you think of my cookin', you'd best get outta here." The kids go outside, preparing for take two. Ma yells "COME AND GET IT—*Kettle style!*" With much attendant yelling, the kids come running, in fast motion no less. Now that's more like it! she says.

Brad Johnson, a poor but stupid lumber mill employee, is crazy in love with Sally Flemming, the boss's rather prissy daughter. Sally drives up to the lumber store in her brand-new Cadillac. She and Brad kiss, and their attraction for each other is palpable. As was typical for films made during that time, their relationship had yet to be consummated. But it is apparent that these two healthy young'uns want nothing more than a good, old-fashioned roll in the hay. Brad and Sally, who have every intention of marrying soon, are wandering around the old Kettle farm, which—except for some goats, geese, and chickens—is currently unoccupied and up for sale. Playing house, as it were, Brad carries Betty over the threshold successfully enough. It's when he steps into the parlor (with Sally still in his muscular arms) that they both fall through some rotted floorboards.

Brad and Sally's romantic relationship bring back special memories for Ma and Pa Kettle.

"Maybe we'd better wait till we're married," Brad says unconvincingly.

The entire Kettle family shows up to, in Ma's words, "gather up the livestock" for the new farm. Seeing two vehicles parked in front of the house, Ma, Pa, and George check it out, holding makeshift weapons. Brad, knowing how their presence could be interpreted, attempts to hide Sally, to no avail. Ma, who remembers the young lady when she was just a girl, asks with deep suspicion, "What're ya' doin' here, Sally? With *him*?"

"It's not what you think, Ma."

"How d'you know what *I'm* thinkin'? Unless we're *both* thinkin' what we *shouldn't* be thinkin'!"

Sally, in an impetuous moment, decides a lie is in order: "We're married!"

Ma is overjoyed. "Land sakes! Why didn't ya' say so in the first place?"

Pa sees the possibility of a business transaction. "So, *that's* why yer lookin' over the place! Why, there isn't a better farm on the whole peninsula." He then goes on to extoll the house's imaginary benefits.

When Sally stalls by saying that this might not be the house for them, Pa generously tells them to stay, rent free, for as long as it takes to make up their minds. Ma is all for this idea. She offers to help clean up the place, after which Pa and George can bring in the old bed from the barn. Just then, a horde of Kettle kids run by them.

"It's a mighty good bed," Pa adds.

Once the family departs, the virtuous Sally says that she will spend the nights in the house alone, while Brad bunks down at the lumber mill.

Ma poses demurely in the faded, rose-covered nightgown Pa purchased for her from a mail-order catalogue when they were first married, thirty years earlier.

We cut to a later scene of Ma and Pa in their new bedroom, settling in for the evening. Pa, as usual, is wearing his long, white nightshirt and derby (he claims it keeps his head warm while he sleeps), and Ma is seated at a vanity table, brushing out her long hair, which clearly has never been cut. She is in an especially sentimental mood, looking back to the time when she and Pa were first married, some thirty years earlier. In honor of the occasion, she is wearing a long, floral nightgown, one that Pa had ordered for her, all by himself, from a mail-order catalogue. "The flowers are a little faded," she says, her voice soft, "but the memories are good. Pa, you always was quite the romantic . . . *Pa?*" And like in every TV sitcom made during the next twenty years, the so-called "romantic" is fast asleep.

Sally's father, Jim Flemming (Claude Akins, right), awakens Ma and Pa in the middle of the night only to learn that his daughter has married without his consent.

The peaceful scene does not last. There is a loud, urgent banging on the front door. "*Ma! Pa! Open up!*" It's Jim Flemming, owner of the lumber yard and Sally's father. Jim demands to know where his daughter is.

Ma castigates him, asking if the poor girl doesn't deserve some privacy on her honeymoon.

"*Honeymoon!* Oh, *no!*"

The lovebirds are still together in the old Kettle house, experiencing some low-comedy moments, including a chicken falling on them through a hole in the ceiling. While attempting to open the bedroom door over its warped floor, Brad pushes too hard, sealing the door shut and sending the pair backward into Ma and Pa's old marriage bed. It collapses on impact.

The morality police—Jim Flemming, Ma, and Pa—force the door open, revealing the fully clothed Brad and Sally lying together within the broken frame.

"I sure thought that bed would hold out longer than that," Pa says with his precise, deadpan delivery.

Picking themselves up and convening with the others in the parlor, Sally admits that she had lied about their being married. She did not believe that her father would approve of her marrying one of his employees, a young fellow of limited means. Mr. Flemming surprises her by saying that he has no objections whatsoever to Brad as a future son-in-law. In fact, he doesn't think *Sally* is good enough for *him*! Jim knows he has spoiled and coddled his only daughter all her life, and by doing so, she is in no way suited to the life of a farmer. Why, she would be crying for a divorce within six months!

Sally, naturally, takes offense at this ungenerous (but likely accurate) assessment of her character. She is determined to prove her father (and Ma) wrong by excelling as a farmer's "wife" during a six-month trial period. As for sleeping arrangements, Pa will stay at the new place with George, Ma will stay with Sally at the old place, and Brad will continue to sleep at the lumber yard. Too busy to do the job himself, Jim Flemming offers to pay Ma and Pa to assist, as well as chaperone, the young couple. They accept the offer, with plans to use the money as the first mortgage payment on their new home.

The alarm clock goes off at four thirty in the morning. Like Bob MacDonald had said to Betty in *The Egg and I*, Ma tells Sally that since this is her first day, she let her sleep in an extra half hour. Now, it's time to rise and shine. The following series of vignettes, also borrowed from *The Egg and I*, play out with tiresome predictability. Sally dresses for her first day of hard labor in a stylish little ensemble that hardly suits the occasion. ("Livestock ain't used to fashion models," Ma says.) She demonstrates complete incompetence in the kitchen, loading the stove with wood too green to burn. No problem, she insists, pouring a bit of kerosene on it. The resulting smoke causes Brad and George to rush inside, believing the house is on fire. By the time Sally gets breakfast on the table, it is burned beyond recognition. ("If she keeps dishin' up meals like *this*," Pa says sagely, "she'll be a widow before she's a bride.") By the time she has scrubbed the kitchen floor, her once-fresh blouse is stained and torn. The *coup de grace* comes when she attempts to hang the wash on the horizontal stove pipe. It breaks in two, sending black soot everywhere as she breaks down in tears. Ma is sweet with her, lending her a hand in getting things back as they were. After that, she suggests that a cold shower will revive them in time to make dinner for the men folk.

Pa (left), always polite, tips his hat to Three Toes (right).

Ma believes the clumsy occupant in the adjoining shower stall is Sally when it's actually Three Toes, a big, black grizzly bear native to the area. Just prior to this is the scene when Sally, in a state of undress, is attempting to change in the bedroom. Hearing someone rattling around in the kitchen, she assumes it is Brad. "Are you hungry, darling?" she calls out. A growl emanates through the closed, locked door. "I'll be right out, dear! *Please* don't do any dishes; just relax for now!" When Ma informs Sally that she was addressing a bear, not her fiancé, what else would she do but faint? A bounty of five hundred dollars is issued for the capture or killing of this supposedly vicious animal.

The following day brings another early-morning wake-up call from Ma. But Sally can hardly move. Her neck is achingly stiff, and she cannot raise her right arm. Ma tells the girl to lie on her stomach.

"What are you going to do to me?" she asks suspiciously.

"I'm gonna rub out your aches—and *pound* some sense into ya'!"

Ma then proceeds to pummel this young woman, bending her like a pretzel as the sound-effects man provides the illusion of cracking bones. She concludes this painful exercise with a loud slap on the girl's bottom.

At first angry at being accosted in so violent a manner, Sally soon realizes that her aches and pains have deserted her. She shyly thanks her benevolent but rough mentor, giving her an appreciative hug. This is followed by the just-as-predictable series of vignettes as the ones in which she makes a mess of things: the requisite montage of advancement. With Ma's tutoring (and torturing),

Team Flemming—(left to right) Pa, Ma, Brad, Sally, and George—reap their rewards at the county fair.

Sally has become a fine cook, turning out six-course breakfasts for her hungry, hardworking fiancé.

When Brad learns he is about to lose his timber lease (a document he needs to start his own lumber business), Sally is determined to employ her newfound culinary gifts to help raise the needed funds, an amount given as five hundred dollars. Her plan works. She wins a fifth of that sum by entering her apple pie in a contest planned for the annual fair. Other contests won by Team Flemming—which is made up of Ma, Pa, Brad, Sally, and George—involve shaving someone with an axe; in this case, Ma shaves Pa's face clean in nineteen seconds, flat. Brad wins a tree-climbing contest (with the help of some grainy stock footage of an

Victims of shivaree, Brad and Sally make the most of their twilight captivity on the lake.

actual tree-scaling exhibition). And Pa takes first place in the log-rolling competition, which is only made possible by having Three Toes breathing down his neck. So terrified is he of being mauled that he beats all the other, younger men in the contest—without even realizing he's a participant! When all is said and done, Team Flemming meets its financial goal.

With each citizen hoping to win the bounty on Three Toes, a group of yahoos sets out into the forest, shotguns in hand. Meanwhile, George lets out the (inaccurate) news that Brad and Sally are married and living up at the old Kettle place. They must have gotten hitched without telling anyone about it, the townspeople conclude.

Engaging in a rustic tradition known as shivaree, a large group of hayseeds invade the alleged newlyweds' home, making as much of a ruckus as possible, and corner the frightened couple. The women line up as they aggressively pass Brad from one to the next, each lady planting a wet one on his handsome face. On the other side of the room, the men are doing the same thing to poor Sally. From there, they whisk the youngsters into the night, where they're handcuffed and set out on a vehicle marked "Honeymoon Express" to spend the remainder of the night on Salmon Lake. Chaperones Ma and Pa have been locked together in the barn, where Ma uses an elaborate pulley system to get them out through a high window and into Sally's hi-tech car, parked just outside. Arriving at Salmon Lake a short time later, Ma and Pa stay in the car, from which they can keep an eye on the stranded, but starry-eyed, lovers. The older couple even does a bit of spooning themselves.

To follow through on the ruse, Ma tells Brad that he cannot very well continue bunking down at the lumber yard—what would people *say*? So, she sets him up as cozily as possible in their old barn, while Ma and Sally continue sharing the indoor bed.

Word arrives that Jim Flemming is ready to give his blessing for his daughter to marry Brad. A huge shipment of wedding gifts from the Flemmings' many wealthy friends arrives at the old farm.

And what a haul it is: a dishwasher, a clothes-washing machine and dryer, a garbage disposal (*"Garbage disposal?!"* says a panicked George), and everything else a busy housewife could want or need. Sally, not surprisingly, is delighted. Once they get the old place wired for electricity, she says, she can begin using these time-saving appliances.

Not so fast, says Brad. "Who *says* we're going to keep all these things? And what will people say when they find out that *I* didn't pay for them?"

Sally objects, calling Brad unfair. Brad, in turn, refers to Sally as "spoiled" and "self-centered."

Well, that's it, says the fair-weather Sally. The wedding is off!

The ladies of the town make a pilgrimage to the Kettle farm to see Sally's much-touted appliances. She generously says that if any of them would like to use these modern luxuries before they are returned to the dealer, they are welcome to do so. Anticipating this, the women had brought along sacks of unwashed laundry. While this assembly line of worker bees experiences the joys of laundering clothes without having to resort to the antiquated washboard, they begin to gossip among themselves. Someone gets the idea that Sally is expecting, and the word begins to spread like chicken pox. One hearing-impaired older lady misinterprets the rumor, and begins to spread the word that *Ma Kettle*, not Sally, is the one in the family way—and this time, she might be expecting twins, or even triplets! The news gets out to the townsmen, who slip Pa a cigar and give him the "you old dog" treatment. Pa, of course, believes this implausible rumor right away. He decides, then and there, to come out of retirement and get to work. In his zeal to prove himself a good provider, he hops aboard Jim Flemming's massive steam shovel and begins making his way through the woods. Not seeing where he is going, Pa somehow manages to back the vehicle toward the edge of a cliff. He steps out of the driver's chair and begins to walk away. It is then that the steam shovel rolls off the precipice and into the deepest part of the river.

Ma (right) berates Pa (center) for causing Jim Flemming's steam shovel to fall from a cliff into the deepest part of the lake. George (left) looks on sympathetically.

Back at the new house, Ma gives Pa holy hell. That steam shovel was worth thousands and thousands of dollars—what was he *thinking?* The truth is, he wasn't thinking—he was merely reacting. Ma is at her breaking point. It's time for Pa to leave. "*Git!*" she says unfeelingly. Pa, a look of horror on his aged face, takes George by the arm and hurries from the house. In a heartbreaking close-up, Ma cries bitter tears.

With the bounty on the bear's hide doubled, Ma and her son Henry take to the woods. Only *they* have a secret weapon: a large cylinder with retractable gates on either side. Ma then sprinkles honey-flavored preserves leading up to the oddly shaped trap. In another part of the woods, Pa and George are working on their own trap: a deep pit dug in the ground, with bits of garbage leading up to it. In a fast-paced action sequence, Pa and Three Toes are cornered in Ma's makeshift invention. When Ma realizes they are both in there, she quickly raises the gate, and both flee. While chasing after Pa, Three Toes (now wearing Pa's derby) falls into George's

Ma rescues Pa from the humane bear trap she and her son had concocted to capture Three Toes.

pit—*with George!* Looking down into the pit, one imagines a terrible fate for the kindly garbage man. What they see instead is even more shocking: Three Toes is cuddling with him. "I think he *loves* me!" George says delightedly. And just like that, he has a new assistant in the sanitation department.

In the wrap-up scene, the newly married Mr. and Mrs. Brad Johnson flee from the old Kettle place in a hail of rice, thrown by well-wishers. The Kettles stand by, with Pa saying that he supposes their chaperoning days are over. "Oh, I don't know about *that*," says Ma. "From now on we're gonna be busy chaperonin' each other!" To put an even finer point on it, she handcuffs their wrists together. And on this "Fifty Shades of Kettle" moment, the film, and the series, sputters out for good.

The Payoff

The box-office take of $1 million was the lowest yet for a Kettle film but still enough for *Old MacDonald's Farm* to make *Variety's* January 8, 1958 list of top box-office hits of 1957. The lukewarm reviews are perhaps best exemplified by this brief mention in the *Buffalo* (NY) *Evening News*, in which the resident critic (billed only as A. S.) states that the film "is dedicated, like most of its predecessors, to the charm of ducks, goats, and pigs in the living room. There is a new Pa Kettle, Parker Fennelly. And Ma, still Marjorie Main, has fun with a bear. Otherwise, the Kettle world is much the same."

Image courtesy of James Bell, Ma and Pa snacks.

PART 3:
THE LEGACY

Chapter 12
Losing Marjorie and Percy

With her movie career now behind her, Marjorie Main went the way of so many of her colleagues: television. She appeared on two episodes of the popular prime-time western *Wagon Train*, "The Cassie Turner Story" (June 4, 1958) and "The Sacramento Story" (June 25, 1958). But the fast pace of television production did not appeal to Marjorie in the least. She opted instead to retire at the age of sixty-six, the same age as Percy Kilbride when he decided to hang up his Al Smith derby for good. She had this parting advice for aspiring actresses: "Be a comedienne. Dramatic actresses are a dime a dozen. Everybody's trying to be Bette Davis or an Ann Blyth. What this country needs is more lady comics . . . Comediennes are as scarce as multi-millionaire boyfriends. If you want to hit the show business jackpot, learn to make 'em laugh instead of trying to make 'em cry."

Marjorie was proud of the impact the Kettle films had made, not just on the United States, but everywhere. "The Kettles are playing all over the world now," she told interviewer Jean McMurphy in 1958. "When I was in Europe a few years ago, I saw my picture on a billboard outside a theater across from my hotel in Venice. I went in to see the show. There I was all right. But Ma was speaking faultless Italian! She was perfectly charming, quite watered down."

Marjorie's ability to make audiences laugh diminished perceptibly after Percy Kilbride retired. An intelligent, solitary man, he spent his final years in a modest apartment in Hollywood, a haven he kept meticulously neat and orderly. This predilection for tidiness intimidated Marjorie, who later said she had often intended to invite Percy to her home for lunch. The fact that there was always

Actor Percy Kilbride Dies; Known To Fans As Pa Kettle

LOS ANGELES (AP) — Drawling Percy Kilbride, Pa Kettle to movie fans, died Friday. He had been ailing since an auto accident injury two months ago. He was 76, and had retired when he reached 65.

Kilbride, veteran of 800 stage roles before making his film debut in 1942, won his greatest fame while co-starring with Marjorie Main in seven films based on the characters Ma and Pa Kettle from "The Egg and I," a novel made into a successful movie.

They played in slapstick fashion a rural couple with a large brood of children.

Last Sept. 17 he and a friend, actor Frank Belmont, 73, were struck by a car at a Hollywood intersection. Belmont was killed. Kilbride underwent brain surgery Nov. 11 and died at 12:45 a.m. Friday at Chase Sanitarium. Death was attributed to hardening of the arteries in the brain and to penumonia.

Kilbride is survived by a sister, Mrs. John L. Crowley of Los Angeles.

A bachelor, Kilbride had lived alone on Social Security since retiring.

He was 61 when the immense popularity of the Kettles boosted him from character actor to star. Lean, angular, slow to speak and slow to grin, he was a natural for the role of a Down

PERCY KILBRIDE
Veteran Actor Dies

East farmer — and played it strictly for laughs.

But he didn't enjoy it. Although the studio made millions from the series, Kilbride complained that the work was too brief and taxes too heavy for him to set much aside. He resisted his final Kettle assignment, on grounds there was no kick in doing the same thing repeatedly, but finally was talked into it. He refused to do more, and other actors starred in two additional films.

Montgomery (AL) Advertiser, December 12, 1964.

Marjorie Main Is Dead at 85; Our Ma Kettle

Los Angeles, April 10 (Special) — Marjorie Main, 85, the fog-horn-voiced queen of hillbilly actresses, who was best known for her portrayal of the weather-beaten Ma Kettle in the "Ma and Pa Kettle" films, died today at St. Vincent's Hospital after a long battle with cancer.

Marjorie Main

She appeared with such stars as Wallace Beery and John Barrymore in films of the 1930s and 40s, but it was her role as Ma Kettle opposite Percy Kilbride (Pa Kettle) that won her the love of millions of moviegoers.

Known as one of the least pretentious of Hollywood stars, she was born in Acton, Ind., Feb. 24, 1890.

She went to Hollywood in 1937 and established herself as a sardonic comedienne, sharp of tongue but with a heart of gold. She made 75 films.

She married Dr. Stanley L. Krebs in 1921. He died in 1935 and she never remarried. The Kettles had 15 children. In fact, the Krebs had none. Miss Main had no known living relatives.

a stack of papers piled high on a desk or table prevented her from extending the invitation.

Percy was extremely regular in his habits, one of which was to take a nightly stroll along Hollywood Boulevard. On September 21, 1964, at 9:10 p.m., he and his friend, eighty-two-year-old retired actor Ralf Belmont, were crossing a busy intersection together when a car came out of nowhere, striking down the two men. Belmont was reported dead at the scene; Kilbride was alive, but unconscious. He lingered for almost two months in the hospital, undergoing brain surgery during his attempted convalescence. On December 11, two months after the accident, Percy Kilbride succumbed to arteriosclerosis and pneumonia; he was seventy-six years old. Because of his status as a veteran of World War I, he was laid to rest in the beautiful Golden Gate National Cemetery in San Bruno, just a few miles from his hometown of San Francisco. His grave is in

New York Daily News, *April 11, 1975.*

Section 2B, Marker 3771-B, near a chain-link fence bordering the freeway. As to his estate, the proceeds were divided by four of his nephews and a sister-in-law.

Kilbride's passing devastated his co-star. "That was one of the saddest days of my life, when Percy was hit, and then when he passed on," Marjorie Main told an interviewer while choking back tears. "He was such a sweet soul."

During her working years, Marjorie had maintained homes in Cheviot Hills—just an hour from the Universal City studio—and in Palm Springs, a three-hour commute—eventually settling in the dry climate of the latter in the hopes of alleviating a long-time sinus condition. Much of her social life was limited to seeing old Hollywood friends and former co-stars on television, which she liked to watch while enjoying her meals. Although she may have been more partial to her dramatic performances, she seemed pleased that her interpretation of Ma Kettle continued to be embraced by the public.

Marjorie was, by her own admission, a terribly lonely individual. Her parents were long dead, she had no siblings, no children—indeed, no family of any kind. When it came time to draft her will, she bequeathed everything to such foundations as the Oxford Group, Moral Re-Armament, and the Leland Stanford Junior University.

In 1974, Marjorie—along with dozens of former MGM stars—gathered for an event to celebrate the Tiffany studio's fiftieth anniversary. A photo shoot and luncheon were scheduled to coincide with the release of the anthology film *That's Entertainment!* Everyone from Fred Astaire and Gene Kelly to Debbie Reynolds and Donald O'Connor were introduced, one at a time, by entertainers Sammy Davis Jr. and Liza Minnelli. A warm ovation greeted the noticeably frail Marjorie as she entered, rather shyly, with the assistance of two escorts. It would be her final public appearance. Marjorie Main—née Mary Tomlinson—succumbed to lung cancer on April 10, 1975, at the age of eighty-five. She is buried next to her husband in the Hollywood Hills Forest Lawn Memorial Park, the Enduring Faith section, lot number 2083.

Rest in peace, Ma and Pa.

Chapter 13
The Kettles in Pop Culture

A screencap from the Kettle-inspired Universal theatrical cartoon Maw and Paw *(1953). Four additional entries were released over the next fifteen years.*

In 1953, when the Ma and Pa Kettle series was still in production, U-I attempted an animated series based on the franchise, to be overseen by Walter Lantz (1899–1994), the American cartoonist best remembered for having created Woody Woodpecker. Perhaps we should add *loosely* before *based*, as the "Maw and Paw" cartoons bear only a superficial resemblance to the originals. At no time is the name Kettle used, nor do the characters resemble, in either appearance or voice, Marjorie Main and Percy Kilbride (they were voiced instead by Grace Stafford and Dal McKinnon). This, evidently, was a way of capitalizing on the popularity of the series without having to compensate either the stars for the use of their likenesses, or Betty MacDonald for permission to use the name.

Maw and Paw, as in the series, have a large brood—about a dozen kids—but the so-called "smart" member of their family is their pet pig, Wilbur. Given the longevity accorded other Lantz characters—Andy Panda, Chilly Willy, and especially Woody Woodpecker—Maw and Paw were featured in only five theatrical cartoons, released between 1953 and 1968: *Maw and Paw* (8/30/53), *Plywood Panic* (9/28/53), *Pig in a Pickle* (8/30/54, later reissued by Castle Films as *The Piggy That Stayed Home*), *Paw's Night Out* (8/16/55), and *Feudin Fightin'-N-Fussin'* (6/1/68). Another Walter Lantz–produced theatrical cartoon with a Kettle connection (however slight) is *The Ostrich Egg and I* (1956). The plot of this hilarious six-minute short concerns a timid man attempting to hide a newly hatched, but still oversized, ostrich from his domineering wife.

To increase its visibility in the television age, Universal (the "International" label was now a thing of the past) began their studio tour, introducing the orange Glamour Tram in 1964. The tram took sightseers around the studio grounds, past many familiar homes (or, more accurately, façades of homes), such as the Hitchcock *Psycho* house, the Munsters' mansion, the Cleavers' home

An approximation of the Kettle farmhouse was erected in Universal's Ark Park as a way of reminding tourists of the famed movie series.

Tourists commune with animals at Universal Studios' Ma and Pa Kettle Animal Farm.

(from *Leave It to Beaver*), and other scenes of interest to television and movie fans. On the outer part of the backlot was the Gausman Ranch, the area where the Kettle films had been shot. Also known as Ark Park, a reference to the Old-Testament story of Noah and the flood, the ranch was home to the many animals that had been featured in Universal productions, including some trained crows from Alfred Hitchcock's terrifying *The Birds* (1963). Bearing the sign "Ma and Pa Kettle's Animal Farm," a mock-up of the old farmhouse from the movies was constructed on the grounds, with hand-painted, intentionally misspelled signs such as "Howdy Naybor." There was also a petting zoo where children (including your authors) communed with the goats, chickens, lambs, and other animals on the site.[47]

---

47 From these humble beginnings came the massively popular Universal Studio Theme Parks, both at its original San Fernando Valley location and in Orlando, Florida. Now occupying the site of the former Kettle Animal Farm is the multi-million-dollar attraction "The Wizarding World of Harry Potter," based on the wildly hyped J.K. Rowling franchise.

Patsy Kelly.   *Andy Devine.*

Also, in 1964, Universal tried to mount a television sitcom featuring Ma and Pa Kettle. Cast in the leads were two veteran character actors, Patsy Kelly (1910–1981) and Andy Devine (1905–1977). Eddie Mayehoff was listed as one of the co-stars, and Irving Lerner was credited as the director. The pilot for the show was apparently filmed but never aired, and the idea for the series was quietly dropped.

With Universal striking out in their attempts to perpetuate the Kettles' reign, it fell to other rustic families to continue the tradition of country-based comedy.

Residing on a farm in the Appalachian Mountains of West Virginia, in the fictional region of "Smokey Corners," is the McCoy clan, headed by Luke (Richard Crenna), a widower in his twenties; his new wife, Kate (Kathleen Nolan); Luke's teenaged sister, Tallahassie (Lydia Reed), who goes by the nickname "Hassie"; and Luke's eleven-year-old brother, Little Luke (Michael Winkelman). The true star of *The Real McCoys* (1957–1963), however, is the cantankerous Grandpa Amos McCoy, played by three-time Academy Award–winning actor Walter Brennan (who, along with Danny Thomas and the ABC show's creator Irving Pincus, was one of the show's executive producers). Other cast members include Andy Clyde and Madge Blake as George and Flora MacMichael, an elderly brother

The cast of The Real McCoys: *(left to right) Lydia Reed, Walter Brennan, Michael Winkelman, Richard Crenna, and Kathleen Nolan.*

The cast of The Beverly Hillbillies *take to the road in their debut season of 1962–1963. Occupying the back seat are Donna Douglas and Irene Ryan; Buddy Ebsen is in the front passenger seat, and Max Baer Jr. is at the wheel.*

and sister, who live on a nearby mountain, and Tony Martinez as the McCoys' Mexican-American farmhand, Pepino Garcia.

One of the writers of *The Real McCoys* was Paul Henning (1911–2005), who had contributed scripts for such classic radio shows as *Fibber McGee and Molly* (1935–1959) and *The George Burns and Gracie Allen Show* (1936–1950). Henning had been raised on a farm in Independence, Missouri, which gave him a personal understanding of rural characters. His scripts treated them with respect, which allowed millions of television viewers to do the same. This type of wholesome, bucolic entertainment—a veritable antidote to the tumult of the 1960s—offered the same type of appeal that could be found in the Kettle series. Henning, in fact, had initially wanted to develop a show based on the Ma and Pa Kettle characters. Instead, he created the enormously popular Clampett family—Jed, Granny, Jethro, and Elly May, better known as *The Beverly Hillbillies*, which debuted on the CBS network in the fall of 1962. (It would remain in prime time until 1971, and in reruns forever.) Jed Clampett (Buddy Ebsen) is a widower with a grown, gorgeous daughter, Elly May (Donna Douglas); Daisy "Granny" Moses (Irene Ryan) is Jed's mother-in-law; and Jethro Bodine (Max Baer Jr.) is the overgrown son of Jed's cousin Pearl (Bea Benaderet). The show's unlikely premise was rendered unforgettable in the series' opening theme, "The Ballad of Jed Clampett."[48] It seems the "poor mountaineer who barely kept his family fed," was out hunting game one day. Missing his target but hitting the earth, "up from the ground came a bubblin' crude" ("Oil, that is. Black gold. Texas tea."). Jed's family members in Missouri insist that their newly mega-rich relative would be better off living in Southern California. Without questioning the logic, or lack thereof, of this idea, Jed, Elly May, Jethro, and an at-first-reluctant Granny, pack up the family's rusty 1921 Oldsmobile touring car and "move to Beverly." ("Hills, that is. Swimming pools. Movie stars.") There, they take up residence in a magnificent forty-room mansion on ten acres (an actual private residence, although in Bel Air, *not* Beverly Hills, at 750 Bel Air Road).

---

48 This expository theme song of *The Beverly Hillbillies* was written by Paul Henning, played by master banjoists Earl Flatt and Lester Scruggs, and sung by the basso profundo Jerry Scoggins.

Irene Ryan (center), who would achieve everlasting fame as Granny on The Beverly Hillbillies, *worked with Marjorie Main (left) in* Ricochet Romance *(1954). Their co-star (at right) is Alfonso Bedoya.*

The cast of Green Acres: *(top row, left to right) Alvy Moore, Tom Lester, and Pat Buttram; (bottom row, left to right) Eva Gabor, Eddie Albert, and Eleanor Audley.*

The original leads of Petticoat Junction, *Bea Benaderet and Edgar Buchanan.*

During the run of *The Beverly Hillbillies*, Henning expanded his fortunes by creating the similarly rustic *Petticoat Junction* (1963–1970), which takes place at "a little hotel called the Shady Rest" ("It is run by Kate, come and be her guest"), and its spinoff, *Green Acres* (1965–1971), both of which were broadcast on CBS. The latter show, in which a city dweller, Oliver Wendell Douglas (Eddie Albert), decides to move with his big-city-loving, country-living-hating wife, Lisa Douglas (Eva Gabor), to a chicken farm in a backwoods community, represents the inverse of the Clampetts' rags-to-riches paradigm. *Green Acres* was a retread of *The Egg and I*, although written and performed in a much broader fashion. The tenacious door-to-door salesman Billy Reed was morphed into the squeaky-voiced Mr. Haney, played by Gene Autry's former sidekick, Pat Buttram.

These shows, predictably enough, were desecrated by critics and embraced by middle America, breaking many pre-existing ratings records during their network reign. Although they showed little sign of slowing down or becoming tiresome to their fan base, they had all succumbed to the infamous "rural purge" of 1971. In the words of Pat Buttram, the network decided to "cancel everything with a tree in it— including *Lassie.*" The CBS network, referred to derisively by urban critics as the "Country Broadcast Station," set out to attract a younger, hipper demographic. Norman Lear's *All in the Family* and its various spinoffs—*Maude, The Jeffersons,* and *Good Times*—with their distinctly urban settings and real-life crises involving abortion, rape, and racial inequality—became the go-to entertainment of the time.

For kids, however, it mattered more what was being shown on television during the daytime than in primetime. Throughout the 1970s, the Kettle films were a staple on local stations' weekend lineups. They were rotated, along with other black-and-white comedies, including those featuring Abbott and Costello and Francis the Talking Mule. Few childhood memories are as fond as

those now-distant weekend mornings, lying on the living room floor with a big bowl of Cap'n Crunch and watching Ma and Pa Kettle. It was truly one of life's greatest pleasures.

With the drastic change in cable TV programming in the eighties, local stations gradually ceased showing the Universal films of the forties and fifties and, as the years passed, they started to become a distant memory. It took the home video revolution of the nineties to bring those family-friendly comedies back into America's collective living room. Between 1994 and 1995, all the Kettle films (as well as other Universal series, from comedies to monster movies, and sometimes a combination of both) were digitally remastered and reissued on videocassette, and later, DVD and Blu-ray.

As a demonstration of the series' ongoing recognition factor, you need only to enter "Ma and Pa Kettle" in a Google search, and 1,380,000 online sources await your perusal. YouTube viewers can watch the Kettles in clips (the one with the 7 x 13 = 28 routine from *Back on the Farm* has gone viral, so to speak, racking up more than a million views) or even—if one has no access to the DVDs—the entire, commercial-free features. A Spanish videographer, Valente Q. Castro, has chosen a unique medium—the children's toy known as Legos—to pay homage to the series. His brief, whimsical films feature "Ma and Pa Legos," with dialogue provided by the original soundtracks. A more accurate attempt to capture Main and Kilbride's image has been achieved by an artist who operates under the name Atelier Denise. Her hand-painted 2-D figurines, available through etsy.com, are made of polymer clay, acrylic paint, and urethane. As she states on her website: "I've portrayed the Kettles in a quasi-'American Gothic' pose, he with the pitchfork at the ready."

Enterprising businesses use the Kettle brand to identify their products. A family in Liverpool, New York, for example, launched their Ma and Pa's Kettle Korn and Popcorn Company in 2000. Another commercial venture, The Egg and I family restaurants, opened for breakfast, brunch, lunch, and dinner in 1988. There are also small towns in the United States that celebrate Ma and Pa Kettle Days, featuring such folksy events as parades, picnics, beauty contests, charity fundraisers, amateur talent shows, and, of course, plenty of socializing and good food. Collectibles, such as original 8x10 stills from the series, appear with regularity on eBay, and reprints of colorful movie posters representing each title are

available from Wal-Mart and other chain stores. If this type of merchandising continues (and we can't think of any reason why it won't), the characters of Ma and Pa Kettle will live on in the public imagination for a long, long time to come.

At the beginning of this study, we asked rhetorically why the Kettle films have been embraced by people all over the world. Having learned about the actors, the writers, directors, and technicians involved in their production, and having reviewed—entry by entry—the films themselves and their legacy in the age of home entertainment—what exactly *have* we learned about the reason behind Ma and Pa Kettle's phenomenal success? Only this: they were real, they were warm, and they were funny.

Image courtesy of Atelier Denise.

Sources

The Internet Movie Database (IMDb) is an invaluable source for filmographies as well as information on the lesser known but indispensable character actors who added distinction to countless films made in the studio era. We are indebted to those dedicated researchers who have supplied IMDb with its countless biographical entries. As for books, magazine, and newspaper articles, the following have been especially helpful:

Cox, Stephen, and John Lofflin. *The Abbott and Costello Story: Sixty Years of "Who's on First?"* Nashville, TN: Cumberland House, 1997.

Crowther, Bosley. "Or Is It Corn? Comparing 'A Run for Your Money' and 'Ma and Pa Kettle Go to Town.'"

Dardis, Tom. *Keaton: The Man Who Wouldn't Lie Down*. New York: Scribner's, 1979.

Eells, George, and Stanley Musgrove. *Mae West*. New York: William Morrow & Co., 1982.

Everson, William K. *The Art of W. C. Fields*. New York: Bonanza Books, 1967.

Findmypast team. "Shivaree: The Traditional Hazing of Our Newly-wed Ancestors." www.findmypast.com, February 11, 2016.

Getz, Leonard. *From Broadway to the Bowery: A History and Filmography of the Dead-End Kids, Little Tough Guys, East Side Kids and Bowery Boys Films, with Cast Biographies*. Jefferson, NC: McFarland & Co., 2006.

Hirschorn, Clive. *The Universal Story: The Complete History of the Studio and Its 2,641 Films*. London W1: Octopus Books, Ltd., 1983.

"Ma and Pa Kettle." *New York Times*, August 28, 1949.

MacDonald, Betty. *The Egg and I*. New York: J. P. Lippincott, 1945.

Maltin, Leonard. *Movie Comedy Teams: The Inside Stories of the Unforgettable Comedians Who Made Millions Laugh!* New York: Signet Film Series, 1970, 1974.

———. *Movies on TV: The Classic Years; More Than 10,000 Movies from the Silent Era Through 1965*. (Second Edition). New York: Penguin Group, 2005.

———. *The Real Stars: The Movie Buff's Bible of Hollywood's Greatest Character Actors*. Philadelphia: Curtis, 1973.

Parish, James Robert. *The Great Movie Series*. "Ma and Pa Kettle," pp. 232–240. New York: A.S. Barnes and Co., Inc., 1971.

———. *The Funsters*. "Marjorie Main." CreateSpace, ©1979, 2014.

———. *The Slapstick Queens*. "Marjorie Main." CreateSpace, ©1972, 2015.

Reynolds, Debbie, and David Patrick Columbia. *Debbie: My Life*. New York: Morrow, 1988.

Quirk, Lawrence J. *Claudette Colbert: An Illustrated Biography*. New York: Crown, 1985.

Telles, Larry. *Helen Gibson: Silent Serial Queen Who Became Hollywood's First Professional Stunt Woman*. Hayden, ID: Bitterroot Mountain LLC, 2013.

Terrace, Vincent. *Encyclopedia of Unaired Television Pilots, 1945–2018*. Jefferson, NC: McFarland & Co., 2018.

Thomas, Bob. "'Pa Kettle' to Quit Family Film Series," Hollywood United Press International (UPI), April 8, 1953.

Tranberg, Charles. *Fred MacMurray: A Biography* (Kindle edition). Duncan, OK: BearManor Media, 2014.

Vogel, Michelle. *Marjorie Main: The Life and Films of Hollywood's Ma Kettle*. Jefferson, NC: McFarland and Co., 2006.

Wellman, Anne. *Betty: The Story of Betty MacDonald, Author of* The Egg and I. Independently published, 2016.

Williamson, J. W. *Hillbillyland: What the Movies Did to the Mountains & What the Mountain Did to the Movies*. Chapel Hill: University of North Carolina Press, 1995.

Index

Abbott and Costello Meet Franken-
    stein 175, 348
Abbott and Costello Meet the
    Mummy 304
Abbott, Bud 14, 26, 171, 351
ABC-TV network 91, 174, 343
Abraham Lincoln (1930) 301
Academy Award 16, 22, 69, 115,
    171, 301, 343
Adventures of Jim Bowie, The 318
Akins, Claude 315, 320, 325
Albert, Eddie 346, 347
Albertson, Jack 270
Albertson, Mabel 266, 270, 279
Aldrich, Fred 315
Aldrich, Robert 238
Allbritton, Louise 12, 32
Allen, Fred 317
"Allen's Alley" 317
Allman, Elvia 35, 298
American Academy of Dramatic
    Arts (Cleveland, OH) 114
Anderson, Glenn E. 12
Andrews, Dana 30
Andy Griffith Show, The 271
Apartment, The 115
Arbuckle, Roscoe "Fatty" 245n
Arc de Triomphe (Paris, France)
    229
Archerd, Army 25
Arglen, George 77, 170, 206, 266,
    272, 298, 315
Arkansas State Teachers College
    300
Arling, Arthur E. 314
Army Air Forces 271
Around the World in Eighty Days
    272

Art Linkletter's House Party 151
Astaire, Fred 60, 339
Astounding B-Monster Archive, The
    172–173
Ates, Roscoe 298
Austin, Lois 170
Autry, Gene 175, 347
Avery, Emile 315

Backus, Jim 113, 114–115
Bacon, Irving 231, 237
Bad Bascomb 24, 79
Baer, Max Jr. 344, 345
Bailey, William 12, 266
Bainter, Fay 29
Baker, Donald 315
Baker, Frank 170
Ball, Alex 170, 206
Ball, Lucille 114, 157
Ball, Susan 153
Bank Dick, The 301–302
Banner Productions 158
Barber, Bobby 298
Barber, Philip 314
Barcroft, Roy 315
Barnacle Bill 24
Barrie, Wendy 22
Barrows, George 315
Barrymore, John 19
Barton, Charles 169, 171–172,
    204
Barton, John 170
Batjac Productions 319
Beauchamp, D. D. 72
Bedtime for Bonzo 158
Beery, Wallace xii, 23–25, 27, 79,
    157
Belding, Dale 77, 113, 149

Belfer, Harold 206
Bells of St. Mary's, The 319
Belmont, Ralf 338
Benaderet, Bea 70, 345, 347
Bennett, Catherine 238
Bennett, Connie Lee 266
Bennett, Enid 238
Bennett, Marjorie 231, 238, 246
Benny, Jack 28, 234
Berkes, Johnny 12, 30, 84
Bernhardt, Sarah 231, 269
Bert, Margaret 315
Besser, Joe 72
Best Things in Life are Free, The 272
Best Years of Our Lives, The 176
Best, James 170, 173–174, 192, 204
Beverly Hillbillies, The 303, 344–345, 346, 347
Bewitched 284n
Big Jack 24
Big Sky, The 301
Big Valley, The 154
Binney, Faire 266
Bishop, Albert 4, 7–8
Bishop, Suzanne 7
Bishop, Wilbur 4, 8
Blake, Madge 343, 345
Blake, Oliver (a.k.a. Oliver Prickett) 149, 155–156, 170, 206, 208, 231, 266
Blesing, Wag 315
Blondie and Dagwood series 158
"Blue Danube, The" 120
Blumberg, Nate J. 14
Blyth, Ann 336
Bogart, Humphrey 22, 239
Bolger, Ray 271
Bonzo Goes to College 158
Booth, Shirley 272

Borden, Eugene 206
Borgani, Nick 206
Born Yesterday 155
Boston Toy Theatre company 316
Bourbon College (Paris, KY) 19
Bow, Clara 171
Bowery Boys, The viii, 22n, 270, 351
Boyle, Robert F. 206, 231
Breen, John 170, 298
Bremer, Lucille 79
Brennan, Walter 343–344
Brissac, Virginia 231, 237, 261
Brocco, Peter 206, 214
Brown, Barbara 113, 149, 154–155, 159, 206, 208
Brown, Helen 298
Brown, Margaret 77, 113, 170, 206, 266, 272
Bruce, Nigel 14, 238
Buchanan, Edgar 347
Buffalo (NY) *Evening News* 333
Burns, Bob 298
Burson, Polly 315
Buttram, Pat 346, 347, 348

Callaway, Cheryl 298
Calliga, George 113, 206
Cameraman, The 157
Capitol Theatre, The (NYC) 168
Capra, Frank 16
Carey, Leslie I. 77, 112, 149, 206, 231, 266, 298, 315
Carle, Frankie 168
Carrillo, Leo 24
Carruthers, Steve 206
Carson, Kit 301
Carter, Douglas 170
Carthay Circle Theater (Los Angeles) 36

"Cassie Turner Story, The" (*Wagon Train* episode) 336
Castro, Valente 349
CBS Radio Network 69, 151
CBS-TV Network 17, 70, 234, 345, 347, 348
Central Park Zoo 118, 119, 134, 135, 137
Chambers, Wheaton 170
Chaplin, Charlie 238
Chapman, Ben 266
Charles, Zachary 170, 172n
Chase, Charley 270
Cheating Cheaters 19
Chefe, Jack 113, 206
Cheshire, Harry 77, 170
Chissell, Noble "Kid" 315
Christie, Howard 77, 314, 320
Christmas in Connecticut 240
Cimarron City 318
Citizen Kane 155
Clark, Billy 170, 206, 266, 272
Clark, Don 315
Clark, Edward 149
Cleopatra (1934) 16, 43n
Clork, Harry 266
Close, Juanita 170
Clyde, Andy 270, 343, 345
Cobb, Edmund 149, 170, 231
Colbert, Claudette 12, 16–17, 35, 37, 39, 41, 41n, 43n, 44, 46, 47, 54, 58, 62, 63, 66, 69, 70, 351
Collins, Ray 113, 149, 155, 161, 206, 208, 220
Colonel Humphrey Flack 236
Columbia Pictures 33, 158, 171–172, 269–270
Combat! 233
Come Back, Little Sheba 272
Come Next Spring 152
Comerford, Janet 298

Comin' Round the Mountain 303
Conaty, James 170
Confessions of a Nazi Spy 208
Conrad, William 114
Conway, Russ 206
Corday, Mara 153–154
Cording, Harry 170
Corman, Roger 273, 302
Corrado, Gino 206, 209
Cosmopolitan Pictures 245n
Costello, Lou viii, 14, 26, 27, 81, 171, 172, 175, 192n, 303, 304, 348, 351
Cowdin, J. Cheever 14
Cowers, Leland T. 316
Crane, Jeannie 29
Crawford, Joan 25, 44
Creed, Roger 315
Crenna, Richard 343, 344
Criss Cross 153
Cristo, Paul 206
Crosby, Bing 319
Crowther, Bosley 28, 147
Curtiss, Edward 298, 314
Custer, Russell 77, 170

D'Arcy, Andre 206, 219
Da Pron, Louis 298
Dale, Esther 12, 31, 77, 83, 170, 204, 266, 270n
Dance with Me, Henry 172
Danny Thomas Show, The 152
Dark Horse, The 34
Darnell, Linda 30
Daughter of Doctor Jekyll 320
Davies, Marion 245n
Davis, Bette 336
Davis, Joan 115
Davis, Sammy Jr. 339
Day at the Races, A 208
Daytime Emmy Awards 233

De Briac, Jean 206
De Corsia, Ted 298, 308
Deacon, Richard 298, 303, 304, 311
Dead End (play and film) 22
Dean, James 114, 237
Dearing, Edgar 231
DeGarro, Harold 170
Dell, Gabriel 21, 22
Delmar, Kenny 317
DeMille, Cecil B. 16, 171, 174
Denise, Atelier 350
DeNormand, George 315
Desilu Studios 157
Desperate Hours, The 239
Destry Rides Again 301
Devine, Andy 14, 343
Devore, Perry 314
DeWeese, Richard 77
Dick Van Dyke Show, The 304
Dickens, Charles 14, 18, 19, 27
Dickson, Helen 113, 266
Dietrich, Marlene 301
Dinner is Served 236
Dirigo, Carmen 12
Disney, Walt 34, 239
Dobkin, Lawrence 206
Dodson, Jack 271
Donald, Peter 317
Donna Reed Show, The 233
Donnelly, Bob 170, 266
Dorr, Lester 170
Double Indemnity 17
Douglas, Donna 344, 345
Dressed to Kill 238
Dressler, Marie xii, 23
Dukes of Hazzard, The 174
Dumont network 236
Dunn, George 315, 318, 321, 328, 332
Dunn, Harvey B. 315

Dunn, Paul 77, 113, 151
Durbin, Deanna 14

Eason, B. Reeves 169
East Side Kids, The 22n, 158
Easton, Robert 298, 303, 307
Eastwood, Clint 234
Ebsen, Buddy 344, 345
Ed Sullivan Show, The (a.k.a. *Toast of the Town*) 272
Eddy, Bonnie Kay 266
Edison, Thomas 47, 101
Egg and I, The (film) 11–17, 27, 30, 35–72, 78, 83, 98n, 114, 149, 151, 175, 172n, 347;
filmography information; (novel) 3, 6–9, 77, 14–15, 110, 232, 236; (radio plays) 35, (TV serial) 70–71; restaurant chain 350; Egg and I Road 10
Eiffel Tower (Paris, France) 225–226, 229
Eldredge, George 170
Eldredge, John 206
Elinor, Carli 206
Elliott, Ross 231, 248, 256, 257
Emert, Oliver 12, 77, 112, 149
Epper, Tony 231
Erskine, Chester 12, 13, 14, 16, 67n
Eyer, Richard Ross ix, 152, 231, 239–240, 298

Fallen Angel 30
"Family Ford, The" 20
Farnum, Franklyn 206
Fawcett, William 298
Faye, Alice 30
Felstead, Charles 12
Fennelly, Catherine 316

Fennelly, Parker 315, 316–318, 321, 333
Ferguson, Frank 170, 175
Feudin Fightin-N-Fussin (Maw and Paw cartoon) 341
Feudin' Fussin' and a-Fightin' (live-action film) 71–72
Fibber McGee and Molly 345
Field, Norman 266
Fields, W. C. 20, 95, 302, 351
Finklehoffe Fred F. 12, 13, 14, 15
Flatt, Earl 345n
Flavin, James 231
Florentine, Diane 12, 77, 113, 151
Forbidden Planet 239
Ford, George 206
Ford, John 174, 258
Forest Lawn Memorial Park, Hollywood Hills 339
Fort Ord army base (Monterey, CA) 153
42ⁿᵈ Street 301
4-H Clubs of America 244, 244n, 249, 263
Fox Pictures 157
Francis the Talking Mule film series 348
Frank, Milo O. Jr. 173
Franklin College (Fairfield, IN) 18
Franklin, Bonnie 298
Freeman, Everett 28
Fuller, Clem 315
Further Adventures of Ma and Pa Kettle, The See *Ma and Pa Kettle* (1949)

Gable, Clark 16
Gabor, Eva 346, 347
Gardner, Jon 206, 266

Garner, Cindy 266
Gausman Ranch (a.k.a. Ark Park) 342
Gausman, Russell A. 12, 77, 112, 149, 169, 206, 231, 266, 298, 314
Gaut, Slim 113, 298
George Burns and Gracie Allen Show, The 115, 116, 303, 345
George Washington Slept Here (play and film) 28–29
George White's Scandals 33
Gereghty, Helen 298, 315
Gershenson, Joseph 149, 169, 206, 266, 298, 314
Gertsman, Maury 77, 169
Get Smart 114
Gibson, Helen 12, 157–158, 170, 190n, 231, 269, 351
Gibson, Hoot 157
Gibson, Kenneth 266
Gilbert, Joe 113, 298
Gilchriest, Gail 302
Gilligan's Island 115, 271
Gilmore, Lowell 266
Gilmour, Arthur D. 266
Gish, Lillian 301
Goetz, William J. 13
Going My Way 319
Golden Gate National Cemetery (Bruno, CA) 338–339
Goldin, Pat 266, 298, 303
Goldstein, Leonard 12, 72, 77, 112, 149, 169, 206, 266, 268
Goldwyn, Samuel 22
Golitzen, Alexander 298, 314
Gone with the Wind 268
Gonzalez, James 206, 266
Good Humor Man, The 273
Goodwin, Harold 149, 157, 206, 266

Gorcey, Leo 22, 22n
Gordon, Dick 113, 206
Gordon, Gale 70
Gordon, Ruth 270
Gosfield, Maurice 113, 116–117
Gould, William 170
Grady, Billy Jr. 149
Graham, A. B. 244n
Graham, Herschel 266
Granby's Green Acres 69–70
Grand Central Terminal (NYC) 118, 125
Grant, John 169, 172, 204
Grapes of Wrath, The (1940 film) 174
Gray, Billy 170
Great Gildersleeve, The 115
Great Lover, The 273
Greatest Show on Earth, The 272
Green Acres 70n, 346, 347
Green, Marshall 314
Griffith, D. W. 301
Griffith, James 170
Grippo, Jan 22n
Guthrie, Carl E. 231

Hagen, Charles 206
Hagney, Frank 315
Hall, Huntz 21, 22
Halls, Ethyl May 315
Halsey, Admiral William "Bull" 234
Halsey, Brett ix, x, xi, 231, 234–236, 239, 243
Hamilton School of Dramatic Expression 18–19
Hamilton, Chuck 206, 298, 315
Hammerstein, Oscar 22, 29
Hammond, Coral 231, 240
Harris, Alan 266
Harris, Sam 206

Harry Fox and His Six Original Beauties 21
Hart, Lorenz 156
Hart, Teddy 149, 155–156, 206, 208, 266
Harvey Girls, The 26
Harvey, Harry 170
Harvey, Jean 315
Hattie, Hilo 266, 272, 294
Haupt, Whitey 231, 240
Hausner, Jerry 149
Hawkins, Timmy 266
Hawks, Howard 301
Hayle, Grace 266
Haymes, Dick 29
Hayward, Jim 298, 308
Hazards of Helen, The 157
Healey, Myron 266, 290
Heigh, Helene 298
Hellman, Lillian 22
Henley, Jack 149, 158, 169, 206, 207–208, 266
Henning, Paul 345, 345n, 347
Herzbrun, Bernard 12, 77, 112, 149, 169, 206, 231, 266
Heskett, Robert Eugene 3–5, 5n, 14
Hickman, George 315
High and the Mighty, The 319
High Sierra 34
Hill, Hallene 170, 172n, 315
Hillside Christian Church 18
Hinds, Samuel S. 12, 61n, 62
Hines, Harry 298, 308
Hitchcock, Alfred 176, 317, 341, 342
Hitler Gang, The 208
Hoagland, George 12, 266
Holden, Joyce 149
Holland, Edna 298
Holland, William 231

Holliday, Judy 155
"Hollywood on Ice" 271
Holmes, Stuart 298
Honeymooners, The 114
Hope, Bob 273
Horsley, David S. 112, 149, 169
Hotel Louis Quatorze (Paris, France) 225
House Divided, A 21
House, Billy 12, 34, 36, 98n
Hudson, Rock 319
Hunnicutt, Arthur 298, 300–301, 303, 305, 313
Hunter, Tab 319
Huston, Walter 21

I Love Lucy 35, 115, 157, 189
I Married a Monster from Outer Space 320
I Married Joan 115
Independent Moving Pictures Company (Imp) 157
Imperio, Rosario 206
Infuhr, Teddy 12, 77, 113, 149, 151, 170, 175–176
Inge, William 272
Ingram, Jack 149
Internet Movie Database (IMDb) 211n, 270, 351
Invisible Boy, The 239
It Ain't Hay 192n
It Came from Outer Space 271
It Happened One Night 16

Jackass Mail 24, 157
Jackson, Gary Lee 170, 206
Jackson, Jackie 113, 170, 206, 266, 272, 273
Jackson, Jimmie 151
Jackson, Robert 152

Jackson, Sherry ix, 113, 149, 150, 152, 170, 206
Janssen, David 234
Jean, Gloria 14
"Jingle Bells" 262
John Loves Mary 270
Johnson, Raymond H. 8
Johnson, Russell 266, 271
Jowett, Corson 206, 266

Kalem Company 157
Kallen, Kitty 168
Kane, Byron 266
Kanin, Garson 155
Kate Smith Evening Hour, The 115
Katzman, Sam 158
Kaufman, George S. 28, 208, 270
Keating, Larry 113, 116
Keaton, Buster 157, 351
Keighley, William 28
Kelley, Alice x, 206, 231, 234, 235, 236–237, 243
Kelly, Gene 339
Kelly, Patsy 343
Kelman, Rickey 315
Kemp, Kenner G. 170, 266
Kennedy, Tom 315
Kenny, Colin 206
Kent, Ted J. 69
Kern, Jerome 22
Kerr, Donald 113, 170
Kettles in the Ozarks, The (1956) ix, 36, 233, 297–313; filmography information 298
Kettles on Old MacDonald's Farm, The (1957) 314–333; filmography information 314–315
Keystone Cops, The 157
Kilbride, Elizabeth Kelly 27
Kilbride, Owen 27

Kilbride, Percy v, x, xii, 12,
  career background of 27–30;
  co-stars' impressions 82–83,
  172–173,235; death of 337,
  338–339; derby of 117–118,
  118n, 143, 336; discontentment
  with role of Pa Kettle 231– 233,
  264, 296, 299, 336; habits of
  29, 82–83, 338; 336–339; 71,
  72, 77, 81, 82–83, 84, 110, 111,
  113, 119, 141n, 147, 149, 150,
  151, 152, 155, 166n, 168, 170,
  172–173, 204, 206, 207–208,
  231–233, 234, 235, 256, 257,
  264, 266, 267–268, 269, 296,
  299, 300, 312, 316, 318, 340,
  348, 349, 350
Kill the Umpire! 273
Killers, The 114
Kings Row 173
Kish, Joe 206
Knight, Fuzzy 12
Kornman, Verna 315
Krasner, Milton 12
Krebs, Dr. Stanley Lefevre 20,
  22, 80
Kruger, Paul 315
Kruschen, Jack 206
KTTV-TV (Los Angeles, CA)
  272
Kunde, Ann 12, 77, 298, 315

Lambs Club 117
Lamont, Charles ix, 77, 81–82,
  92n, 112, 118–119, 157, 206,
  231, 268, 298
Lamour, Dorothy 296
Lancaster, Burt 153, 272
Lantz, Walter 340–341
Lassie 348
Lava, William 231

Lawrence, Walter 298
"Lazy Mary" 210
Le Baron, Eddie 206
Leary, Donna 77, 113, 170 206,
  266, 272, 273
Leary, Nolan 12, 77, 170
Lease, Rex 77, 113, 149, 170, 175
Leave It to Beaver 304, 342
Leeds, Peter 113, 149
Leland Stanford Junior University
  339
Lenard, Kay 231, 233–234, 298,
  300
Leon, Peggy 298
Leonard, Lu 298
Lerner, Irving 343
Lesser, Sol 268
Levitt, Ruby R. 169, 231, 266,
  298, 314
Lewis, Al 77
Lewis, Jerry 114
Life of Riley, The 153
Limelight 238
Linder, Jenny 170, 206, 266, 272
Lockwood, King 206
Long, Richard 12, 32, 47, 77, 83,
  93, 113, 118, 149, 150, 153–154,
  172
Lontoc, Leon 266, 291
Lost in Space 152
Lowe's State Building (NYC)
  151
Lung, Charles 266
Luukiuluana 266
Lux Radio Theatre 35, 69

Ma and Pa Kettle (1949) 76–111;
  filmography information 77–78
Ma and Pa Kettle at Home (1954)
  ix, x, 150, 230–264;
  filmography information 231

Ma and Pa Kettle at the Fair
(1952) ix, x, 149, 158, 169–204,
264, 313;
filmography information 169–170
Ma and Pa Kettle at Waikiki
(1955) ix, 150, 157, 158,
265–296;
filmography information 266–267
Ma and Pa Kettle Back on the Farm
(1951) ix, 148–168, 212, 349;
filmography information 149
"Ma and Pa Kettle Days" 350
Ma and Pa Kettle Go to Town
(1950) 112–147, 149, 154, 158,
208, 229, 351;
filmography information 112–113
Ma and Pa Kettle on Vacation
(1953) 157, 158, 205–229, 269;
filmography information 206–207
Ma and Pa Kettle's Animal Farm
342
Ma and Pa's Kettle Korn and
Popcorn Company 350
MacBride, Donald 12, 33–34
MacDonald, Betty 2–10; lawsuit
against 6–9; 12, 13, 15, 15n, 16,
33, 35, 69, 77, 110, 340, 352
MacDonald, Donald 231, 240
MacMurray, Fred 12, 17, 35, 37,
41n, 60, 69, 352
MacRae, Gordon 272
Mad Libs (party game) 114
Main, Marjorie (a.k.a. Mary
Tomlinson) career background
of 18–27; co-stars' impressions of 79–82, 152, 153, 158,
172–173, 235, 239, 302; death
of 338–339; devotion to husband 20, 22, 80; germaphobia of
79–80, 158, 302; professionalism of 27, 81–82, 204; v, viii, x,

xii, xiii, 12, 36, 49, 69, 71, 72,
77, 78, 80, 81, 82, 83, 110, 111,
113, 118, 120n, 147, 149, 150,
151, 152, 153, 157–158, 170,
172–173, 190n, 204, 206, 207,
210, 231, 232, 233, 234, 235,
239, 240, 266, 267, 269, 276,
278n, 286, 295, 298, 299, 300,
302, 313, 315, 316, 318, 321,
323, 324, 325, 328, 332, 333,
336, 338, 339, 340, 346, 348,
349, 350, 352
Maltin, Leonard viii, 263, 352
Man from Planet X, The 304
Man in the Attic 272
Man Who Cried Wolf, The 23
Mannheimer, Albert 155
March, Hal 113, 115–116
Margolis, Herbert H. 77, 314,
318
Marlowe, Frank 170, 266
Martell, Alphonse 206
Martinez, Tony 345
Marx Brothers, The 33, 208
Mason, Sydney 170
Maud Scheerer Shakespeare Play-
ers 316
Mauu, Charles 266
Maw and Paw (Maw and Paw
cartoon) 341
Maw and Paw cartoon series
340–341; *see also individual titles*
Mayer, Louis B. 13
Mayehoff, Eddie 343
Maytime 320
McCarthy, J. Harvey 36
McDonough, Betty 231, 298
McFarland, Frank 170
McGraw, Charles 113, 114
McGuire, Annie 8–9
McKinney, Mira 298

McKinnon, Dal 340
McMurphy, Jean 336
Meade, Claire 170
Meader, William 298
"Me and My Shadow" 71
Meeker, Russell 315
Meet Danny Wilson 273
Meet Me in St. Louis 26, 79
Menzies, William Cameron 268
Mercury Theatre on the Air 155
Merkel, Una 298, 301–302, 305
Metro-Goldwyn-Mayer (MGM) 25
Meyer, Torben 206
Midwestern Practical Nurses Association 83
Miguel, Timothy A. 266
Miller, Bodil 206, 209
Miller, Patrick 231, 240
Mills, Frank 315
Min and Bill 23
Mini-Skirt Mob, The 152
Minnelli, Liza 339
Miracle of Our Lady of Fatima, The 152
Mitchum, Robert 124
Mole People, The 315
Monogram Pictures 22n, 30, 270, 304
Monsieur Verdoux 238
Montgomery, George 319
Mook, Beverly 77, 113, 170, 206, 266, 272
Moore, Ida 12, 34, 77
Moots, Donna Cregan 231, 240
Moral Re-Armament 339
Moreno, Rita 206, 218n
Morgan, Boyd "Red" 315
Morgan, Dennis 240
Morheim, Louis 77
Morley, Jay A. Jr. 298

Morris, Richard 169, 204
Morrow, Patricia 231, 240, 298, 315
Mothers-in-Law, The 304
Movies on TV (Maltin, ed.) 263, 352
Mowbray, Alan x, 231, 234, 236, 239, 248, 256, 257
Mower, Jack 206, 298
Mr. Imperium 80
Mr. Wise Guy 158
Mrs. O'Malley and Mr. Malone 78, 79
Mrs. Piggle-Wiggle (MacDonald) 9
"Mudder/Fodder" comedy routine 192n
Muhl, Edward 315
Munsters, The 341
Music in the Air 22
Music Mates, The 271
My Favorite Wife 33–34
My Man Godfrey 236
My Sister Eileen 174
My Three Sons 17

Nanny and the Professor 154
Nardelli, George 266
Natteford, Jack 269
Nayfack, Nicholas 239
Nearest and Dearest 154
Nelson, Lori ix, 170, 172–173, 192, 204, 234, 266, 272
Nelson, Robert 231
Neumann, Dorothy 266
Neury, Roger 206
New York Times, The 23, 110, 118, 147, 168, 203–204, 351
Niblo, Fred 238
Nicholson, Emrich 77, 112, 149
Night at the Opera, A 208
Night in Casablanca, A 208

Nolan, Kathleen 343, 344
Noose Hangs High, The 192n
Norris Industries 237
Norris, Ken 237
Novak, Eva 315
Novello, Jay 206
Nugent, Carol 231, 240
Nugent, Judy 231, 240

O'Brien, Dave 298, 305
O'Brien, Margaret 79–80
O'Brien, William H. 113, 170, 315
O'Connor, Donald 71–72, 339
O'Connor, Frank 13, 170
O'Madigan, Isabel 12, 31, 77, 172n
O'Malley, Lillian 298
O'Neal, Anne 149, 159
Odell, Rosemary 77, 112, 149, 169, 206, 266
Olivier, Laurence 14
Orbom, Eric 170, 266
Ostrich Egg and I, The 341
Oxford Group 339

Padden, Sarah 298
Pagett, Eddie 298
Pagett, Gary 231, 240
Palace Theatre (NYC) 20, 110, 203
Palance, Jack 272
Palmer, Byron 266, 271
Panorama Theater (Los Angeles, CA) 312
Paramount Pictures 171
Paris, Manuel 207
Parker Fennelly Duo, The 316
Parnell, Emory 77, 84–85, 98n, 149, 170, 180, 204, 231
Pasadena Playhouse, The 33, 156

Pat and Mike 270
Paw's Night Out (Maw and Paw cartoon) 341
Peary, Harold 115
Penn, Arthur 174
Pepperidge Farm 316
Perry Mason 155
Persson, Eugene 13, 77, 113, 151, 170
Peter Pan (1953 Disney animated film) 34
Peters, Ralph 266
Petticoat Junction 347
Phi Eta Sigma fraternity 303
Pierce, Jack P. 12
Pig in a Pickle (Maw and Paw cartoon) 341
Piltz, George 266
Pincus, Irving 343
Pious, Minerva 317
Pitman, George 298
Plague and I, The (MacDonald) 9
Plumer, Rose 77, 170
Plywood Panic (Maw and Paw cartoon) 341
Pogue, Mel 170
Ponder Heart, The 302
Portanova, Mike 298
Potel, Victor 12, 30–31, 84
Poule, Ezelle 267
Price, Roger 114
Pritchard, Robert 149, 231, 298
Psycho (1960 Hitchcock film) 341

Quiz Kids 303

Ragaway, Martin 112, 113–114, 169, 172
Randall, Meg 77, 85, 93, 113, 118, 149, 153
Rathbone, Basil 14, 238

Ray, Aldo 319
Raynor, William 314, 318
RCA Observational Tower (NYC) 129
Real McCoys, The 343–345
Rebel Without a Cause 114, 237
Red Mill, The 245n
Red Pony, The 273
Reed, Lydia 343–344
Reeves, Richard 267, 290
Rekwart, Waclaw 207
Revenge of the Creature 173, 234
Reynolds, Debbie 80, 339, 352
Richmond, Felice 298
Ricochet Romance 233, 346
Ridge, Walter 298
Ridgeway, Suzanne 207
Risdon, Elizabeth 12
Robert Mitchell Boy Choir 319
Roberts, Mark 207
Robinson, Dewey 77
Robinson, George 206, 298
Robinson, Robert 170
Rochelle, Edwin 170
Rogers, Roy 175
Rogers, Will xii, 318
Roman, Ric 267
Romeo and Juliet 250n
Rondell, Ronnie Jr. 170, 207, 267, 272
Room Service 33
Roope, Fay 266, 279
Ross, Stan 231
Rowling, J. K. 342n
Roy Rogers Show, The 239
Roy, John 207
Royal Geographic Society 236
Ruman, Sig 206, 208
Runyon, Damon 123
Rutledge, Ann 301
Ryan, Dick 170

Ryan, Irene 344, 345, 346

"Sacramento Story, The" (*Wagon Train* episode) 336
San Francisco Chronicle, The 233
Sardo, Cosmo 267
Saroyan, William 301
Sawyer, Joe 298
Saxe, Carl 315
Saylor, Syd 170
Schine Theaters chain 267–268, 296
Schoengarth, Russell F. 12, 77, 112, 149
Schreiner, Elana 77, 113, 170, 207, 267, 272
Schwarzwald, Milton 77, 112
Scoggins, Jerry 345n
Screen Actors Guild 236
Scruggs, Lester 345n
Sedgwick, Edward 149, 151, 152, 156, 157
Sgt. Bilko (*The Phil Silvers Show*) 114, 116–117
Shadow of the Thin Man 270
Shakespeare, William 14, 19, 20, 250n, 260, 269, 316
Shaw, Frank 12
Shaw, Tom 266
Sheldon, Kathryn 298
Sherlock Holmes and the Spider Woman 176
Sherlock Holmes Universal film series 14, 176, 238
Sholem, Lee 266, 268, 269
"Silent Night" 262
Simpson, Russell 170, 174
Sinatra, Frank 125, 273
Skelton, Red 114, 157
Skinner, Frank 12, 35

Sloane, J. P. ix, 113, 149, 150, 151–152
Smith, Al 117, 336
Smith, Edna 315
Smith, John 315, 318–319, 322
Smith, Loring 266, 270, 279
Snow White and the Seven Dwarfs (Disney animated feature, 1937) 34
Solid Gold Cadillac, The 270
Somers, Cap 315
Sommers, Jay 70, 70n
Sorority Girl 273
Sotto, Marilyn 314
Soule, Olan 113, 116, 135
Sowards, George 77, 170, 298, 315
Spellbound 176
Spence, Sandra 267
Spiker, Ray 298
Spite Marriage 157
Spitz, Leo 13
Spooks Run Wild 158
"S'posin'" 71
St. Oegger, Joan 112, 149, 170, 206, 231, 266, 298
Stafford, Grace 340
Stalag 17 208
Stanwyck, Barbara 17, 23, 154, 240
Star Trek: The Original Series 153
State Fair 29
Stein, Herman 206
Steinbeck, John 174
Stella Dallas 23
Stern, Leonard 112, 113, 114, 169, 172
Stine, Clifford 266, 314
Stoddard, Samuel ix, 229, 263, 296
Sturgess, Olive ix, 298, 302, 305

Sullivan, Brick 113, 170
Sullivan, Charles 170
Summer Stock 25, 26
Sutton, Grady 302
Swanson, Gloria 22
Sweeney, Alfred 298
Sweeney, Bob 115
Sweet and Lowdown 320

Taft, Sara 170, 315
Take Me Out to the Ballgame 273
Talbott, Gloria 315, 319–320, 322
Talbott, Lori 319
Tale of Two Cities, A (Dickens) 27
Taming of the Shrew (Shakespeare) 19
Tamkin, David 12
Tarzan's Magic Fountain 268
Tarzana Medical Center (Tarzana, CA) 154
Taylor, Forrest 170
Terrell, Ken 207, 231
That's Entertainment! 339
Theater Guild 236
They Came to Blow Up America 208
Thicker Than Water 154
This is Hollywood 35
This is Your Music 272
This Island Earth 271
Thomas, Bob 231
Thomas, Danny 152, 343
Thompson, Glenn 315
Thornton, Claudette 266
Three Stooges Meet Hercules, The 272
Three Stooges, The viii, 270
Three Toes (Grizzly bear) 320–321, 327, 330, 332, 333
"Tiger Rag" 87, 87n, 120, 281

Time of Their Lives, The 172
Time of Your Life, The 301
Tobacco Road 301
Toland, Gregg 22
Tomack, Sid 298, 308
Tonight We Sing 271–272
Tony Award 218n, 302
Tree Grows in Brooklyn, A 176, 320
Trevor, Claire 22
Trial of Mary Dugan, The 25–26
Triesault, Ivan 206
Trouble Along the Way 152
Trouble with Harry, The 317–318
Tryon, Thomas 320
Tugboat Annie 23
Turner, Leslie 298
Tuttles of Tahiti, The 176
20th Century-Fox studios 13, 29, 30, 69n, 85, 272
Tyler, Harry 78, 298

U.S. Air Force Reserves 237
Ullman, Elwood 266, 269–270
Union Pacific 171
Universal Pictures Corporation x, xiii, xiv, 13–14, 21, 22n, 32, 38n, 157, 158, 172, 173, 176, 238, 315, 341–343, 351
Universal-International Pictures (U-I) 12, 13–14, 21, 22n, 26, 27, 32, 72, 77, 78, 93, 110, 112, 152, 158, 168, 169, 176, 203, 206, 208, 222, 231, 234, 238, 266, 298, 299, 314
University of Texas (Austin) 303

Vallin, Rick 231
Van Enger, Charles 112, 149
Variety Weekly 69, 296, 333
Vidor, King 245n

Vincent, Sailor 315
Virginian, The (1914) 174
Vogel, Virgil W. 266, 314, 315
Vogue Films 157
von Zell, Harry 149

Wagon Train 336
Wagon Wheels 171
Waldorf-Astoria Hotel (NYC) 118, 119, 121, 126, 127, 133, 138, 140
Walls, Joe 298
Walters, Glen 315
Warner Bros. 22n, 28, 151, 158, 173, 240
Warner Theater (Los Angeles, CA) 203
"War of the Worlds" broadcast of 1938 155
Waterman, Willard 113, 115
We're No Angels 319
Weaver, Tom 315
Weiner, Leonard 206, 231
Welden, Ben 267, 290
Weldon, Joan 272
Welles, Orson 155
Wellman, William 171
West, Mae 20, 139, 351
West, Vera 12
Westmore, Bud 112, 149, 169, 206, 231, 266, 298, 314
Wexler, Paul 298, 311
What Ever Happened to Baby Jane? 238
WHB radio network (Kansas City, MO) 82
Where's Charley? 271
White Woman 28
Whitmore, James 78, 79, 80
"Who's on First?" comedy routine 172, 351

WHN (NYC radio station) 151
Wiard, Judy 267
Wicked Age, The 20
Wickes, Mary 231, 238–239
Wild on the Beach 152
Wild Wild West, The 153
Wilde, Lois 267
Wilder, Billy 17, 115, 208
Wilkerson, Guy 231
Wilkins, William J. 7
Williams, Lawrence A. 267
Willock, Dave 207
Wills, Chill 233
Wills, Henry 315
Willson, Henry 319
Wilson, Richard 231, 298
Wind, The 301
Wings 171
Winkelman, Michael 343, 344
Winninger, Charles 29
Wistful Widow of Wagon Gap, The 26, 151

Withers, Isabel 315
Wizarding World of Harry Potter, The (theme park exhibit) 342n
Woman's Face, A 25
"Wonderful Race at Rimrock, The" (Beauchamp) 72
Woollcott, Alexander 208
Worden, Hank 231
Wyler, William 21, 22, 176, 239
Wyoming 23

Yaconelli, Zacharias 207
Yakima Indian Reservation 84
Yarnell, Sally 267
Young and the Restless, The 233
Yowlachie, Chief (a.k.a. Daniel Simmons) 77, 84, 113

Zane, Nancy 231, 240

Made in the USA
Middletown, DE
10 March 2021